THE DAYS ARE JUST PACKED

Other Books by Bill Watterson

Calvin and Hobbes
Something Under the Bed Is Drooling
Yukon Ho!
Weirdos from Another Planet
The Revenge of the Baby-Sat
Scientific Progress Goes "Boink"
Attack of the Deranged Mutant Killer Monster Snow Goons

Treasury Collections

The Calvin and Hobbes Lazy Sunday Book
The Authoritative Calvin and Hobbes
The Indispensable Calvin and Hobbes

THE DAYS ARE JUST PACKED

A Calvin and Hobbes Collection by Bill Watterson

IS THE COAST CLEAR? GIVE ME A BOOST!
WHAT'S THE PLAN?
WE WAIT FOR SUSIE TO WALK UNDERNEATH THIS TREE AND THEN WE DROP THE WATER BALLOON ON HER!
WHAT IF SHE DOESN'T WALK BY?
THEN WE JUST SIT IN THE TREE ALL DAY.
I LOVE SUMMER.
THE DAYS ARE JUST **PACKED**.

WARNER BOOKS

A Warner Book

First published in Great Britain in 1993 by Warner Books
Reprinted 1993
Second Reprint 1993

Calvin and Hobbes is a cartoon feature created by Bill Watterson, syndicated
internationally by Universal Press Syndicate and first published in the United States
by Andrews and McMeel.

The moral right of the author has been asserted.

A CIP catalogue record for this book
is available from the British Library

ISBN 0 7515 0761 X

Printed and bound in Great Britain by
BPCC Hazell Books Ltd
Member of BPCC Ltd

Warner Books
A Division of
Little, Brown and Company (UK) Limited
Brettenham House
Lancaster Place
London WC2E 7EN

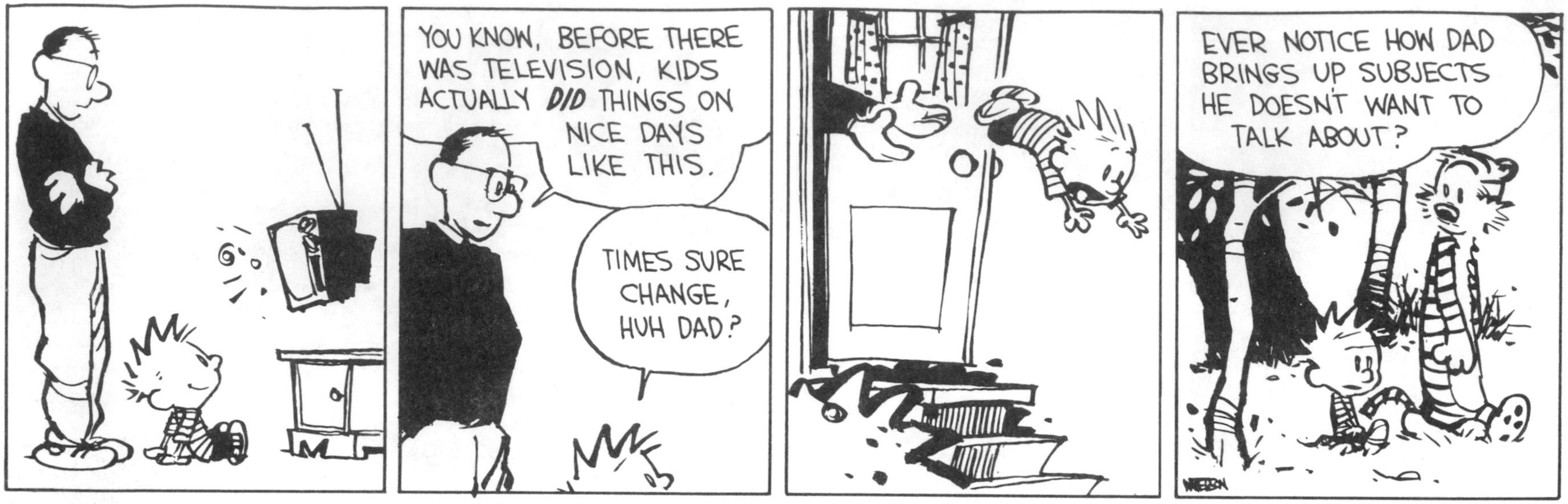
YOU KNOW, BEFORE THERE WAS TELEVISION, KIDS ACTUALLY DID THINGS ON NICE DAYS LIKE THIS.
TIMES SURE CHANGE, HUH DAD?
EVER NOTICE HOW DAD BRINGS UP SUBJECTS HE DOESN'T WANT TO TALK ABOUT?

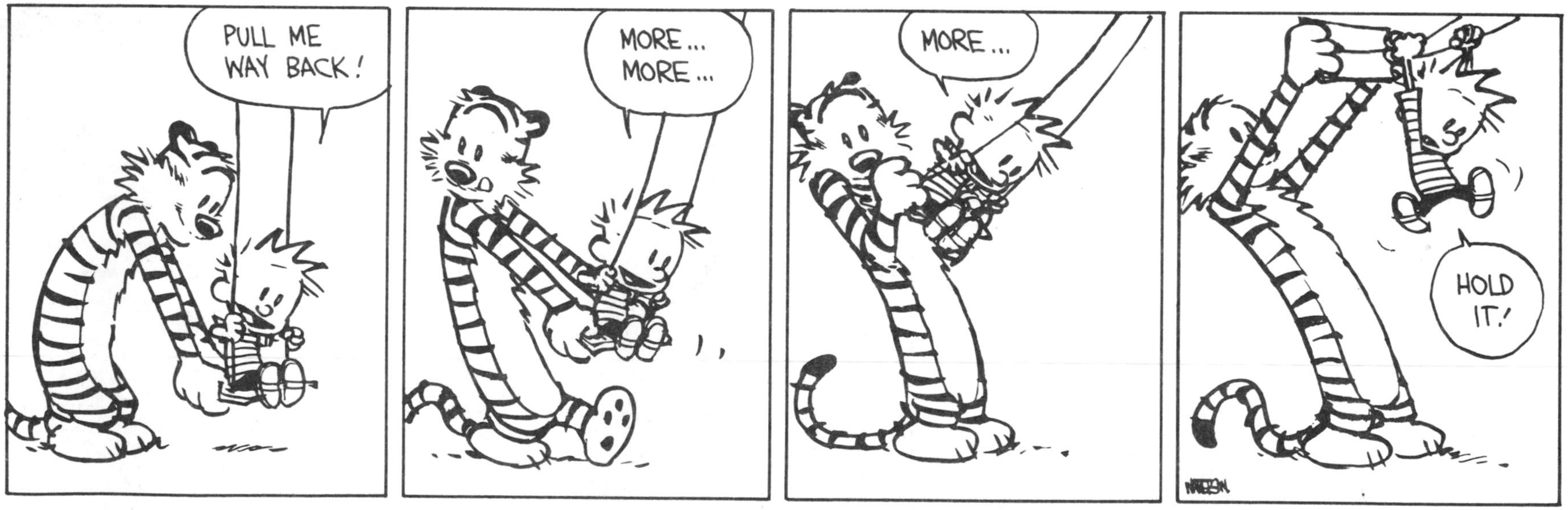
PULL ME WAY BACK!
MORE... MORE...
MORE...
HOLD IT!

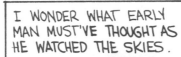

calvin and HObbEs

by WATTERSON

THERE'S VENUS. THERE'S MARS, AND THERE'S JUPITER.

AND I'M *STUCK* HERE.

ON A CLEAR NIGHT LIKE THIS, YOU REALIZE HOW INCOMPREHENSIBLY VAST THE UNIVERSE REALLY IS.

I WONDER WHAT EARLY MAN MUST'VE THOUGHT AS HE WATCHED THE SKIES.

HE'D SEE HE WAS AN INFINITESIMAL PART OF CREATION, BUT HE'D HAVE NO UNDERSTANDING OF PLANETS OR STARS OR COMETS OR ANYTHING.

IMAGINE HOW BIG AND MYSTERIOUS THE NIGHT WOULD'VE SEEMED TO HIM! I'LL BET HE FELT VERY FRAGILE AND AFRAID, DON'T YOU THINK?

...HOBBES? HOBBES ??

...H-HELLO?... ANYB-BODY ??

NUGH!...

WUMP!

I'LL BET *THAT'S* WHAT HE FELT LIKE! SABER-TOOTH TIGER FOOD!

FROM NOW ON, I'M GOING TO STAY INSIDE AT NIGHT AND WATCH TV.

7

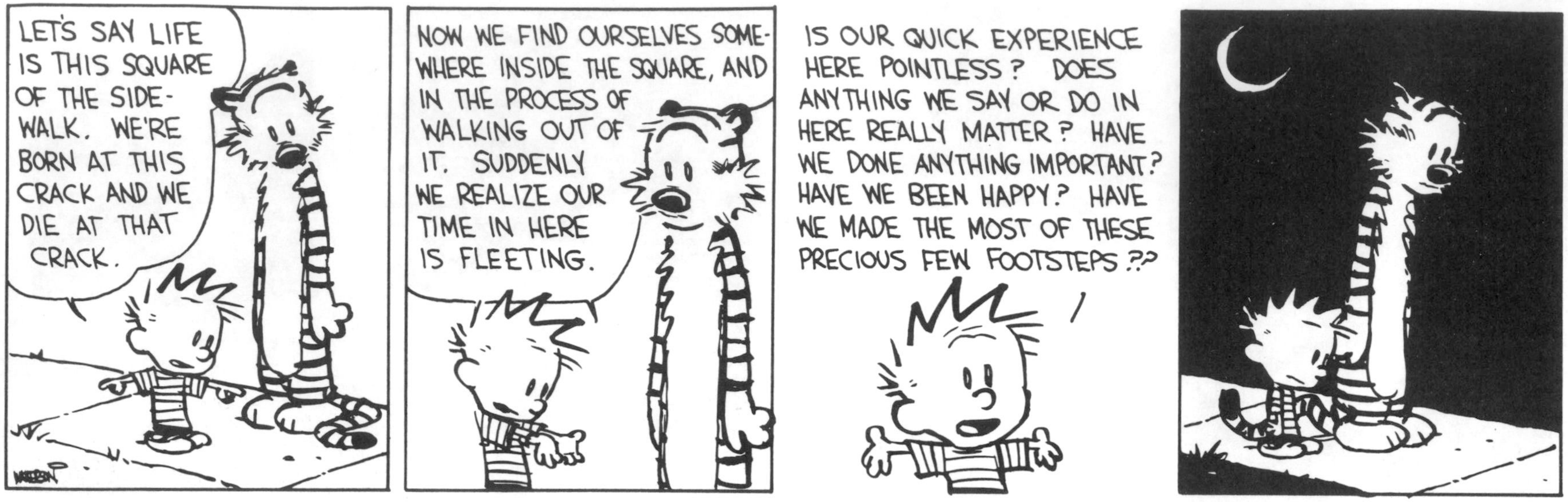
LET'S SAY LIFE IS THIS SQUARE OF THE SIDE-WALK. WE'RE BORN AT THIS CRACK AND WE DIE AT THAT CRACK.
NOW WE FIND OURSELVES SOMEWHERE INSIDE THE SQUARE, AND IN THE PROCESS OF WALKING OUT OF IT. SUDDENLY WE REALIZE OUR TIME IN HERE IS FLEETING.
IS OUR QUICK EXPERIENCE HERE POINTLESS? DOES ANYTHING WE SAY OR DO IN HERE REALLY MATTER? HAVE WE DONE ANYTHING IMPORTANT? HAVE WE BEEN HAPPY? HAVE WE MADE THE MOST OF THESE PRECIOUS FEW FOOTSTEPS??

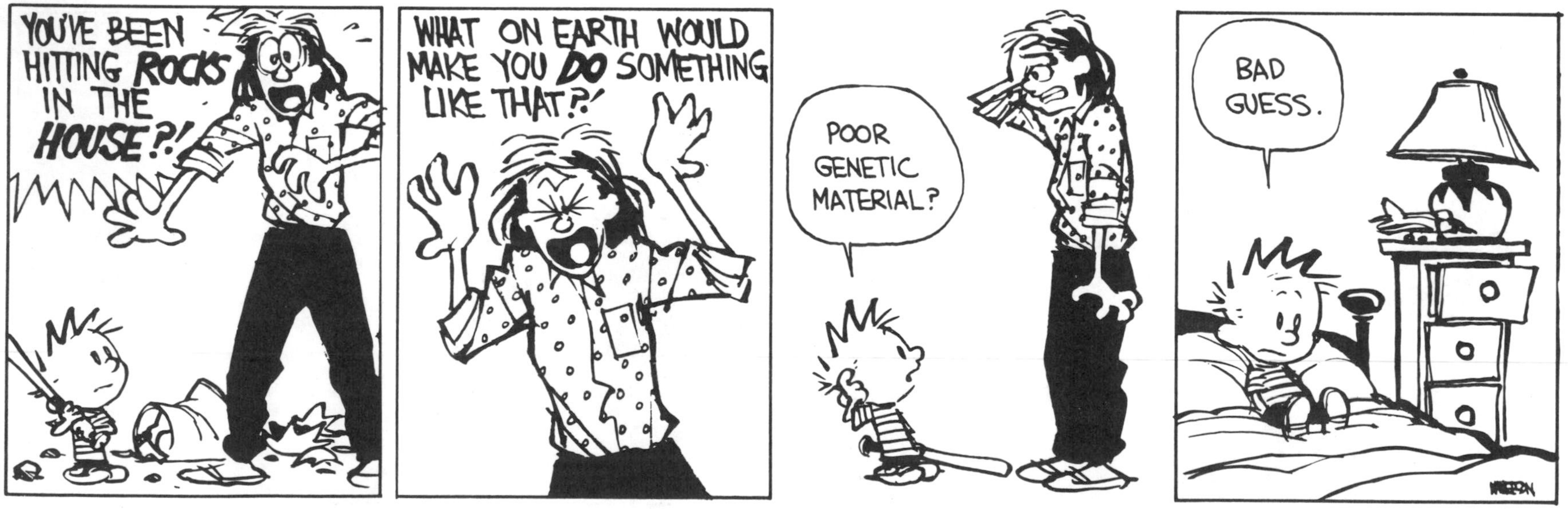
YOU'VE BEEN HITTING ROCKS IN THE HOUSE?!
WHAT ON EARTH WOULD MAKE YOU DO SOMETHING LIKE THAT?!
POOR GENETIC MATERIAL?
BAD GUESS.

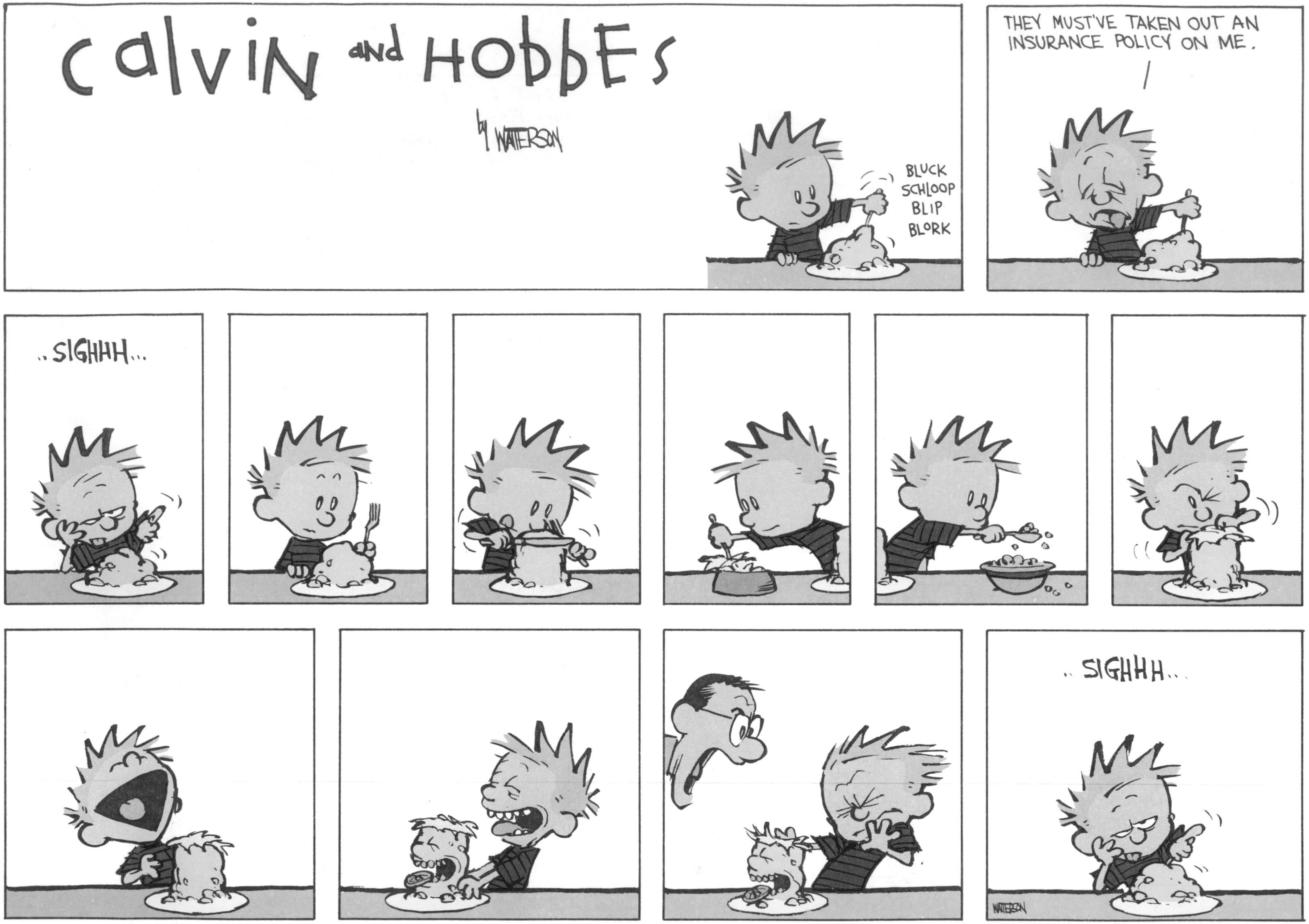
Calvin and HOBBES
by WATTERSON
BLUCK
SCHLOOP
BLIP
BLORK
THEY MUST'VE TAKEN OUT AN INSURANCE POLICY ON ME.
.. SIGHHH...
.. SIGHHH...
WATTERSON

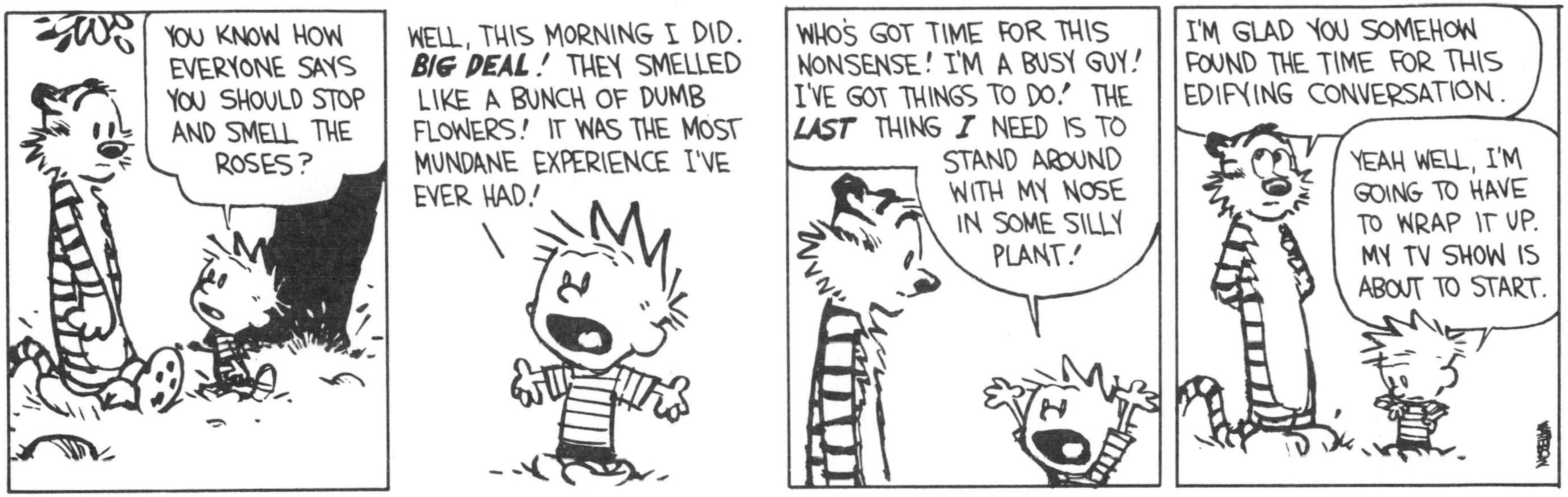
YOU KNOW HOW EVERYONE SAYS YOU SHOULD STOP AND SMELL THE ROSES?
WELL, THIS MORNING I DID. BIG DEAL! THEY SMELLED LIKE A BUNCH OF DUMB FLOWERS! IT WAS THE MOST MUNDANE EXPERIENCE I'VE EVER HAD!
WHO'S GOT TIME FOR THIS NONSENSE! I'M A BUSY GUY! I'VE GOT THINGS TO DO! THE LAST THING I NEED IS TO STAND AROUND WITH MY NOSE IN SOME SILLY PLANT!
I'M GLAD YOU SOMEHOW FOUND THE TIME FOR THIS EDIFYING CONVERSATION.
YEAH WELL, I'M GOING TO HAVE TO WRAP IT UP. MY TV SHOW IS ABOUT TO START.

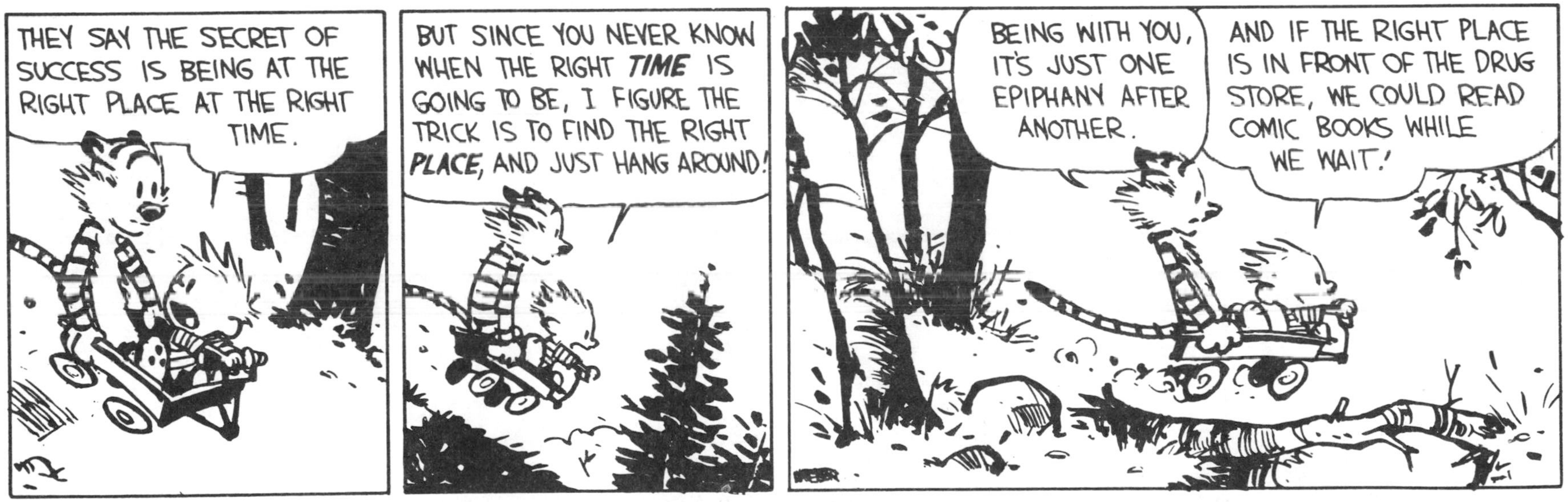
THEY SAY THE SECRET OF SUCCESS IS BEING AT THE RIGHT PLACE AT THE RIGHT TIME.
BUT SINCE YOU NEVER KNOW WHEN THE RIGHT TIME IS GOING TO BE, I FIGURE THE TRICK IS TO FIND THE RIGHT PLACE, AND JUST HANG AROUND!
BEING WITH YOU, IT'S JUST ONE EPIPHANY AFTER ANOTHER.
AND IF THE RIGHT PLACE IS IN FRONT OF THE DRUG STORE, WE COULD READ COMIC BOOKS WHILE WE WAIT!

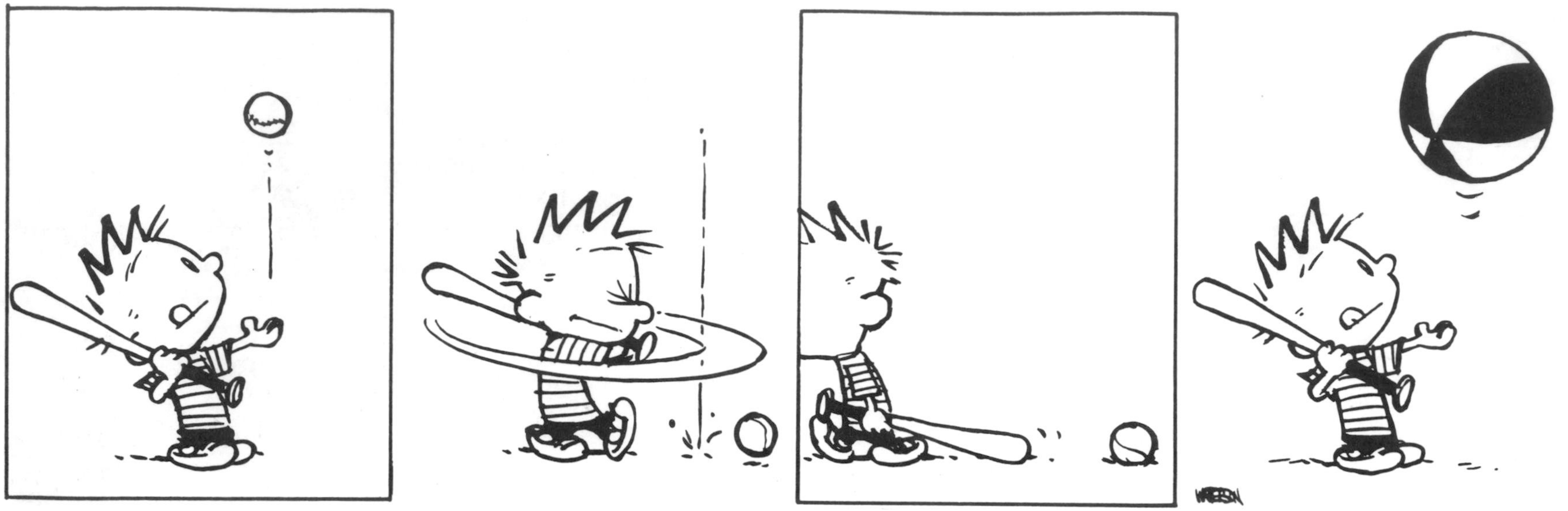

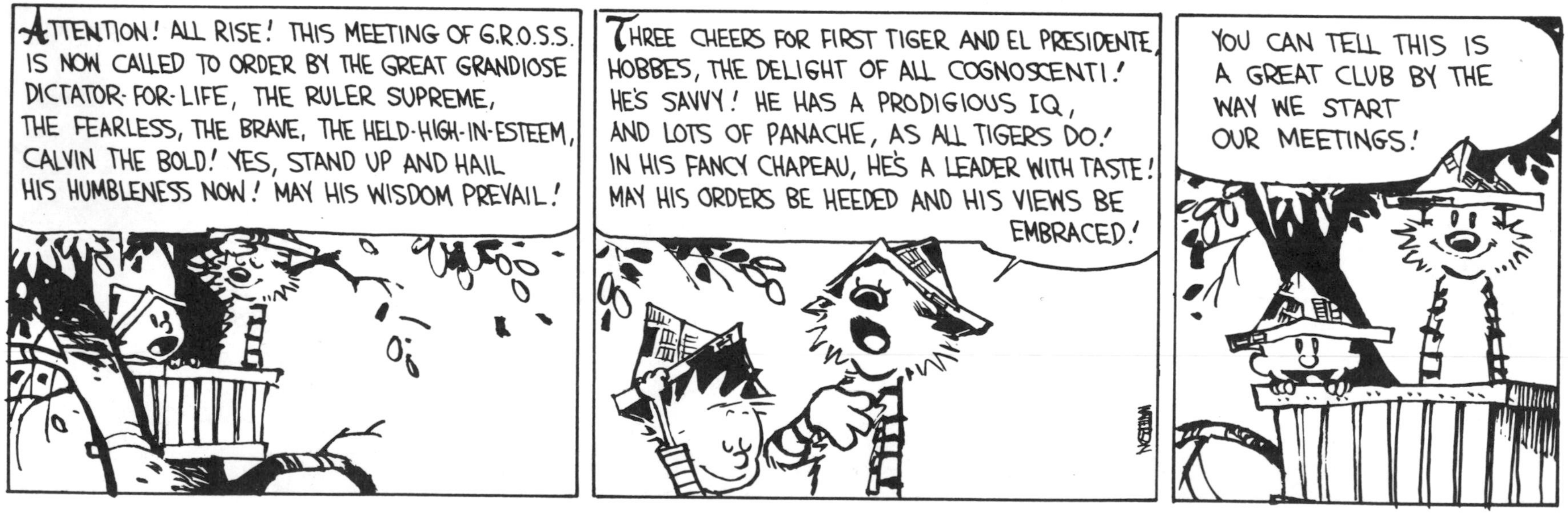
ATTENTION! ALL RISE! THIS MEETING OF G.R.O.S.S. IS NOW CALLED TO ORDER BY THE GREAT GRANDIOSE DICTATOR-FOR-LIFE, THE RULER SUPREME, THE FEARLESS, THE BRAVE, THE HELD-HIGH-IN-ESTEEM, CALVIN THE BOLD! YES, STAND UP AND HAIL HIS HUMBLENESS NOW! MAY HIS WISDOM PREVAIL!
THREE CHEERS FOR FIRST TIGER AND EL PRESIDENTE, HOBBES, THE DELIGHT OF ALL COGNOSCENTI! HE'S SAVVY! HE HAS A PRODIGIOUS IQ, AND LOTS OF PANACHE, AS ALL TIGERS DO! IN HIS FANCY CHAPEAU, HE'S A LEADER WITH TASTE! MAY HIS ORDERS BE HEEDED AND HIS VIEWS BE EMBRACED!
YOU CAN TELL THIS IS A GREAT CLUB BY THE WAY WE START OUR MEETINGS!

THIS MEETING OF THE GET RID OF SLIMY GIRLS CLUB IS NOW IN SESSION! FIRST TIGER HOBBES WILL PRESENT OUR FINANCIAL REPORT.

WAIT, WE DIDN'T SING THE G.R.O.S.S. ANTHEM.

WE SING THAT AT THE END OF THE MEETING.

I WANT TO SING IT NOW.

WE CAN'T. WE HAVE TO FOLLOW PROPER PROTOCOL! SEE? IT SAYS ON THE AGENDA THAT WE SING THE ANTHEM LAST!

OHHOHH GROHOSS ♪ BEST CLUB IN THE COSMOS..

STOP THAT, YOU ANARCHIST!

YOU GET TWO DEMERITS FOR SINGING THE CLUB ANTHEM BEFORE IT WAS ON THE AGENDA!

WELL YOU GET FIVE DEMERITS FOR NOT TAKING OFF YOUR HAT DURING ITS HALLOWED REFRAIN!

YOU CAN'T GIVE ME DEMERITS! I OUTRANK YOU.

HA! YOU'RE JUST A FIGUREHEAD! YOUR DUTIES ARE CEREMONIAL! I HAVE ALL THE REAL RESPONSIBILITIES!

WHAT?! I'M DICTATOR-FOR-LIFE! I HAVE TEN TIMES THE IMPORTANCE OF A LOWLY FIRST TIGER! A HUNDRED TIMES! A MILLION TIMES!

IF YOU'RE SO IMPORTANT, HOW COME YOU SING THE SOPRANO PART OF OUR ANTHEM?

THAT'S JUST TILL MY VOICE CHANGES!

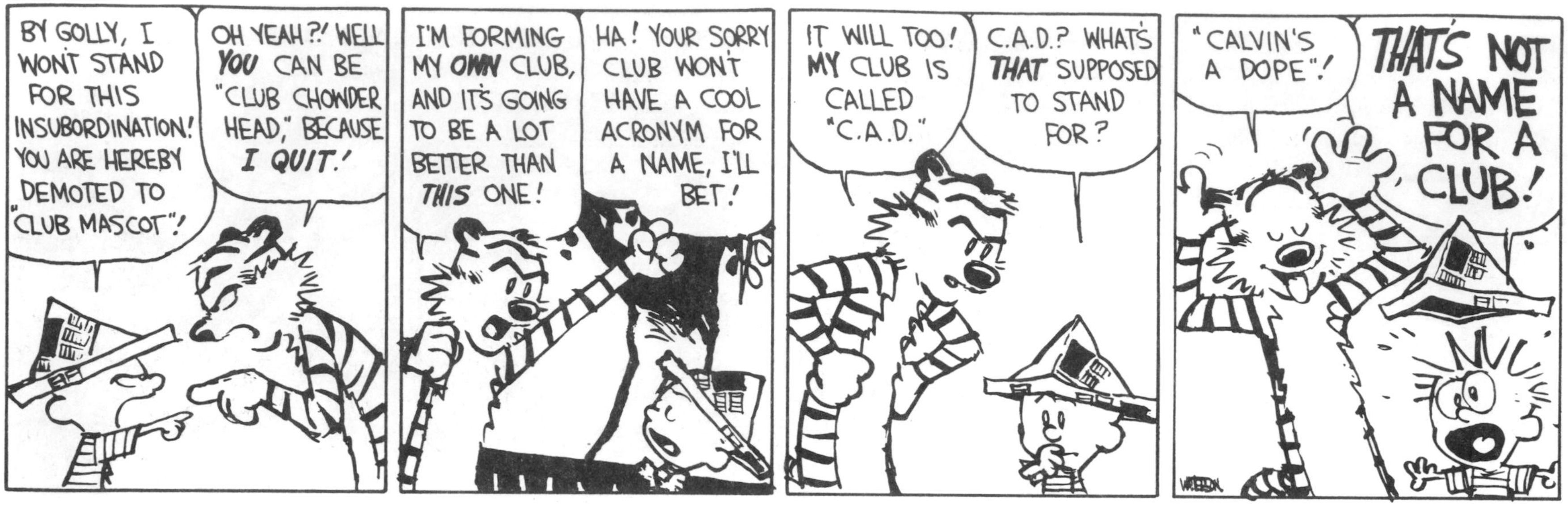
BY GOLLY, I WON'T STAND FOR THIS INSUBORDINATION! YOU ARE HEREBY DEMOTED TO "CLUB MASCOT"!
OH YEAH?! WELL YOU CAN BE "CLUB CHOWDER HEAD," BECAUSE I QUIT!
I'M FORMING MY OWN CLUB, AND IT'S GOING TO BE A LOT BETTER THAN THIS ONE!
HA! YOUR SORRY CLUB WON'T HAVE A COOL ACRONYM FOR A NAME, I'LL BET!
IT WILL TOO! MY CLUB IS CALLED "C.A.D."
C.A.D.? WHAT'S THAT SUPPOSED TO STAND FOR?
"CALVIN'S A DOPE"!
THAT'S NOT A NAME FOR A CLUB!

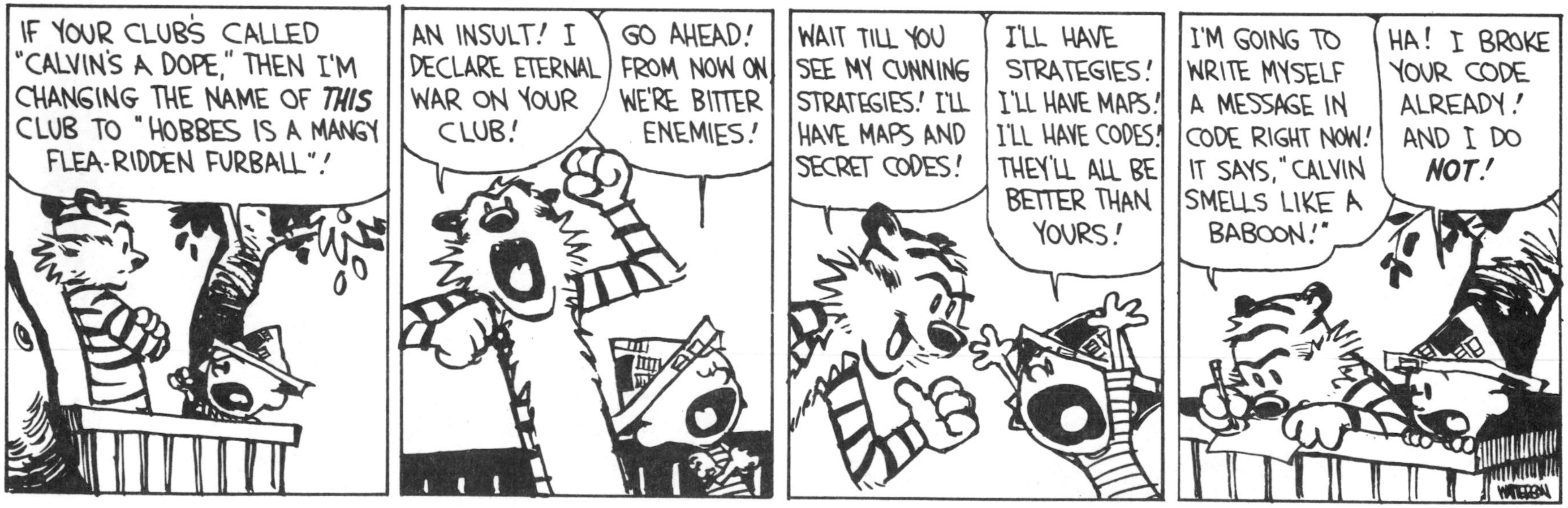
IF YOUR CLUB'S CALLED "CALVIN'S A DOPE," THEN I'M CHANGING THE NAME OF THIS CLUB TO "HOBBES IS A MANGY FLEA-RIDDEN FURBALL"!
AN INSULT! I DECLARE ETERNAL WAR ON YOUR CLUB!
GO AHEAD! FROM NOW ON WE'RE BITTER ENEMIES!
WAIT TILL YOU SEE MY CUNNING STRATEGIES! I'LL HAVE MAPS AND SECRET CODES!
I'LL HAVE STRATEGIES! I'LL HAVE MAPS! I'LL HAVE CODES! THEY'LL ALL BE BETTER THAN YOURS!
I'M GOING TO WRITE MYSELF A MESSAGE IN CODE RIGHT NOW! IT SAYS, "CALVIN SMELLS LIKE A BABOON!"
HA! I BROKE YOUR CODE ALREADY! AND I DO NOT!

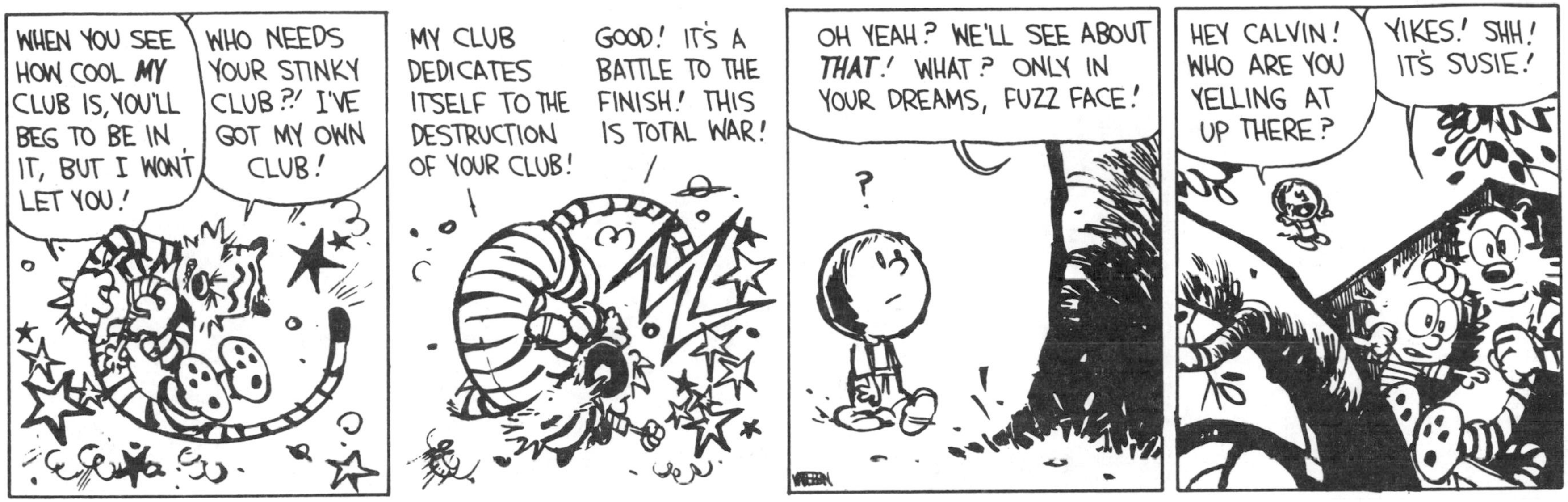
WHEN YOU SEE HOW COOL MY CLUB IS, YOU'LL BEG TO BE IN IT, BUT I WON'T LET YOU!
WHO NEEDS YOUR STINKY CLUB?! I'VE GOT MY OWN CLUB!
MY CLUB DEDICATES ITSELF TO THE DESTRUCTION OF YOUR CLUB!
GOOD! IT'S A BATTLE TO THE FINISH! THIS IS TOTAL WAR!
OH YEAH? WE'LL SEE ABOUT THAT! WHAT? ONLY IN YOUR DREAMS, FUZZ FACE!
?
HEY CALVIN! WHO ARE YOU YELLING AT UP THERE?
YIKES! SHH! IT'S SUSIE!

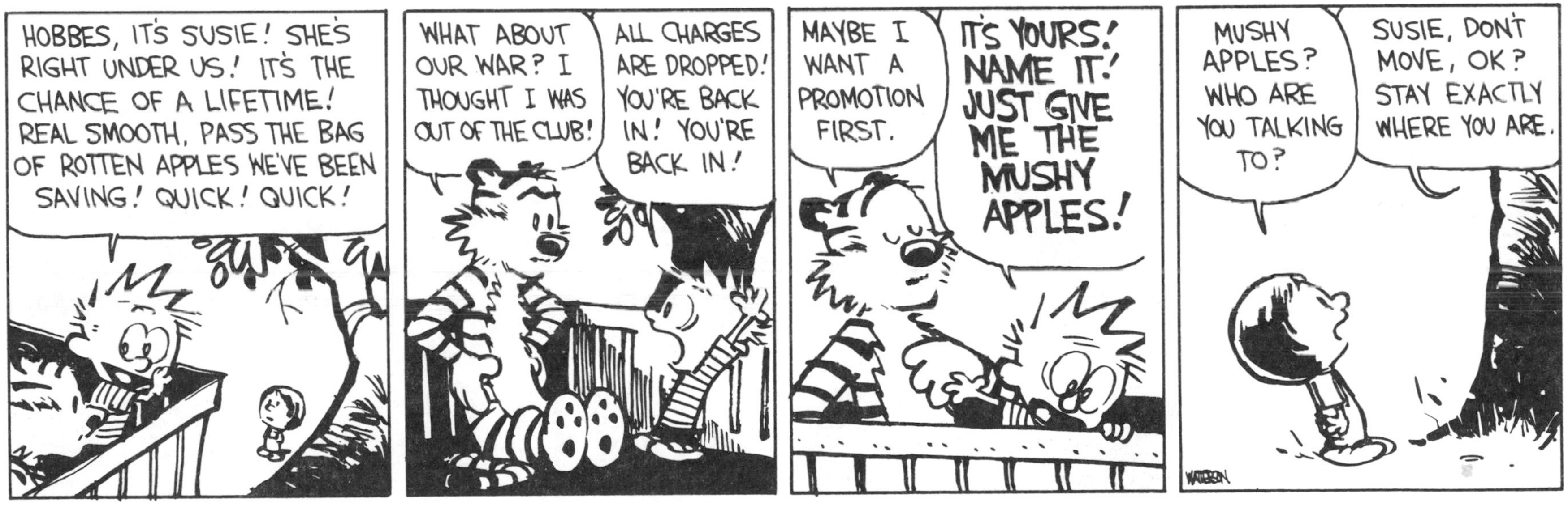
HOBBES, IT'S SUSIE! SHE'S RIGHT UNDER US! IT'S THE CHANCE OF A LIFETIME! REAL SMOOTH, PASS THE BAG OF ROTTEN APPLES WE'VE BEEN SAVING! QUICK! QUICK!
WHAT ABOUT OUR WAR? I THOUGHT I WAS OUT OF THE CLUB!
ALL CHARGES ARE DROPPED! YOU'RE BACK IN! YOU'RE BACK IN!
MAYBE I WANT A PROMOTION FIRST.
IT'S YOURS! NAME IT! JUST GIVE ME THE MUSHY APPLES!
MUSHY APPLES? WHO ARE YOU TALKING TO?
SUSIE, DON'T MOVE, OK? STAY EXACTLY WHERE YOU ARE.

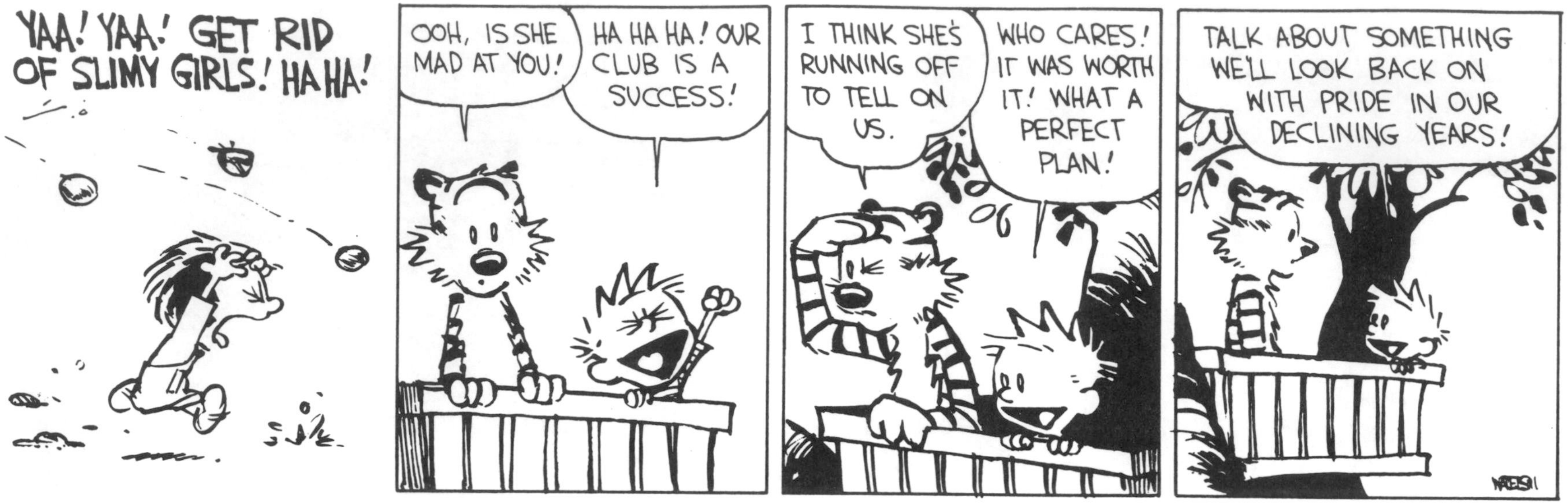
YAA! YAA! GET RID OF SLIMY GIRLS! HA HA!
OOH, IS SHE MAD AT YOU!
HA HA HA! OUR CLUB IS A SUCCESS!
I THINK SHE'S RUNNING OFF TO TELL ON US.
WHO CARES! IT WAS WORTH IT! WHAT A PERFECT PLAN!
TALK ABOUT SOMETHING WE'LL LOOK BACK ON WITH PRIDE IN OUR DECLINING YEARS!

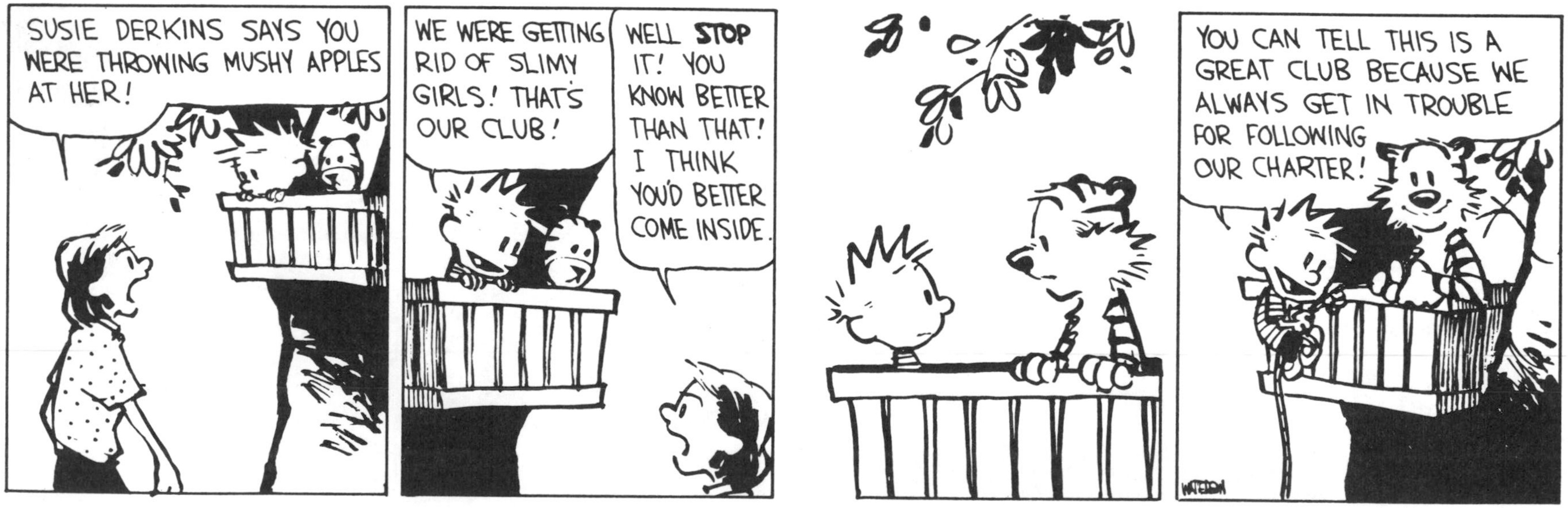
SUSIE DERKINS SAYS YOU WERE THROWING MUSHY APPLES AT HER!
WE WERE GETTING RID OF SLIMY GIRLS! THAT'S OUR CLUB!
WELL STOP IT! YOU KNOW BETTER THAN THAT! I THINK YOU'D BETTER COME INSIDE.
YOU CAN TELL THIS IS A GREAT CLUB BECAUSE WE ALWAYS GET IN TROUBLE FOR FOLLOWING OUR CHARTER!

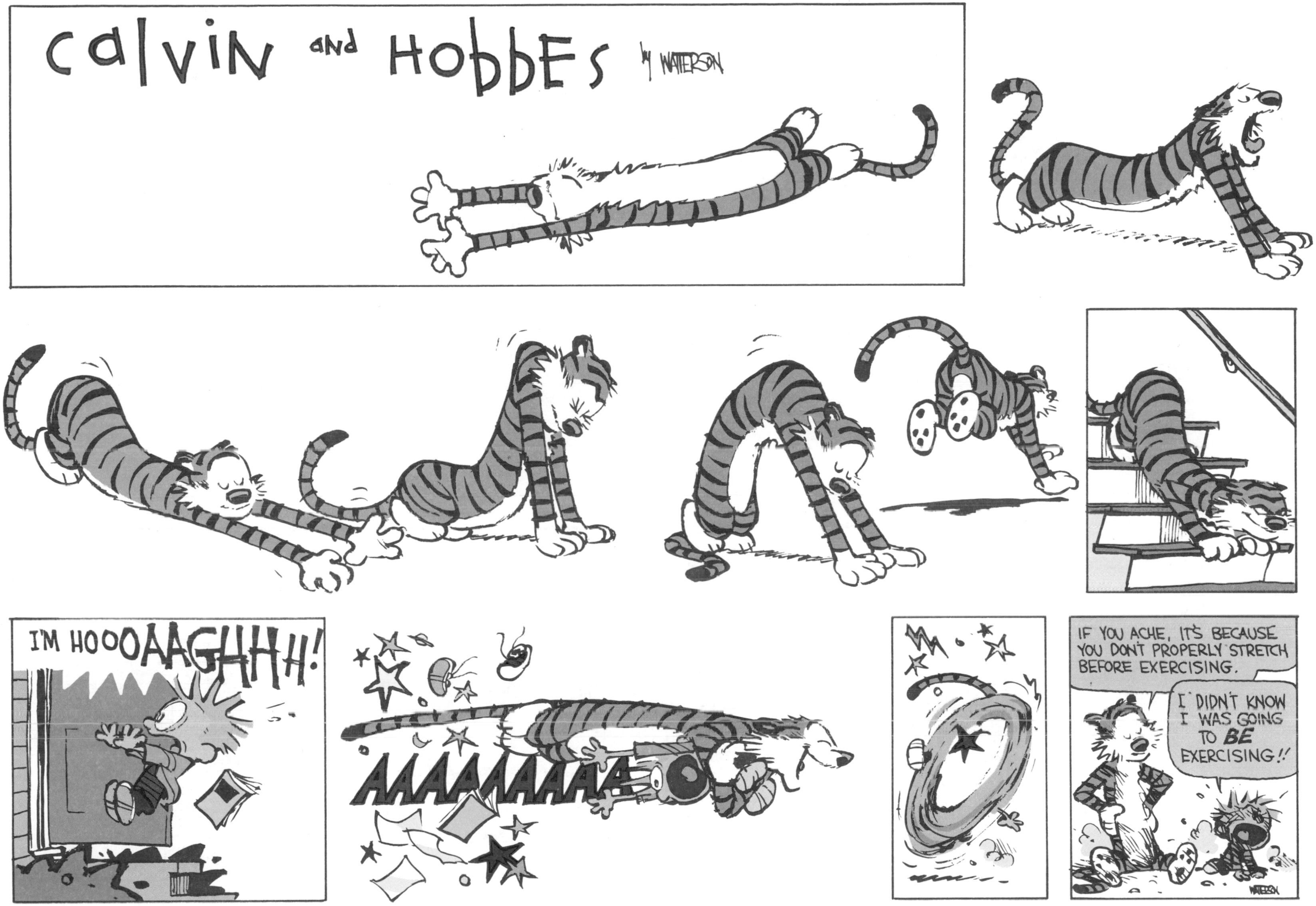

calvin and HOBBES
by WATTERSON
I'M HOOOAAGHHHH!
AAAAAAAAA
IF YOU ACHE, IT'S BECAUSE YOU DON'T PROPERLY STRETCH BEFORE EXERCISING.
I DIDN'T KNOW I WAS GOING TO BE EXERCISING!!
WATTERSON

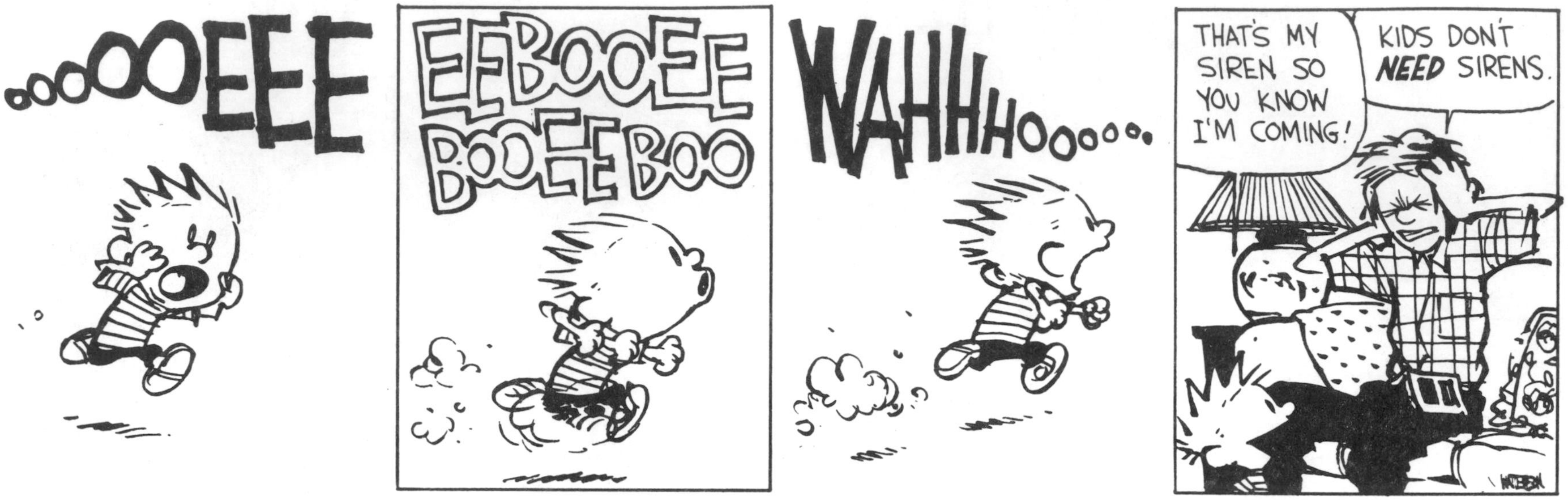
oooOOEEE
EEBOOEE BOOEEBOO
WAHHHOoooo
THAT'S MY SIREN SO YOU KNOW I'M COMING!
KIDS DON'T **NEED** SIRENS.

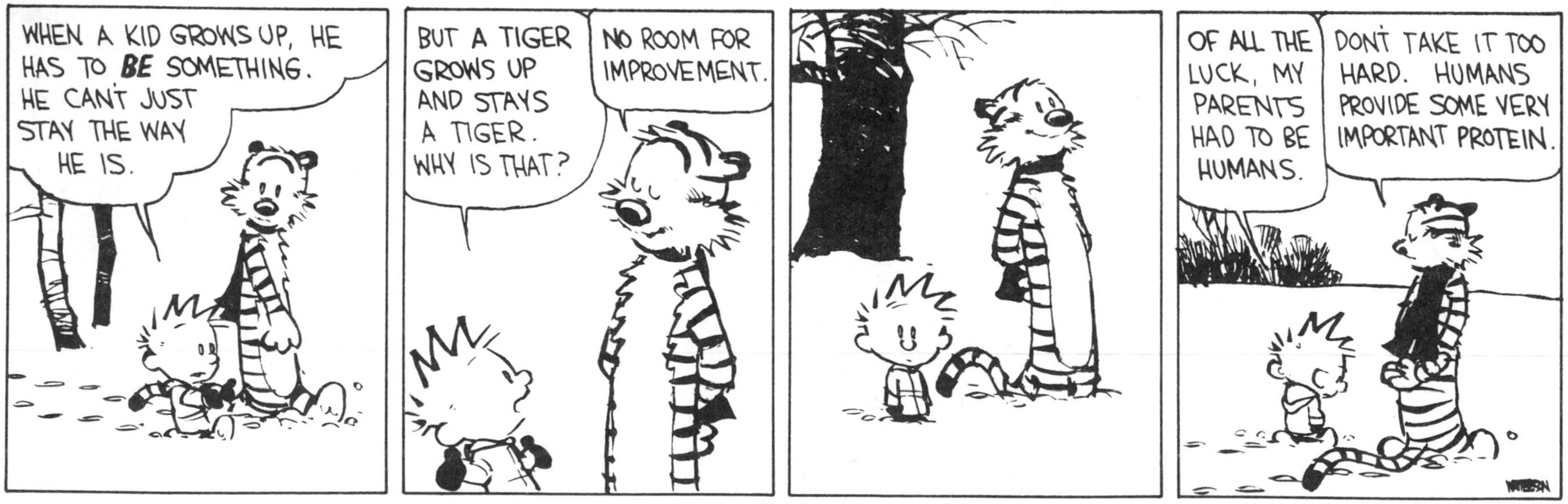
WHEN A KID GROWS UP, HE HAS TO **BE** SOMETHING. HE CAN'T JUST STAY THE WAY HE IS.
BUT A TIGER GROWS UP AND STAYS A TIGER. WHY IS THAT?
NO ROOM FOR IMPROVEMENT.
OF ALL THE LUCK, MY PARENTS HAD TO BE HUMANS.
DON'T TAKE IT TOO HARD. HUMANS PROVIDE SOME VERY IMPORTANT PROTEIN.

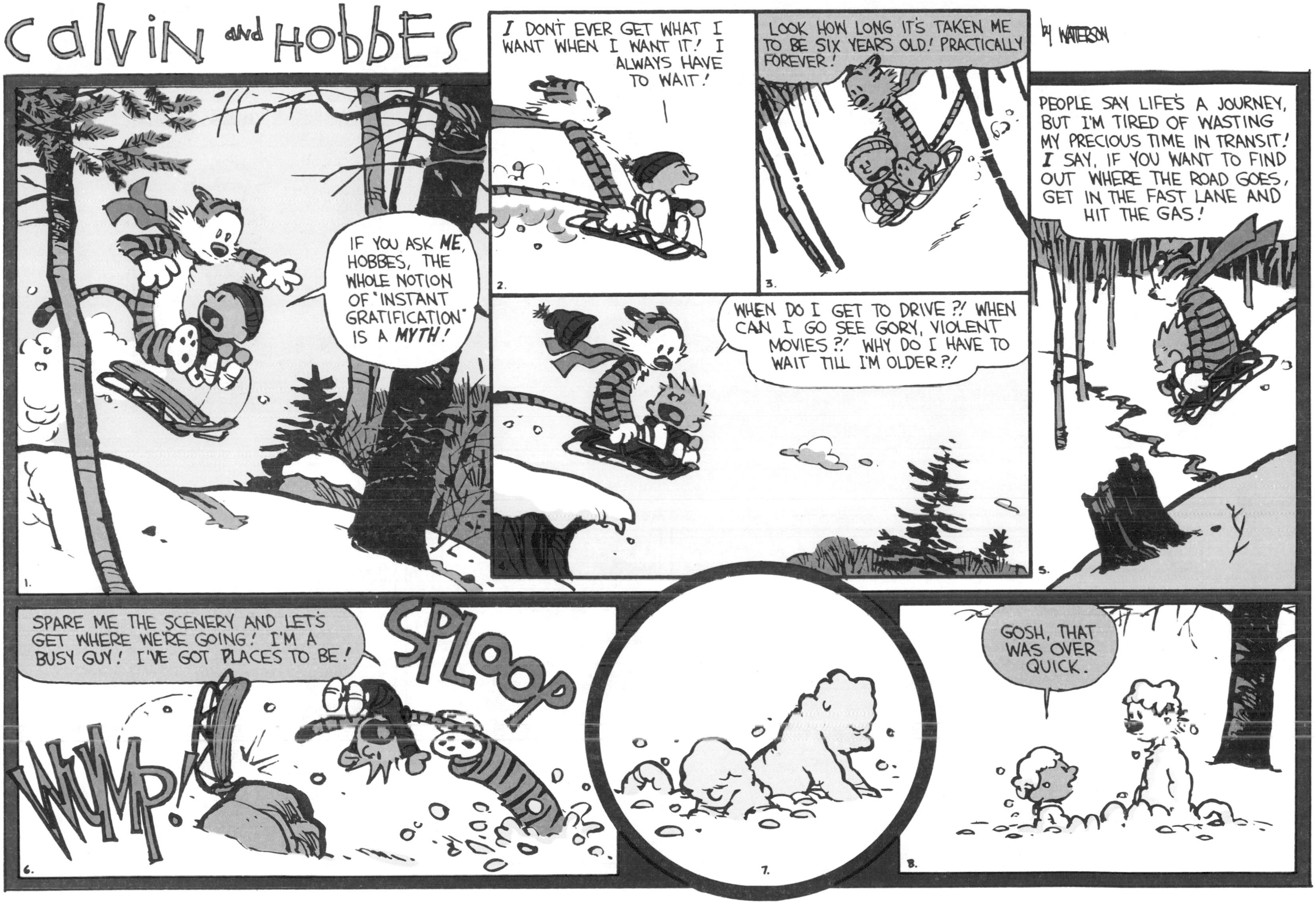
Calvin and HobbEs
by WATTERSON
IF YOU ASK ME, HOBBES, THE WHOLE NOTION OF "INSTANT GRATIFICATION" IS A MYTH!
I DON'T EVER GET WHAT I WANT WHEN I WANT IT! I ALWAYS HAVE TO WAIT!
LOOK HOW LONG IT'S TAKEN ME TO BE SIX YEARS OLD! PRACTICALLY FOREVER!
WHEN DO I GET TO DRIVE?! WHEN CAN I GO SEE GORY, VIOLENT MOVIES?! WHY DO I HAVE TO WAIT TILL I'M OLDER?!
PEOPLE SAY LIFE'S A JOURNEY, BUT I'M TIRED OF WASTING MY PRECIOUS TIME IN TRANSIT! I SAY, IF YOU WANT TO FIND OUT WHERE THE ROAD GOES, GET IN THE FAST LANE AND HIT THE GAS!
SPARE ME THE SCENERY AND LET'S GET WHERE WE'RE GOING! I'M A BUSY GUY! I'VE GOT PLACES TO BE!
SPLOOP
WUMP!
GOSH, THAT WAS OVER QUICK.

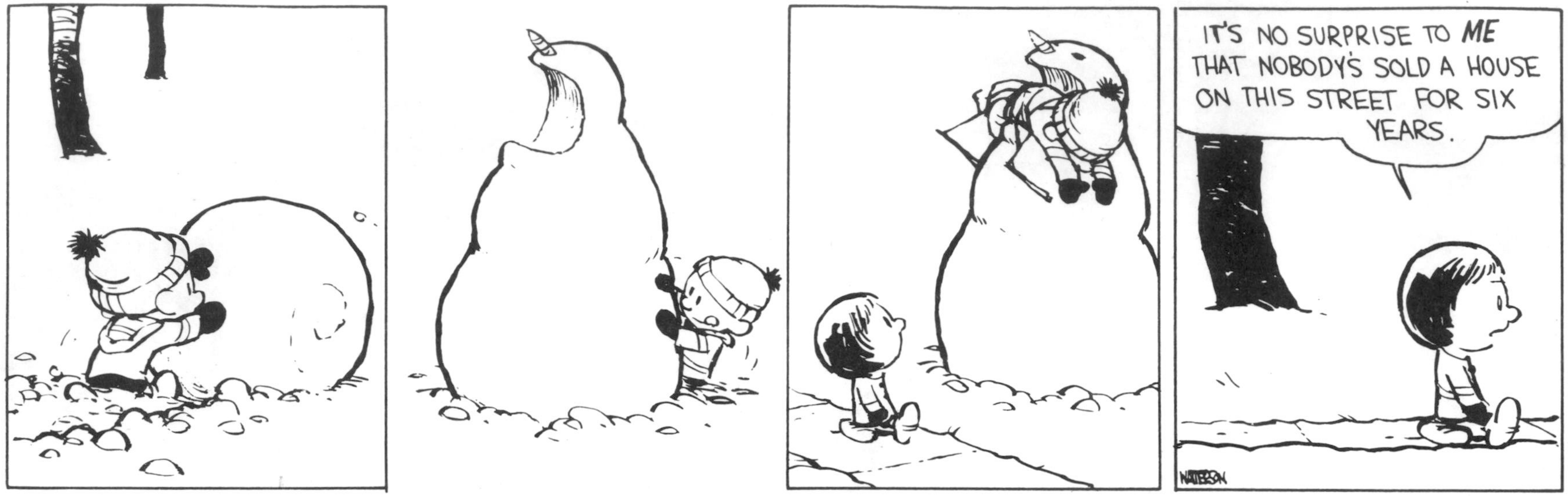

IT'S NO SURPRISE TO ME THAT NOBODY'S SOLD A HOUSE ON THIS STREET FOR SIX YEARS.

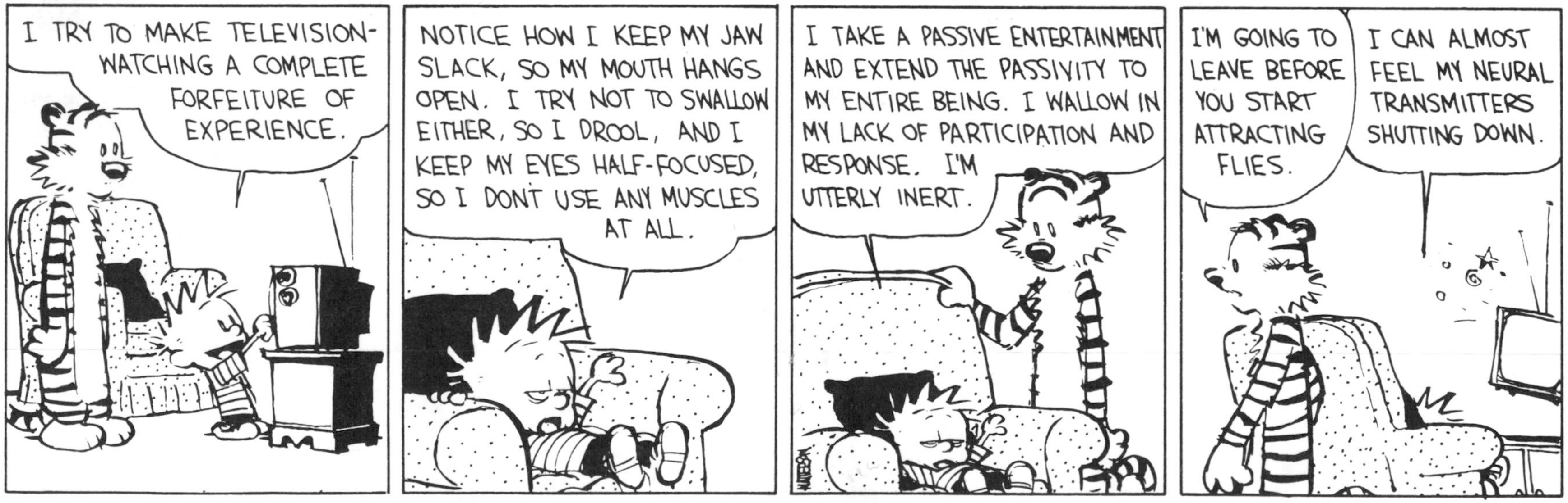

I TRY TO MAKE TELEVISION-WATCHING A COMPLETE FORFEITURE OF EXPERIENCE.
NOTICE HOW I KEEP MY JAW SLACK, SO MY MOUTH HANGS OPEN. I TRY NOT TO SWALLOW EITHER, SO I DROOL, AND I KEEP MY EYES HALF-FOCUSED, SO I DON'T USE ANY MUSCLES AT ALL.
I TAKE A PASSIVE ENTERTAINMENT AND EXTEND THE PASSIVITY TO MY ENTIRE BEING. I WALLOW IN MY LACK OF PARTICIPATION AND RESPONSE. I'M UTTERLY INERT.
I'M GOING TO LEAVE BEFORE YOU START ATTRACTING FLIES.
I CAN ALMOST FEEL MY NEURAL TRANSMITTERS SHUTTING DOWN.

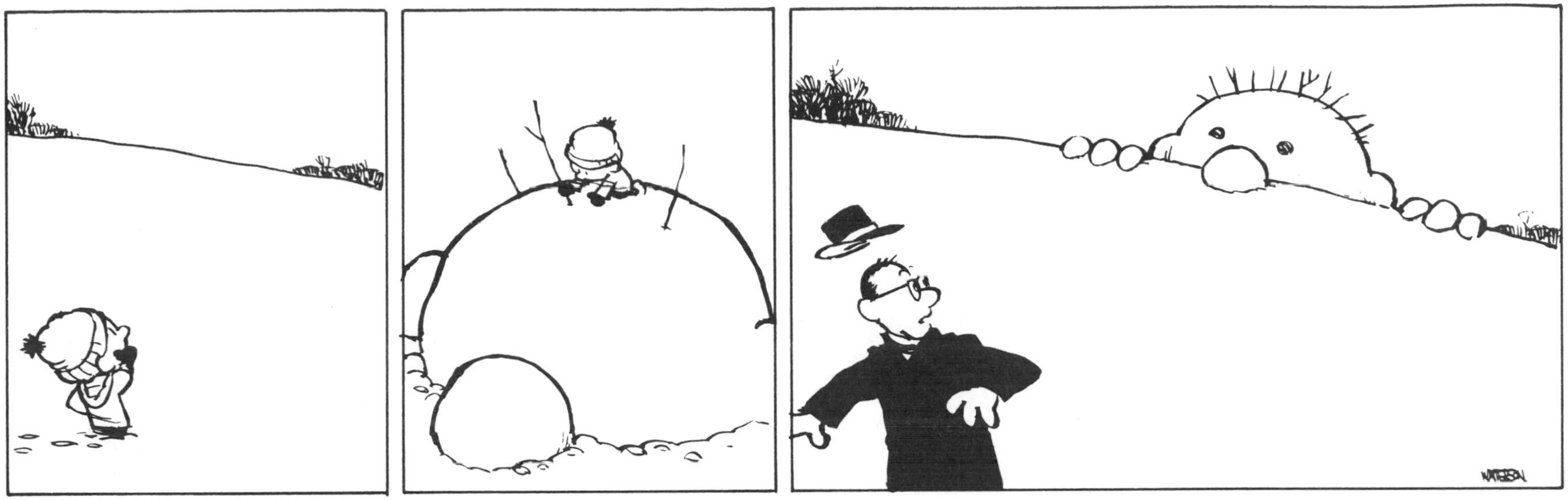

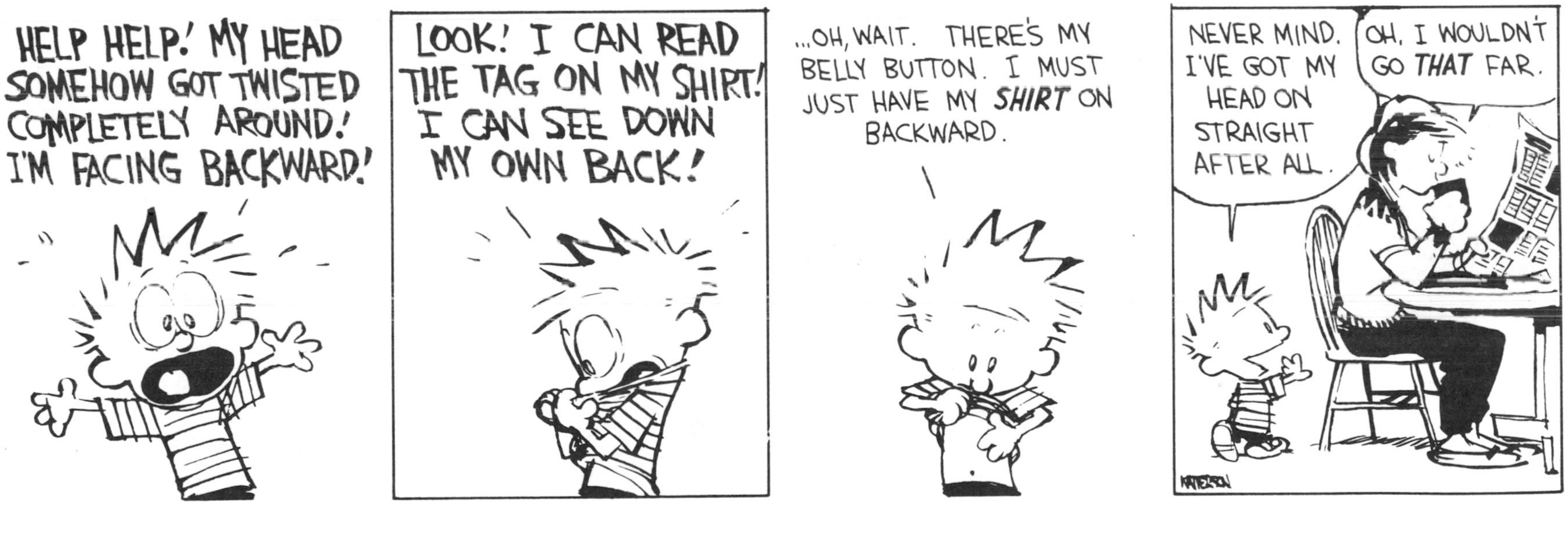

HELP HELP! MY HEAD SOMEHOW GOT TWISTED COMPLETELY AROUND! I'M FACING BACKWARD!
LOOK! I CAN READ THE TAG ON MY SHIRT! I CAN SEE DOWN MY OWN BACK!
...OH, WAIT. THERE'S MY BELLY BUTTON. I MUST JUST HAVE MY *SHIRT* ON BACKWARD.
NEVER MIND. I'VE GOT MY HEAD ON STRAIGHT AFTER ALL.
OH, I WOULDN'T GO *THAT* FAR.

OH SURE!
NICE TRY!

DARN, DARN, DARN DARN, DARN!

 AREN'T YOU SUPPOSED TO BE DOING HOMEWORK NOW?

I QUIT DOING HOMEWORK. HOMEWORK IS BAD FOR MY SELF-ESTEEM.

IT IS?

SURE! IT SENDS THE MESSAGE THAT I DON'T KNOW ENOUGH! ALL THAT EMPHASIS ON RIGHT ANSWERS MAKES ME FEEL BAD WHEN I GET THEM WRONG.

SO INSTEAD OF TRYING TO LEARN, I'M JUST CONCENTRATING ON LIKING MYSELF THE WAY I AM.

YOUR SELF-ESTEEM IS ENHANCED BY REMAINING AN IGNORAMUS?

PLEASE! LET'S CALL IT "INFORMATIONALLY IMPAIRED."

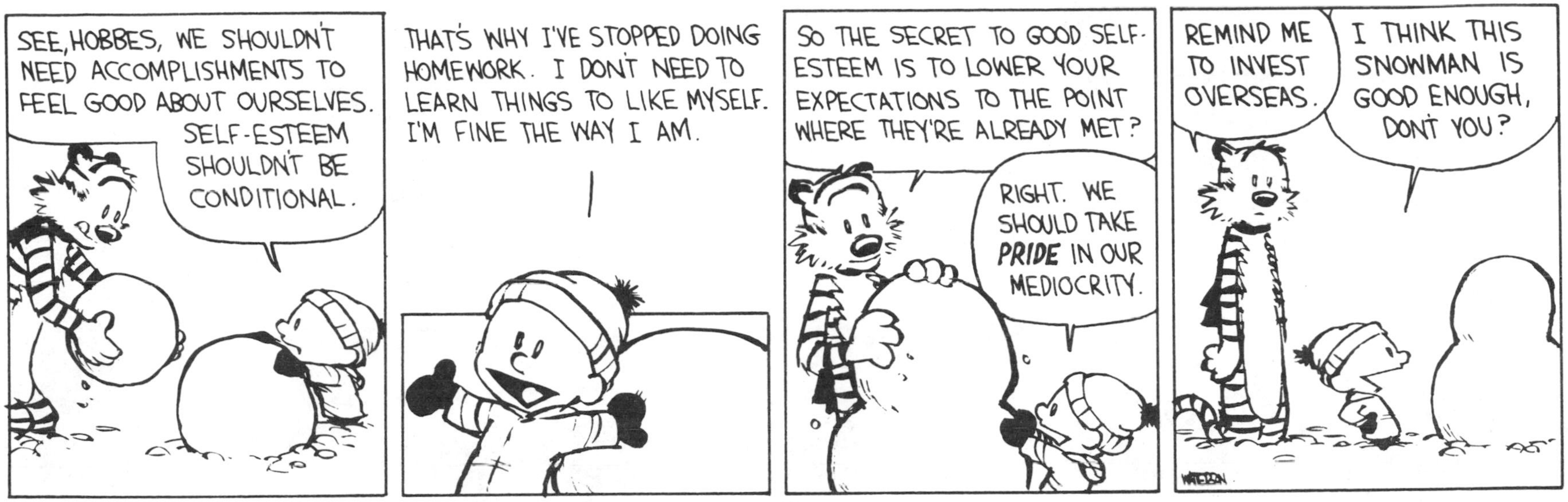
SEE, HOBBES, WE SHOULDN'T NEED ACCOMPLISHMENTS TO FEEL GOOD ABOUT OURSELVES.
SELF-ESTEEM SHOULDN'T BE CONDITIONAL.
THAT'S WHY I'VE STOPPED DOING HOMEWORK. I DON'T NEED TO LEARN THINGS TO LIKE MYSELF. I'M FINE THE WAY I AM.
SO THE SECRET TO GOOD SELF-ESTEEM IS TO LOWER YOUR EXPECTATIONS TO THE POINT WHERE THEY'RE ALREADY MET?
RIGHT. WE SHOULD TAKE PRIDE IN OUR MEDIOCRITY.
REMIND ME TO INVEST OVERSEAS.
I THINK THIS SNOWMAN IS GOOD ENOUGH, DON'T YOU?

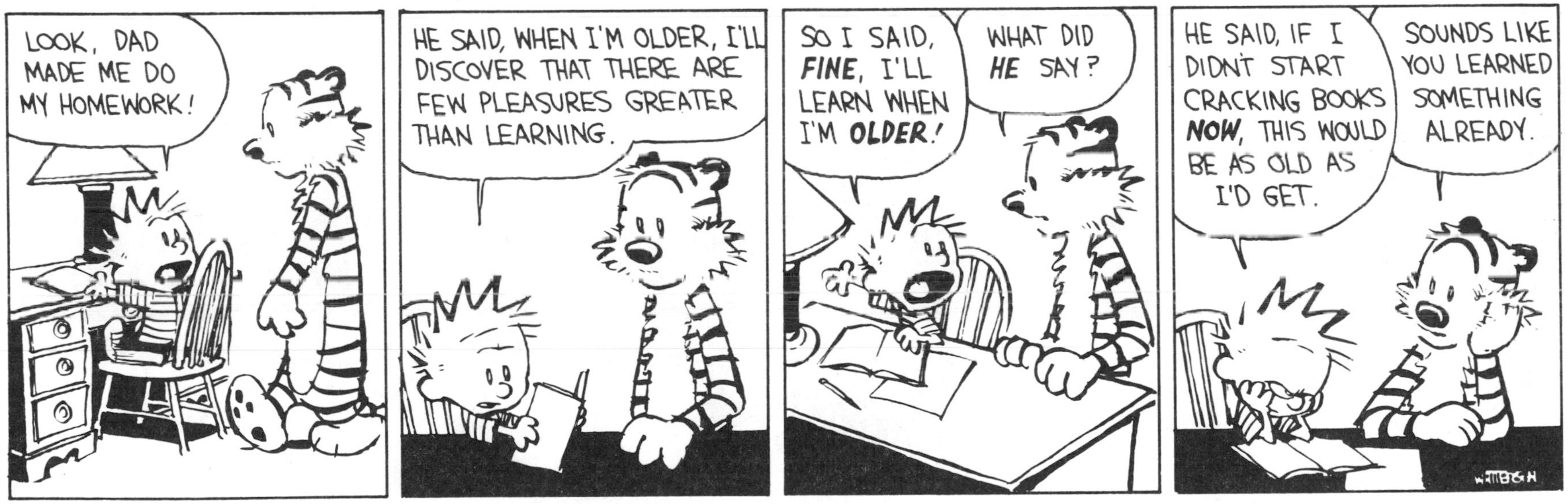
LOOK, DAD MADE ME DO MY HOMEWORK!
HE SAID, WHEN I'M OLDER, I'LL DISCOVER THAT THERE ARE FEW PLEASURES GREATER THAN LEARNING.
SO I SAID, FINE, I'LL LEARN WHEN I'M OLDER!
WHAT DID HE SAY?
HE SAID, IF I DIDN'T START CRACKING BOOKS NOW, THIS WOULD BE AS OLD AS I'D GET.
SOUNDS LIKE YOU LEARNED SOMETHING ALREADY.

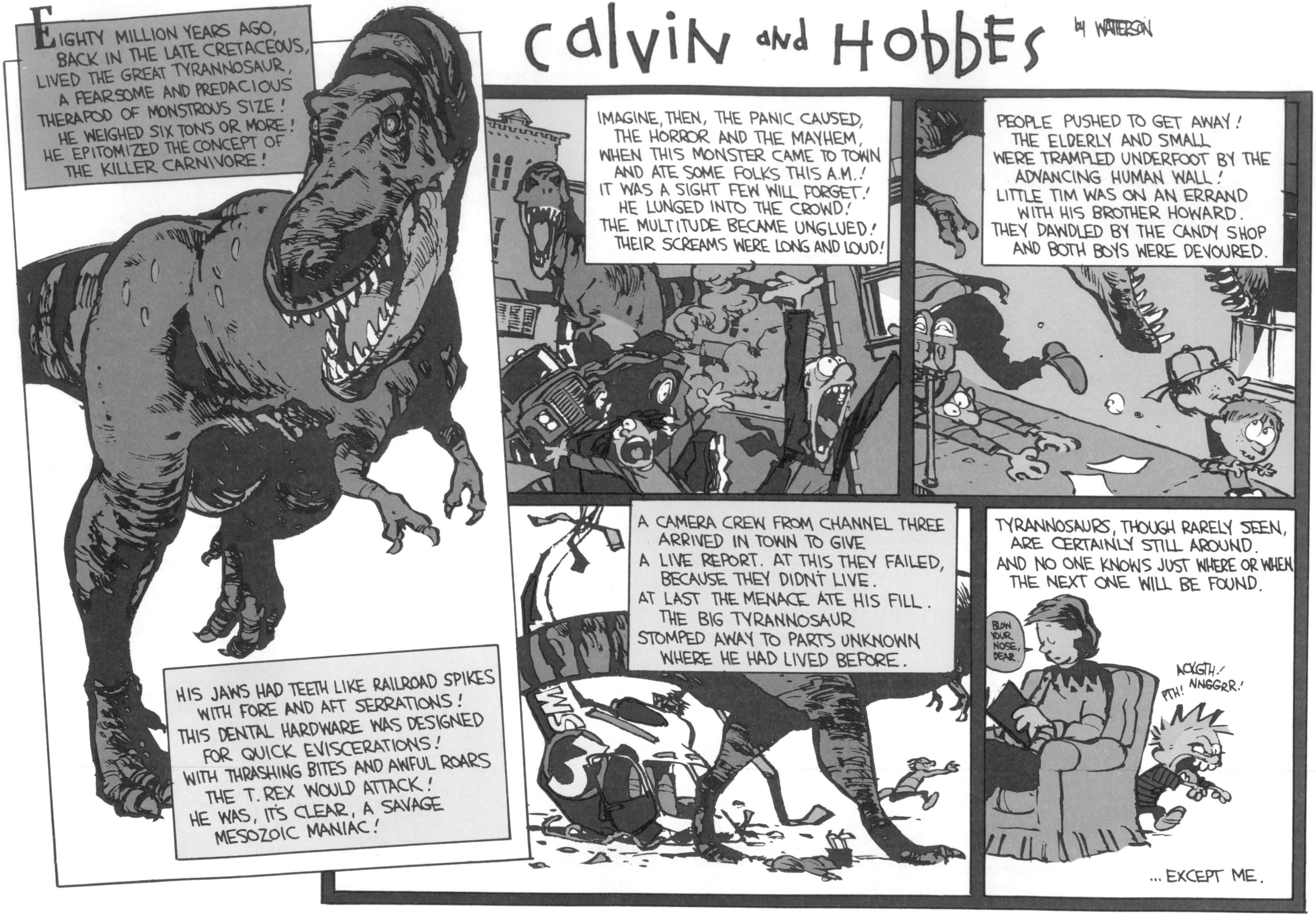
Calvin and Hobbes
by WATTERSON
EIGHTY MILLION YEARS AGO, BACK IN THE LATE CRETACEOUS, LIVED THE GREAT TYRANNOSAUR, A FEARSOME AND PREDACIOUS THERAPOD OF MONSTROUS SIZE! HE WEIGHED SIX TONS OR MORE! HE EPITOMIZED THE CONCEPT OF THE KILLER CARNIVORE!
HIS JAWS HAD TEETH LIKE RAILROAD SPIKES WITH FORE AND AFT SERRATIONS! THIS DENTAL HARDWARE WAS DESIGNED FOR QUICK EVISCERATIONS! WITH THRASHING BITES AND AWFUL ROARS THE T. REX WOULD ATTACK! HE WAS, IT'S CLEAR, A SAVAGE MESOZOIC MANIAC!
IMAGINE, THEN, THE PANIC CAUSED, THE HORROR AND THE MAYHEM, WHEN THIS MONSTER CAME TO TOWN AND ATE SOME FOLKS THIS A.M.! IT WAS A SIGHT FEW WILL FORGET! HE LUNGED INTO THE CROWD! THE MULTITUDE BECAME UNGLUED! THEIR SCREAMS WERE LONG AND LOUD!
PEOPLE PUSHED TO GET AWAY! THE ELDERLY AND SMALL WERE TRAMPLED UNDERFOOT BY THE ADVANCING HUMAN WALL! LITTLE TIM WAS ON AN ERRAND WITH HIS BROTHER HOWARD. THEY DAWDLED BY THE CANDY SHOP AND BOTH BOYS WERE DEVOURED.
A CAMERA CREW FROM CHANNEL THREE ARRIVED IN TOWN TO GIVE A LIVE REPORT. AT THIS THEY FAILED, BECAUSE THEY DIDN'T LIVE. AT LAST THE MENACE ATE HIS FILL. THE BIG TYRANNOSAUR STOMPED AWAY TO PARTS UNKNOWN WHERE HE HAD LIVED BEFORE.
TYRANNOSAURS, THOUGH RARELY SEEN, ARE CERTAINLY STILL AROUND. AND NO ONE KNOWS JUST WHERE OR WHEN THE NEXT ONE WILL BE FOUND.
BLOW YOUR NOSE, DEAR.
ACKGTH! NNGGRR! PTH!
... EXCEPT ME.

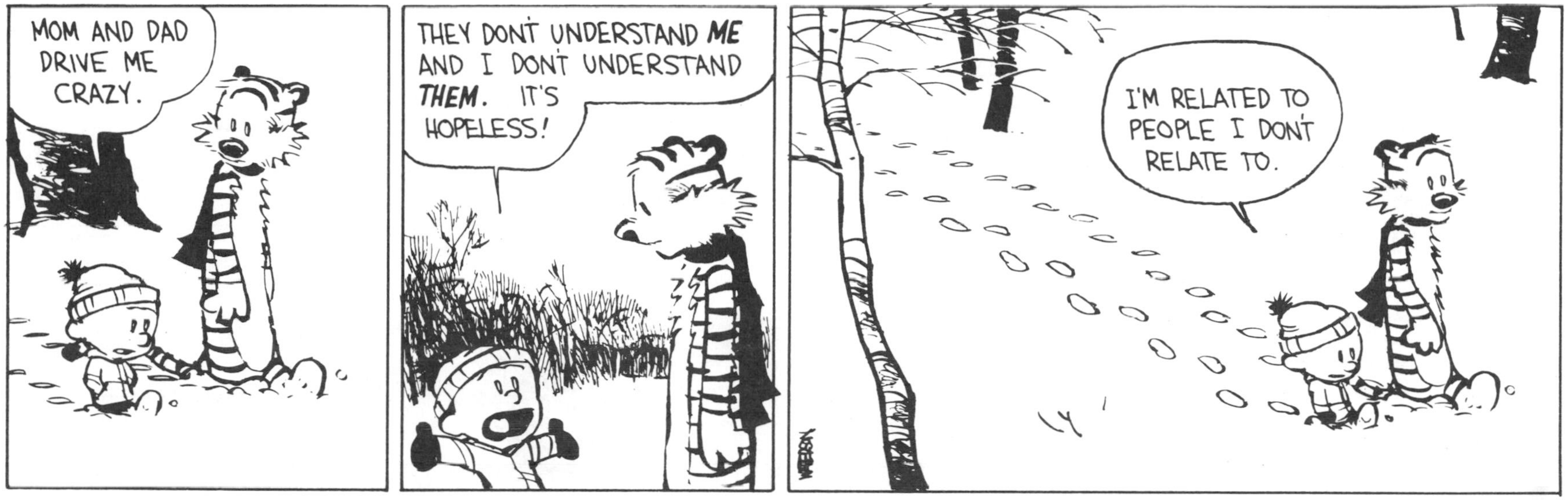
MOM AND DAD DRIVE ME CRAZY.
THEY DON'T UNDERSTAND **ME** AND I DON'T UNDERSTAND **THEM**. IT'S HOPELESS!
I'M RELATED TO PEOPLE I DON'T RELATE TO.
WATTERSON

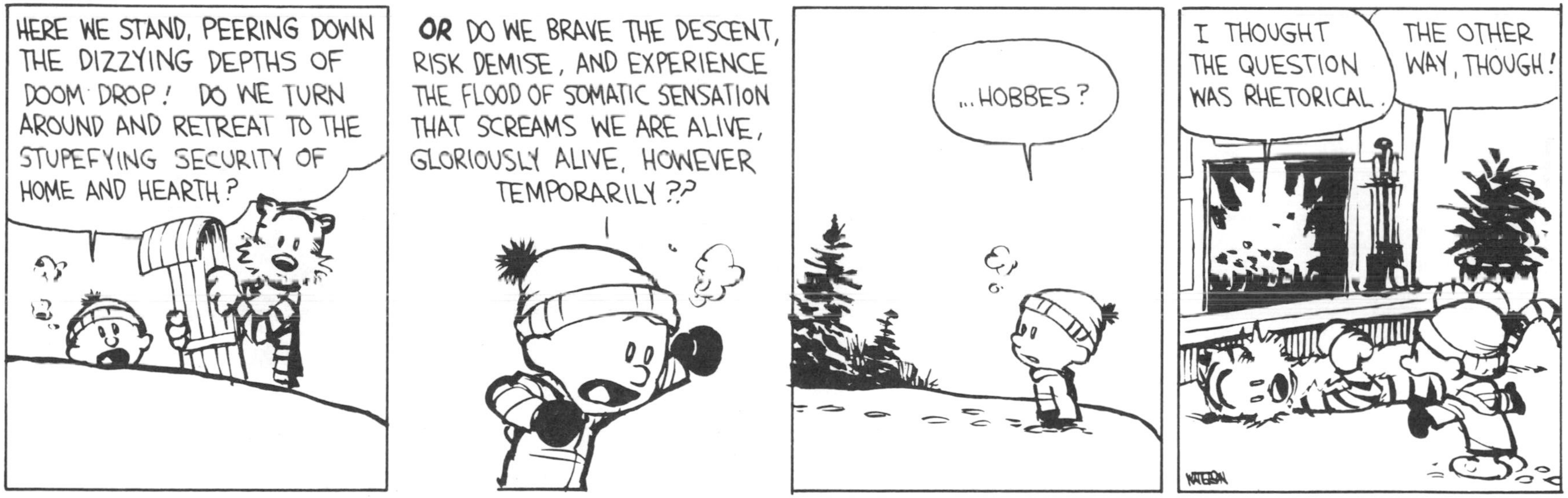
HERE WE STAND, PEERING DOWN THE DIZZYING DEPTHS OF DOOM DROP! DO WE TURN AROUND AND RETREAT TO THE STUPEFYING SECURITY OF HOME AND HEARTH?
OR DO WE BRAVE THE DESCENT, RISK DEMISE, AND EXPERIENCE THE FLOOD OF SOMATIC SENSATION THAT SCREAMS WE ARE ALIVE, GLORIOUSLY ALIVE, HOWEVER TEMPORARILY??
...HOBBES?
I THOUGHT THE QUESTION WAS RHETORICAL.
THE OTHER WAY, THOUGH!
WATTERSON

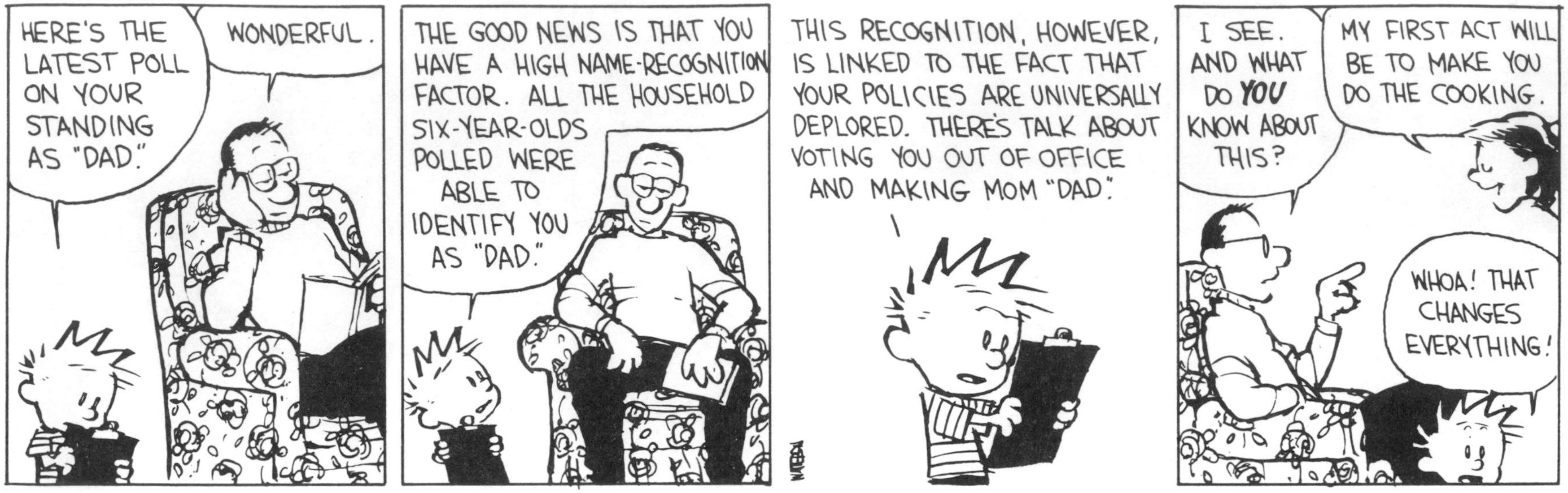
HERE'S THE LATEST POLL ON YOUR STANDING AS "DAD."
WONDERFUL.
THE GOOD NEWS IS THAT YOU HAVE A HIGH NAME-RECOGNITION FACTOR. ALL THE HOUSEHOLD SIX-YEAR-OLDS POLLED WERE ABLE TO IDENTIFY YOU AS "DAD."
THIS RECOGNITION, HOWEVER, IS LINKED TO THE FACT THAT YOUR POLICIES ARE UNIVERSALLY DEPLORED. THERE'S TALK ABOUT VOTING YOU OUT OF OFFICE AND MAKING MOM "DAD."
I SEE. AND WHAT DO *YOU* KNOW ABOUT THIS?
MY FIRST ACT WILL BE TO MAKE YOU DO THE COOKING.
WHOA! THAT CHANGES EVERYTHING!

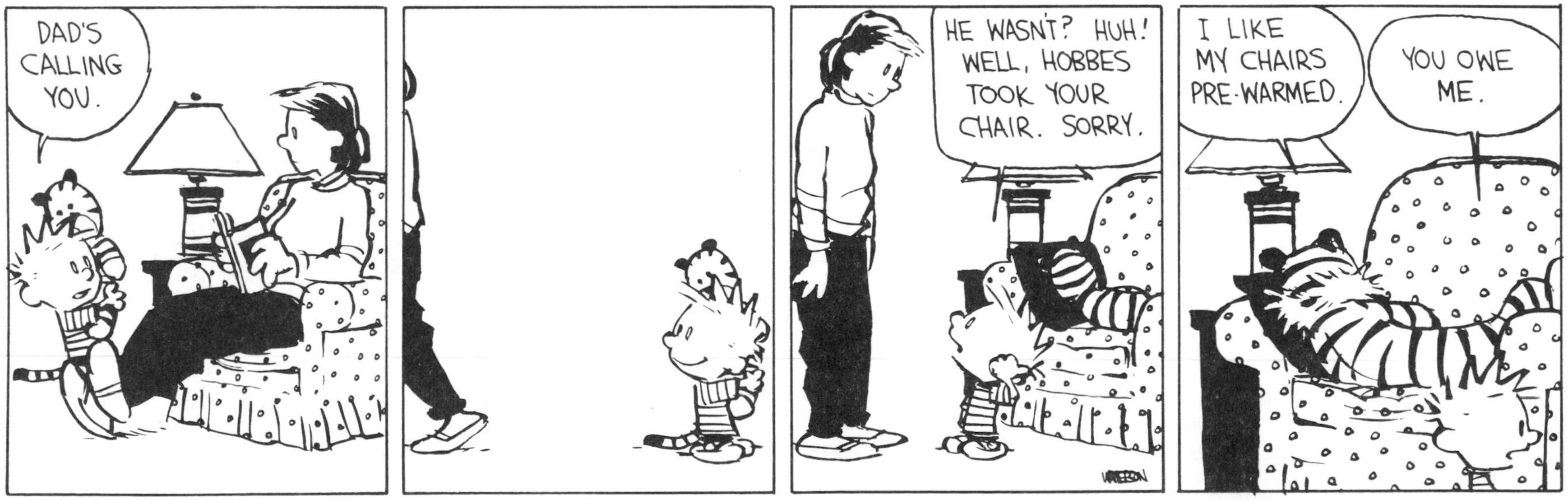
DAD'S CALLING YOU.
HE WASN'T? HUH! WELL, HOBBES TOOK YOUR CHAIR. SORRY.
I LIKE MY CHAIRS PRE-WARMED.
YOU OWE ME.

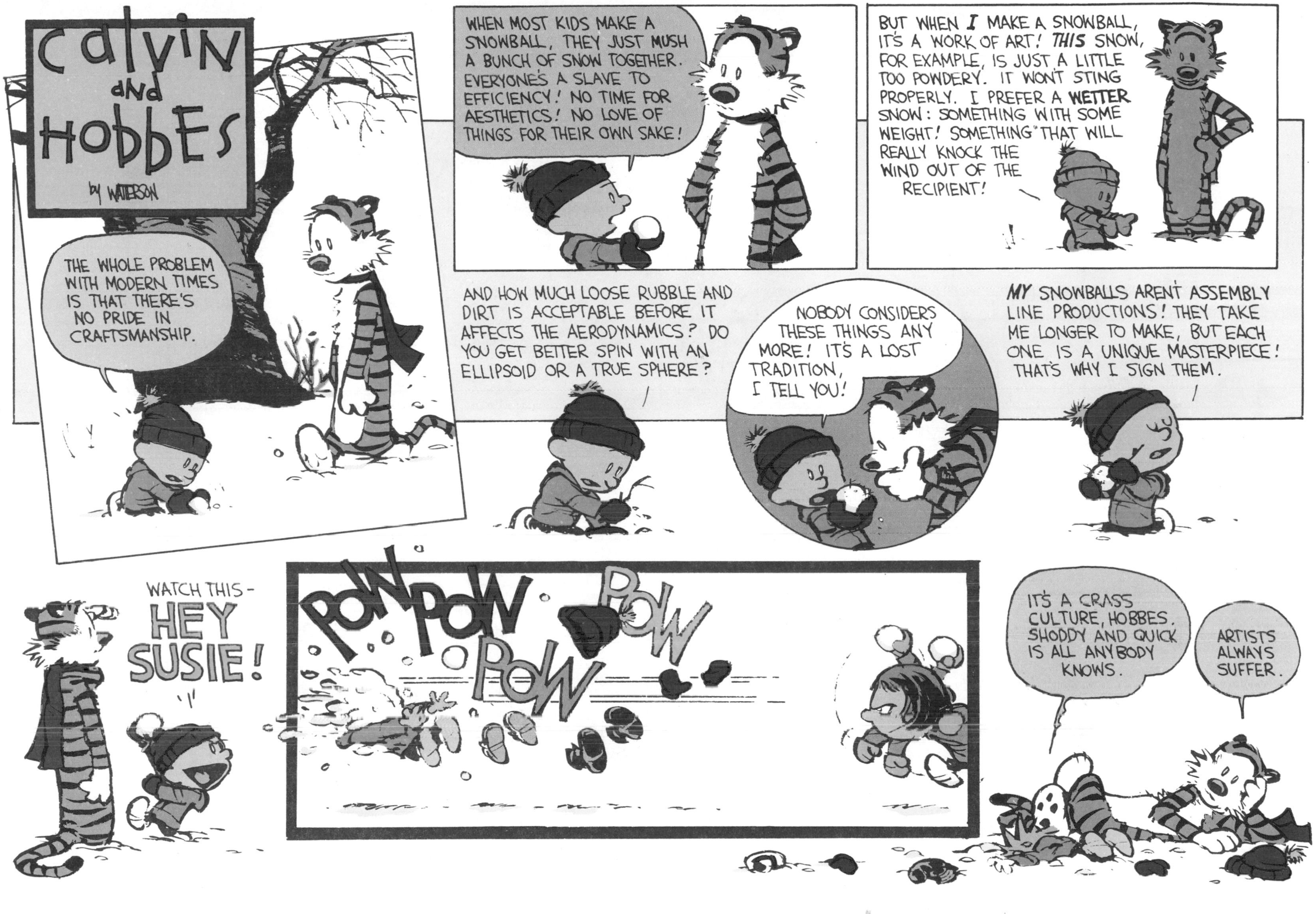
CALVIN AND HOBBES
by WATTERSON
THE WHOLE PROBLEM WITH MODERN TIMES IS THAT THERE'S NO PRIDE IN CRAFTSMANSHIP.
WHEN MOST KIDS MAKE A SNOWBALL, THEY JUST MUSH A BUNCH OF SNOW TOGETHER. EVERYONE'S A SLAVE TO EFFICIENCY! NO TIME FOR AESTHETICS! NO LOVE OF THINGS FOR THEIR OWN SAKE!
BUT WHEN I MAKE A SNOWBALL, IT'S A WORK OF ART! THIS SNOW, FOR EXAMPLE, IS JUST A LITTLE TOO POWDERY. IT WON'T STING PROPERLY. I PREFER A WETTER SNOW: SOMETHING WITH SOME WEIGHT! SOMETHING THAT WILL REALLY KNOCK THE WIND OUT OF THE RECIPIENT!
AND HOW MUCH LOOSE RUBBLE AND DIRT IS ACCEPTABLE BEFORE IT AFFECTS THE AERODYNAMICS? DO YOU GET BETTER SPIN WITH AN ELLIPSOID OR A TRUE SPHERE?
NOBODY CONSIDERS THESE THINGS ANY MORE! IT'S A LOST TRADITION, I TELL YOU!
MY SNOWBALLS AREN'T ASSEMBLY LINE PRODUCTIONS! THEY TAKE ME LONGER TO MAKE, BUT EACH ONE IS A UNIQUE MASTERPIECE! THAT'S WHY I SIGN THEM.
WATCH THIS-
HEY SUSIE!
POW POW POW POW
IT'S A CRASS CULTURE, HOBBES. SHODDY AND QUICK IS ALL ANYBODY KNOWS.
ARTISTS ALWAYS SUFFER.

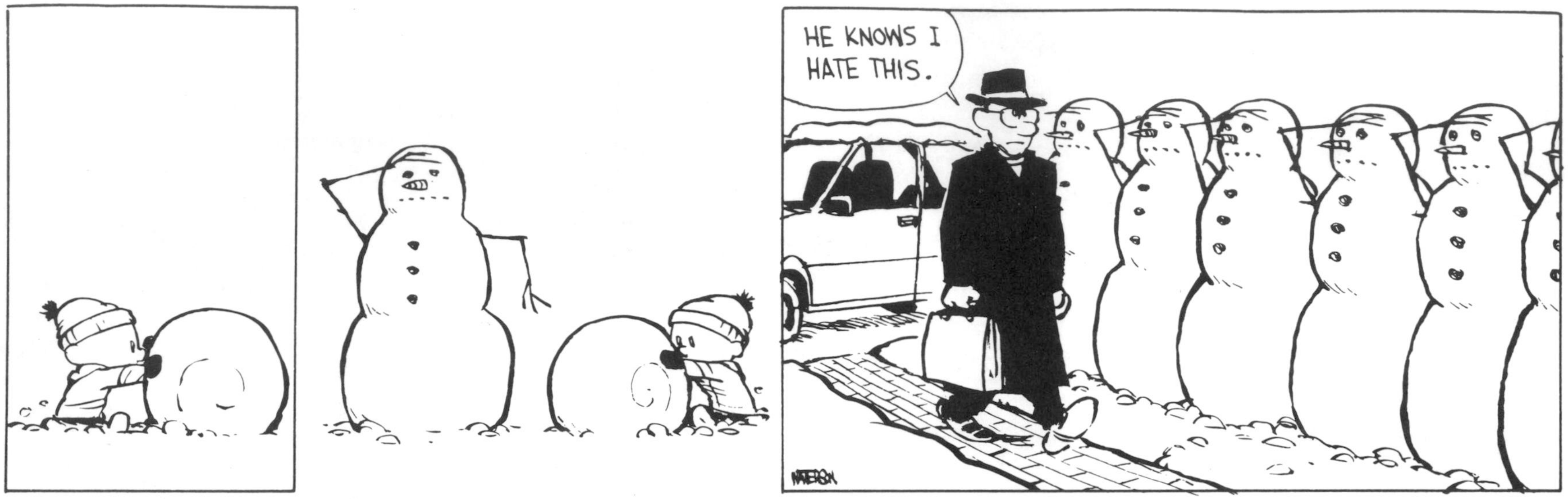
HE KNOWS I HATE THIS.

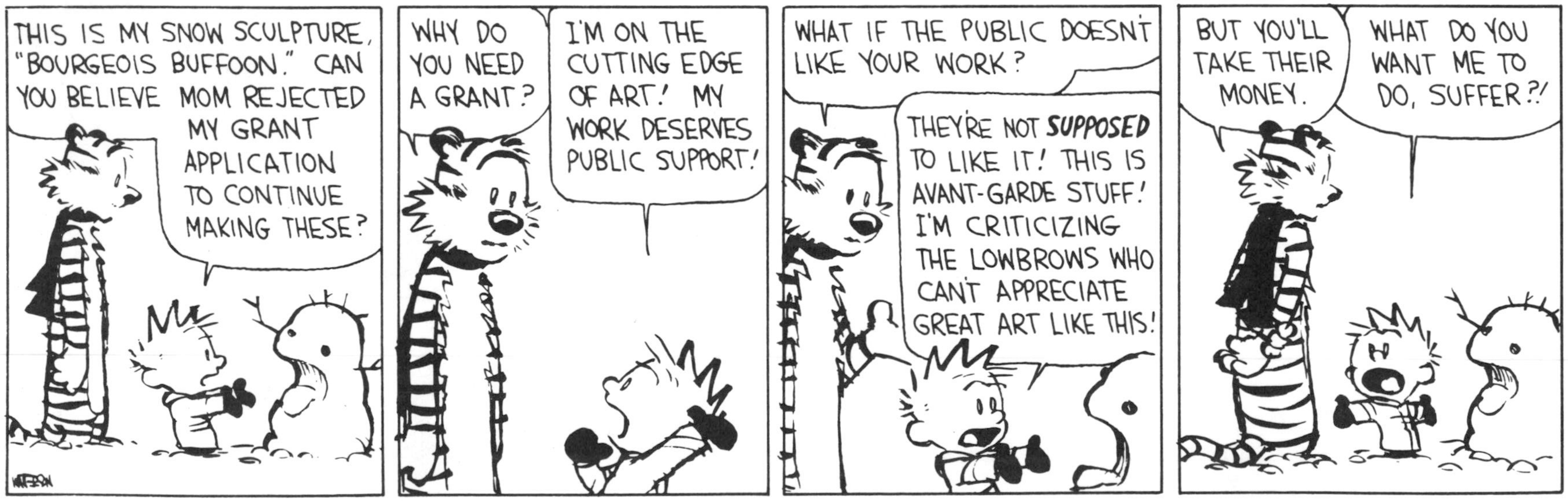
THIS IS MY SNOW SCULPTURE, "BOURGEOIS BUFFOON." CAN YOU BELIEVE MOM REJECTED MY GRANT APPLICATION TO CONTINUE MAKING THESE?
WHY DO YOU NEED A GRANT?
I'M ON THE CUTTING EDGE OF ART! MY WORK DESERVES PUBLIC SUPPORT!
WHAT IF THE PUBLIC DOESN'T LIKE YOUR WORK?
THEY'RE NOT SUPPOSED TO LIKE IT! THIS IS AVANT-GARDE STUFF! I'M CRITICIZING THE LOWBROWS WHO CAN'T APPRECIATE GREAT ART LIKE THIS!
BUT YOU'LL TAKE THEIR MONEY.
WHAT DO YOU WANT ME TO DO, SUFFER?!

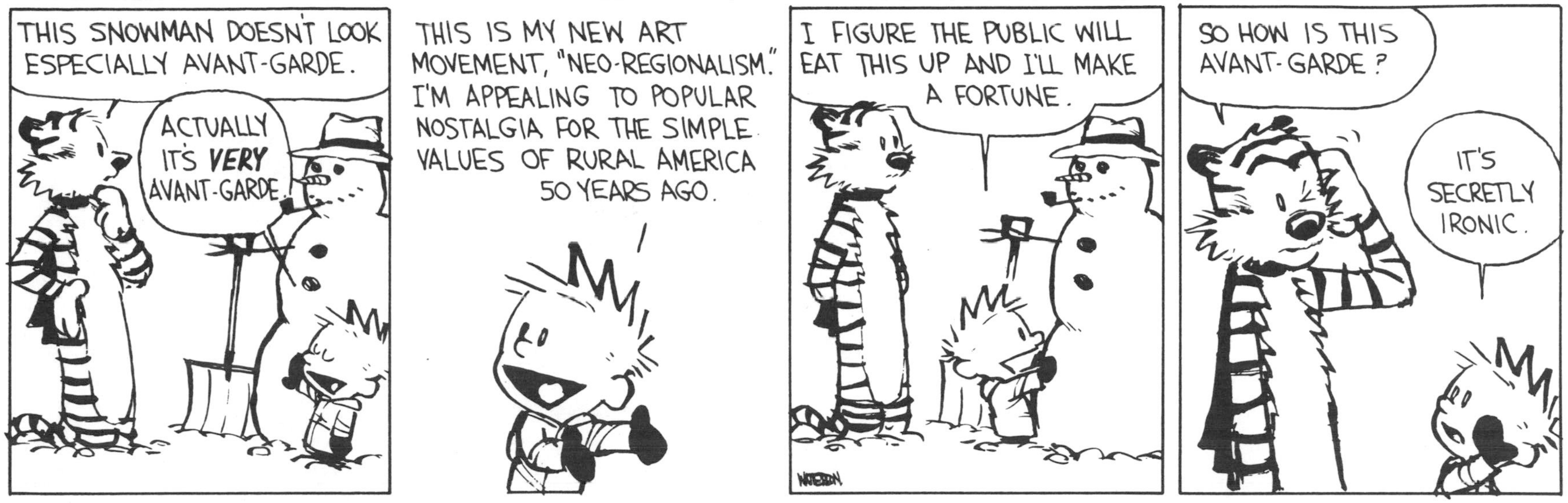
THIS SNOWMAN DOESN'T LOOK ESPECIALLY AVANT-GARDE.
ACTUALLY IT'S **VERY** AVANT-GARDE.
THIS IS MY NEW ART MOVEMENT, "NEO-REGIONALISM." I'M APPEALING TO POPULAR NOSTALGIA FOR THE SIMPLE VALUES OF RURAL AMERICA 50 YEARS AGO.
I FIGURE THE PUBLIC WILL EAT THIS UP AND I'LL MAKE A FORTUNE.
SO HOW IS THIS AVANT-GARDE?
IT'S SECRETLY IRONIC.

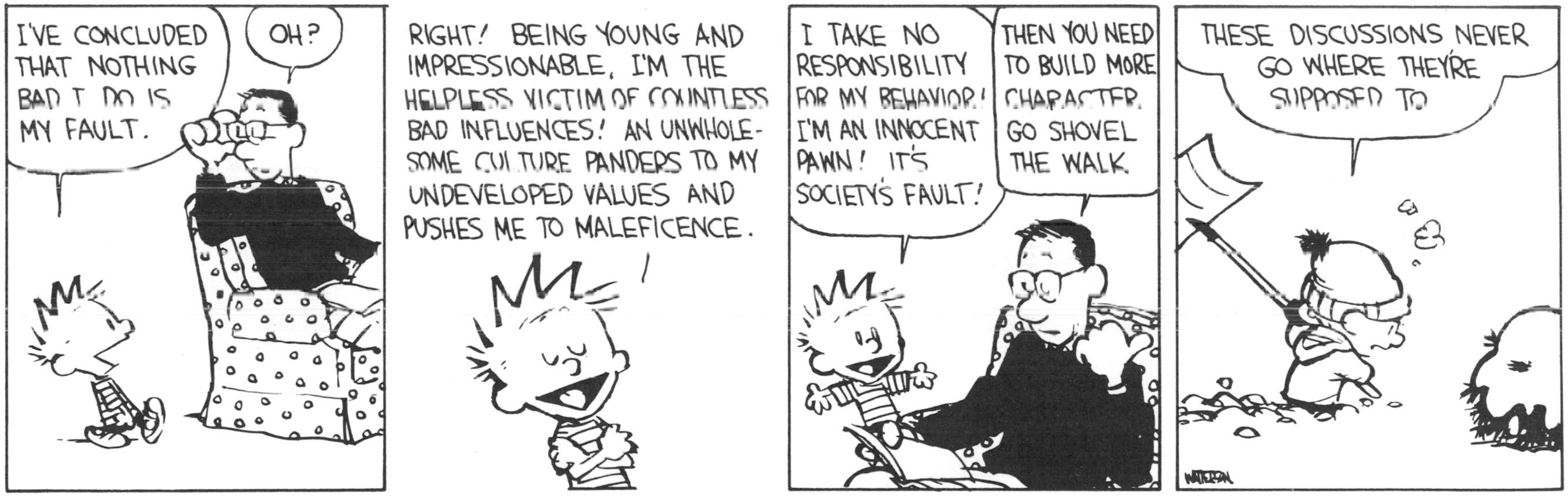
I'VE CONCLUDED THAT NOTHING BAD I DO IS MY FAULT.
OH?
RIGHT! BEING YOUNG AND IMPRESSIONABLE, I'M THE HELPLESS VICTIM OF COUNTLESS BAD INFLUENCES! AN UNWHOLESOME CULTURE PANDERS TO MY UNDEVELOPED VALUES AND PUSHES ME TO MALEFICENCE.
I TAKE NO RESPONSIBILITY FOR MY BEHAVIOR! I'M AN INNOCENT PAWN! IT'S SOCIETY'S FAULT!
THEN YOU NEED TO BUILD MORE CHARACTER. GO SHOVEL THE WALK.
THESE DISCUSSIONS NEVER GO WHERE THEY'RE SUPPOSED TO.

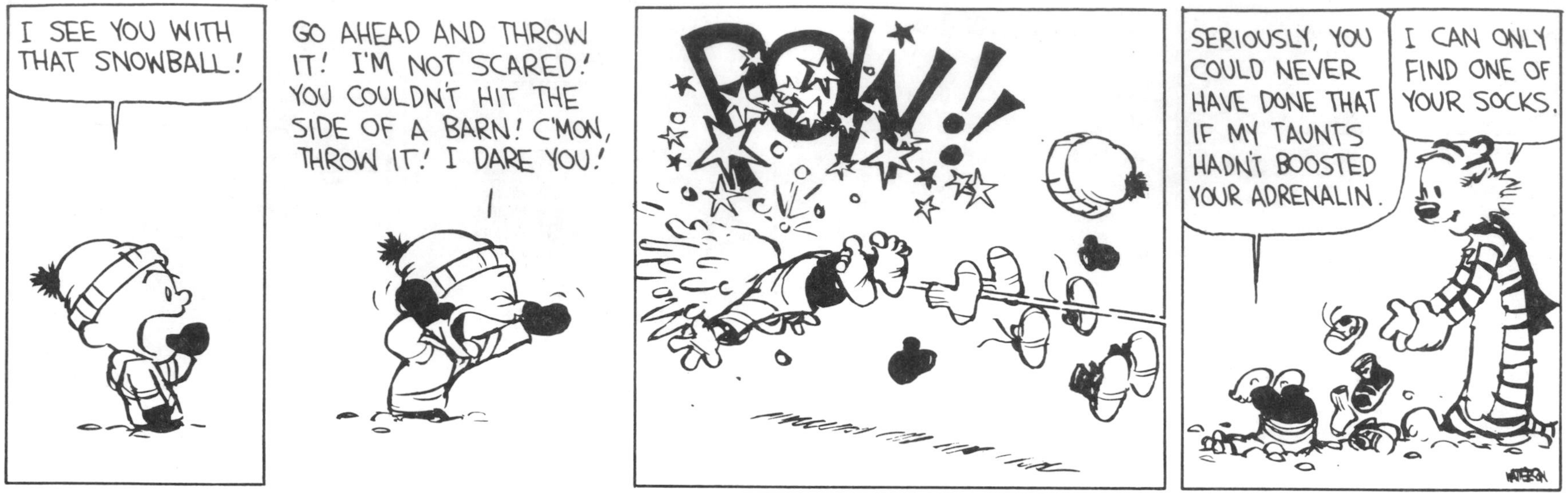
I SEE YOU WITH THAT SNOWBALL!
GO AHEAD AND THROW IT! I'M NOT SCARED! YOU COULDN'T HIT THE SIDE OF A BARN! C'MON, THROW IT! I DARE YOU!
POW!!
SERIOUSLY, YOU COULD NEVER HAVE DONE THAT IF MY TAUNTS HADN'T BOOSTED YOUR ADRENALIN.
I CAN ONLY FIND ONE OF YOUR SOCKS.

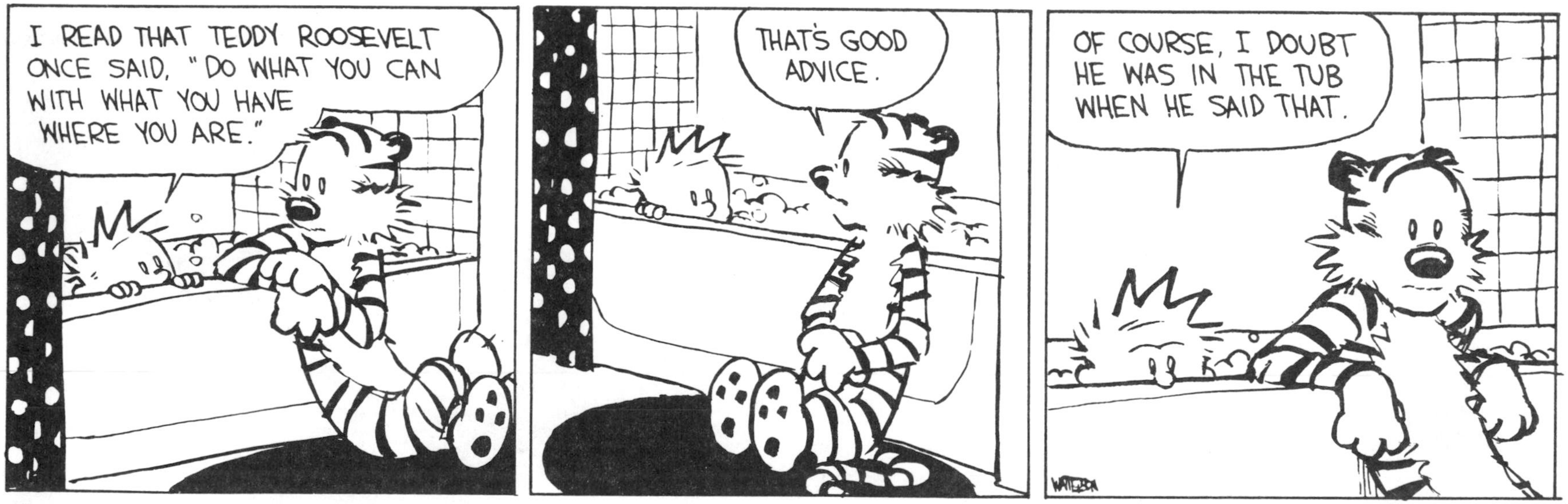
I READ THAT TEDDY ROOSEVELT ONCE SAID, "DO WHAT YOU CAN WITH WHAT YOU HAVE WHERE YOU ARE."
THAT'S GOOD ADVICE.
OF COURSE, I DOUBT HE WAS IN THE TUB WHEN HE SAID THAT.

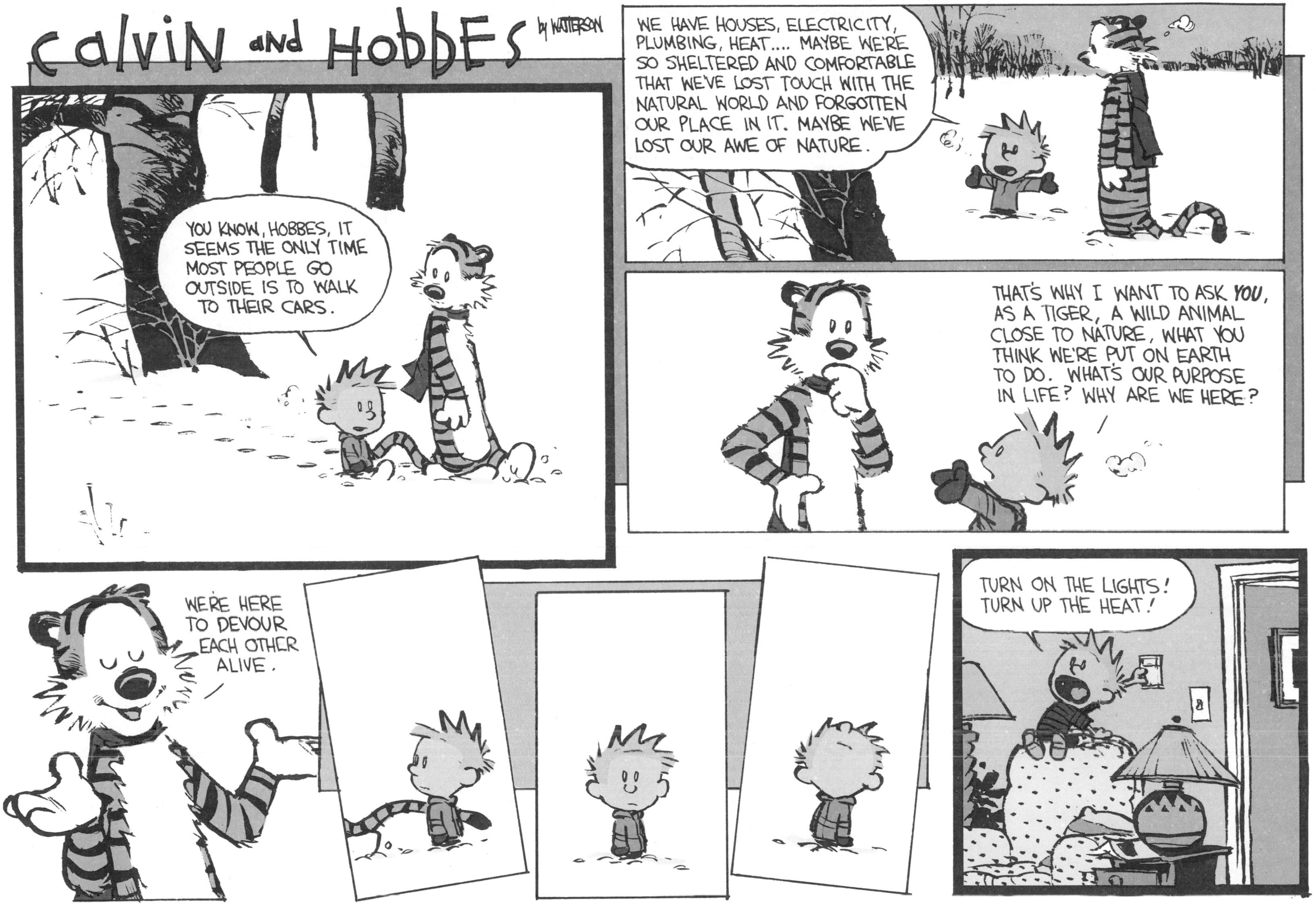
Calvin and Hobbes
by WATTERSON
YOU KNOW, HOBBES, IT SEEMS THE ONLY TIME MOST PEOPLE GO OUTSIDE IS TO WALK TO THEIR CARS.
WE HAVE HOUSES, ELECTRICITY, PLUMBING, HEAT.... MAYBE WE'RE SO SHELTERED AND COMFORTABLE THAT WE'VE LOST TOUCH WITH THE NATURAL WORLD AND FORGOTTEN OUR PLACE IN IT. MAYBE WE'VE LOST OUR AWE OF NATURE.
THAT'S WHY I WANT TO ASK YOU, AS A TIGER, A WILD ANIMAL CLOSE TO NATURE, WHAT YOU THINK WE'RE PUT ON EARTH TO DO. WHAT'S OUR PURPOSE IN LIFE? WHY ARE WE HERE?
WE'RE HERE TO DEVOUR EACH OTHER ALIVE.
TURN ON THE LIGHTS! TURN UP THE HEAT!

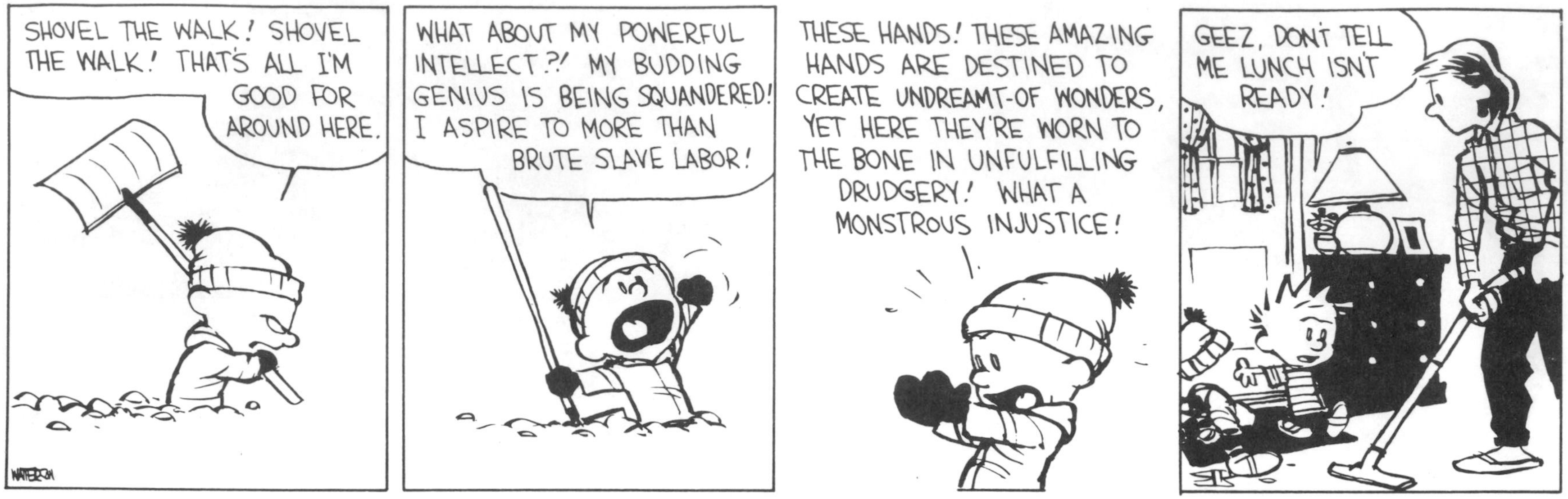
SHOVEL THE WALK! SHOVEL THE WALK! THAT'S ALL I'M GOOD FOR AROUND HERE.
WHAT ABOUT MY POWERFUL INTELLECT?! MY BUDDING GENIUS IS BEING SQUANDERED! I ASPIRE TO MORE THAN BRUTE SLAVE LABOR!
THESE HANDS! THESE AMAZING HANDS ARE DESTINED TO CREATE UNDREAMT-OF WONDERS, YET HERE THEY'RE WORN TO THE BONE IN UNFULFILLING DRUDGERY! WHAT A MONSTROUS INJUSTICE!
GEEZ, DON'T TELL ME LUNCH ISN'T READY!

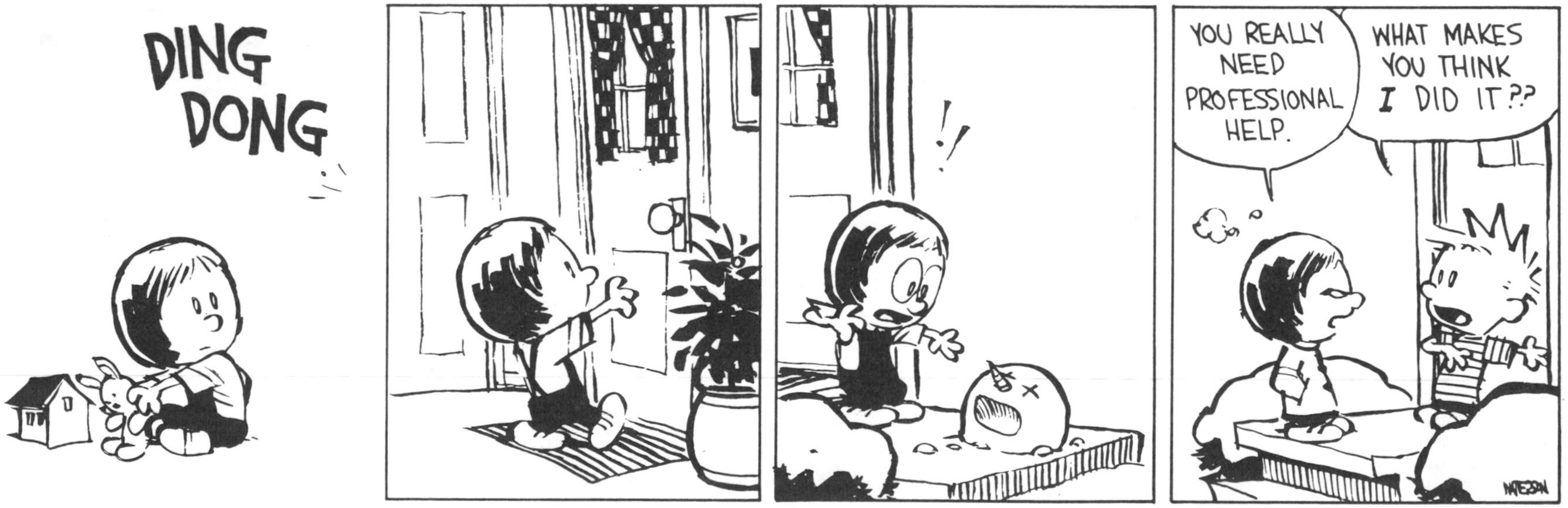
DING DONG
YOU REALLY NEED PROFESSIONAL HELP.
WHAT MAKES YOU THINK I DID IT??

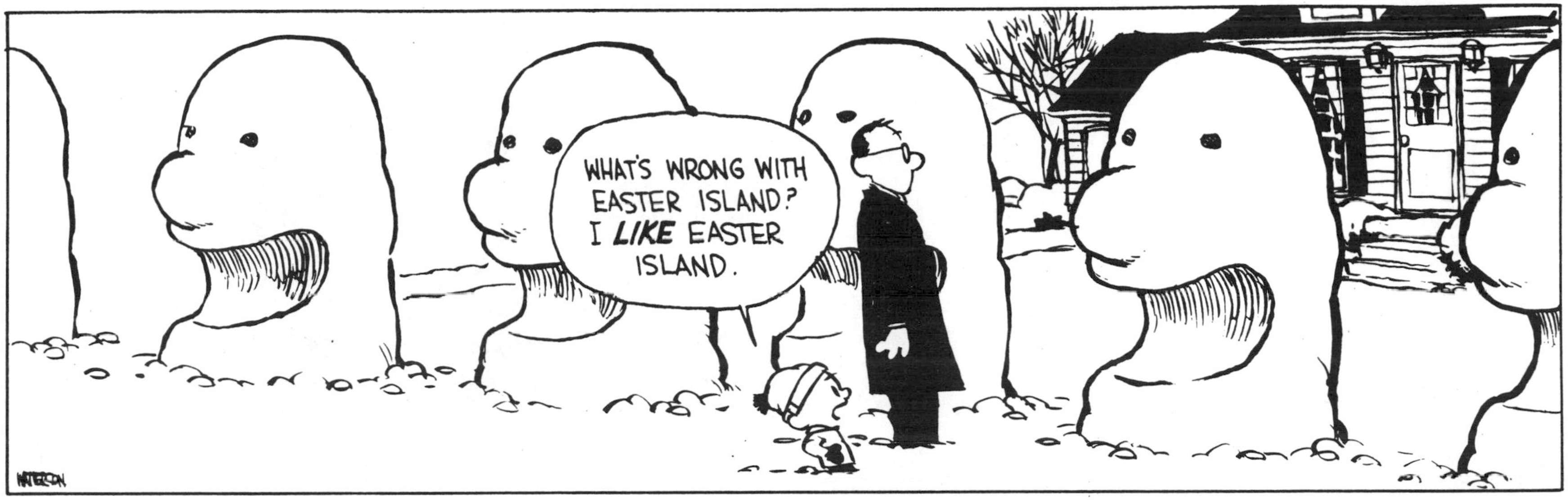
WHAT'S WRONG WITH EASTER ISLAND? I **LIKE** EASTER ISLAND.

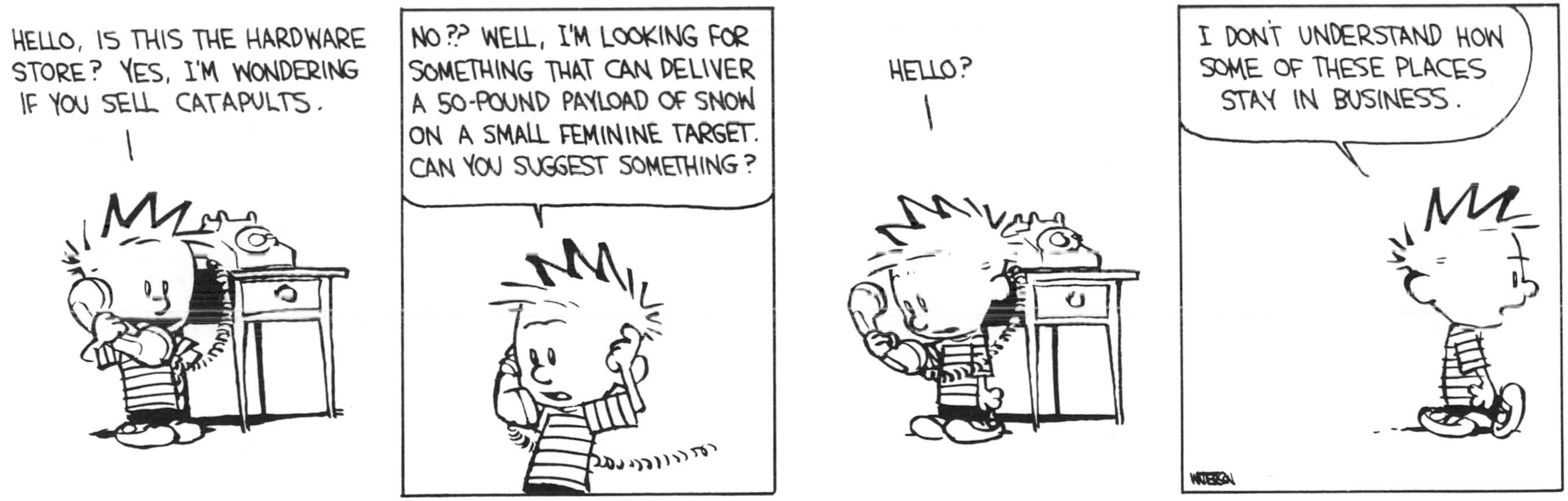
HELLO, IS THIS THE HARDWARE STORE? YES, I'M WONDERING IF YOU SELL CATAPULTS.
NO?? WELL, I'M LOOKING FOR SOMETHING THAT CAN DELIVER A 50-POUND PAYLOAD OF SNOW ON A SMALL FEMININE TARGET. CAN YOU SUGGEST SOMETHING?
HELLO?
I DON'T UNDERSTAND HOW SOME OF THESE PLACES STAY IN BUSINESS.

I DON'T THINK YOU HAVE ENOUGH TO DO.

I WON! I DID IT! I WON! I WON!
I'M THE CHAMPION! I'M THE BEST THERE IS! I'M THE TOP OF THE HEAP! HA HA HA!
IS THIS ALL THERE IS??

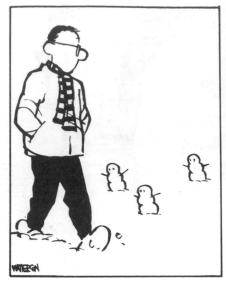

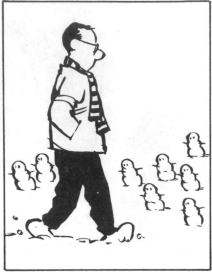

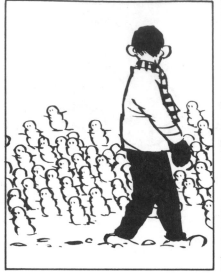

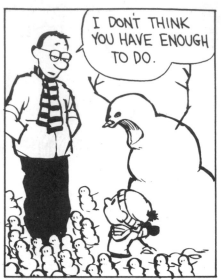

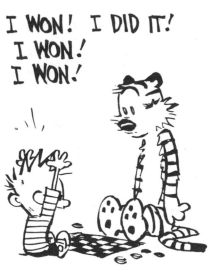

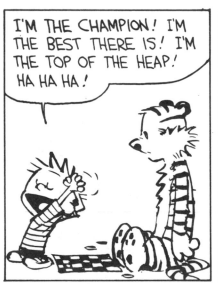

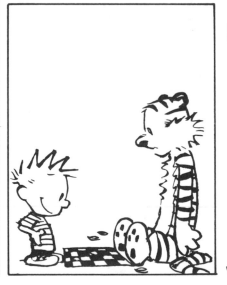

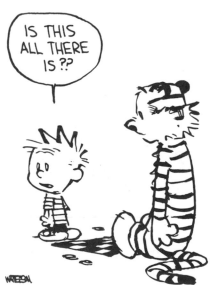

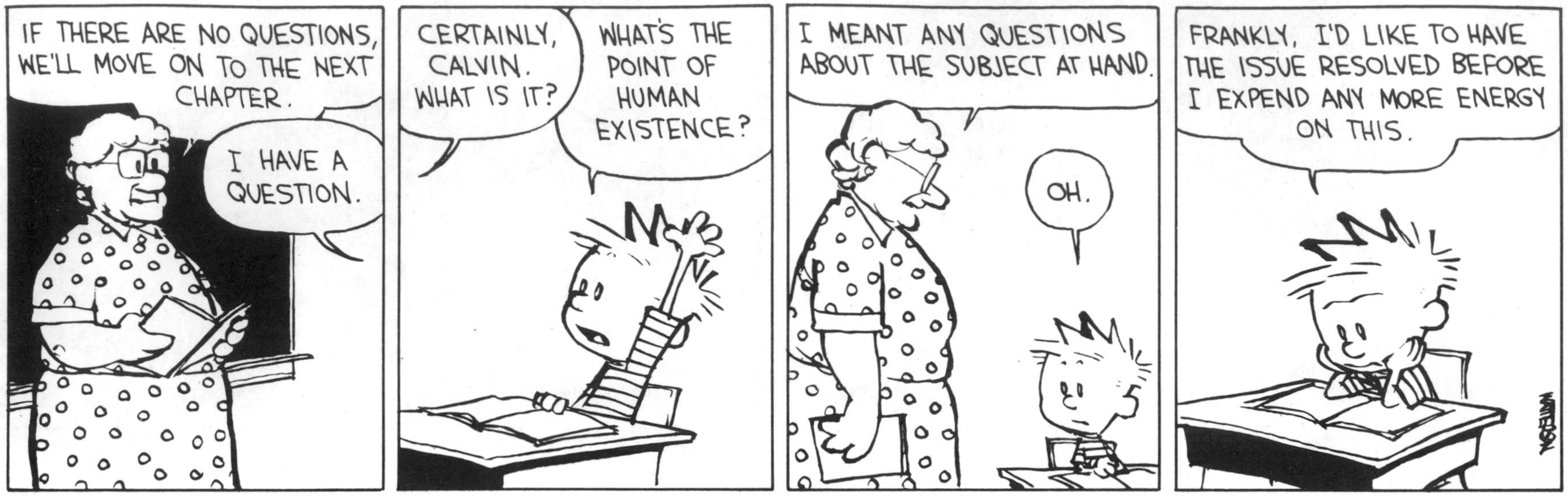
IF THERE ARE NO QUESTIONS, WE'LL MOVE ON TO THE NEXT CHAPTER.
I HAVE A QUESTION.
CERTAINLY, CALVIN. WHAT IS IT?
WHAT'S THE POINT OF HUMAN EXISTENCE?
I MEANT ANY QUESTIONS ABOUT THE SUBJECT AT HAND.
OH.
FRANKLY, I'D LIKE TO HAVE THE ISSUE RESOLVED BEFORE I EXPEND ANY MORE ENERGY ON THIS.
WATERSON

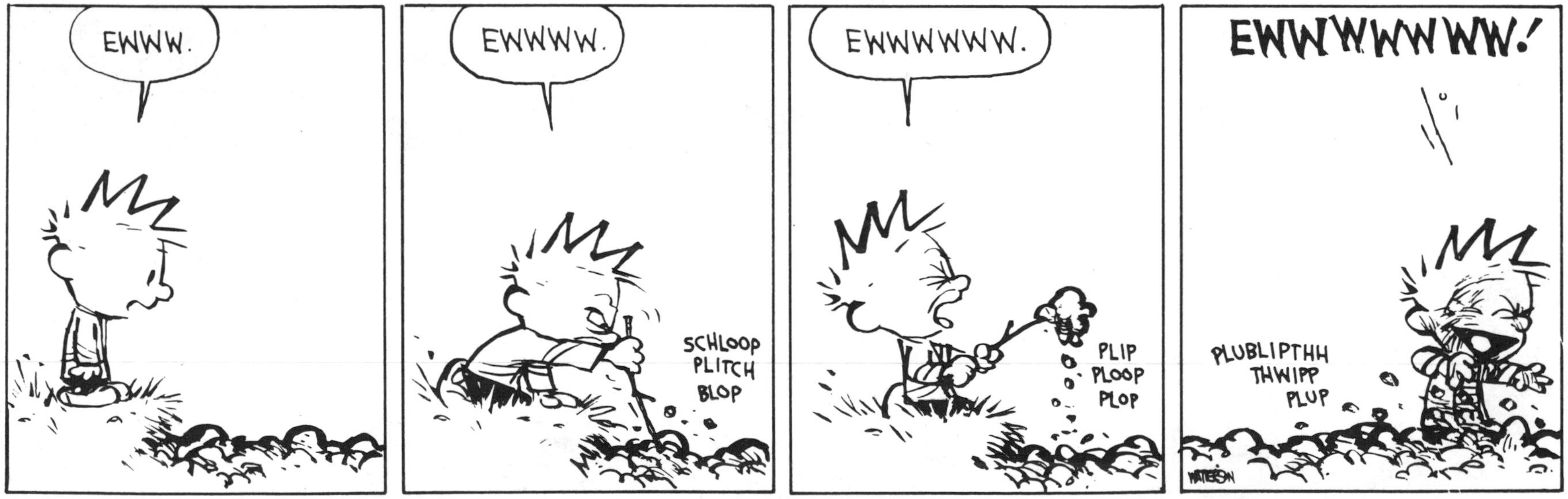
EWWW.
EWWWW.
SCHLOOP
PLITCH
BLOP
EWWWWWW.
PLIP
PLOOP
PLOP
EWWWWWWW!
PLUBLIPTHH
THWIPP
PLUP
WATERSON

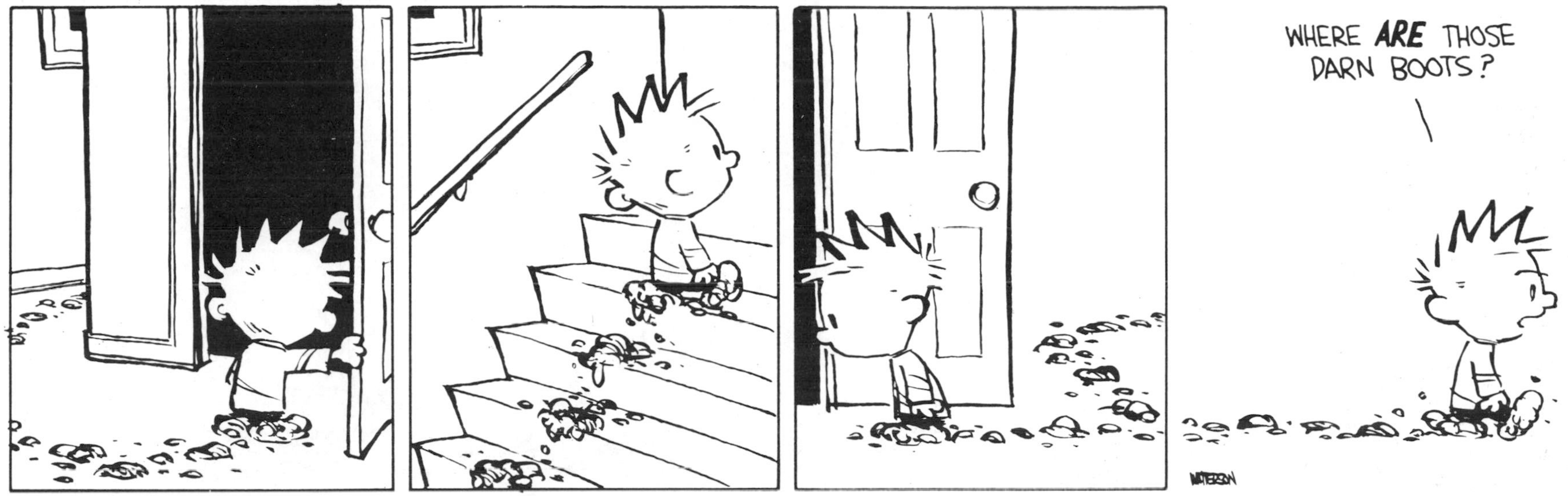
WHERE ARE THOSE DARN BOOTS?
WATTERSON

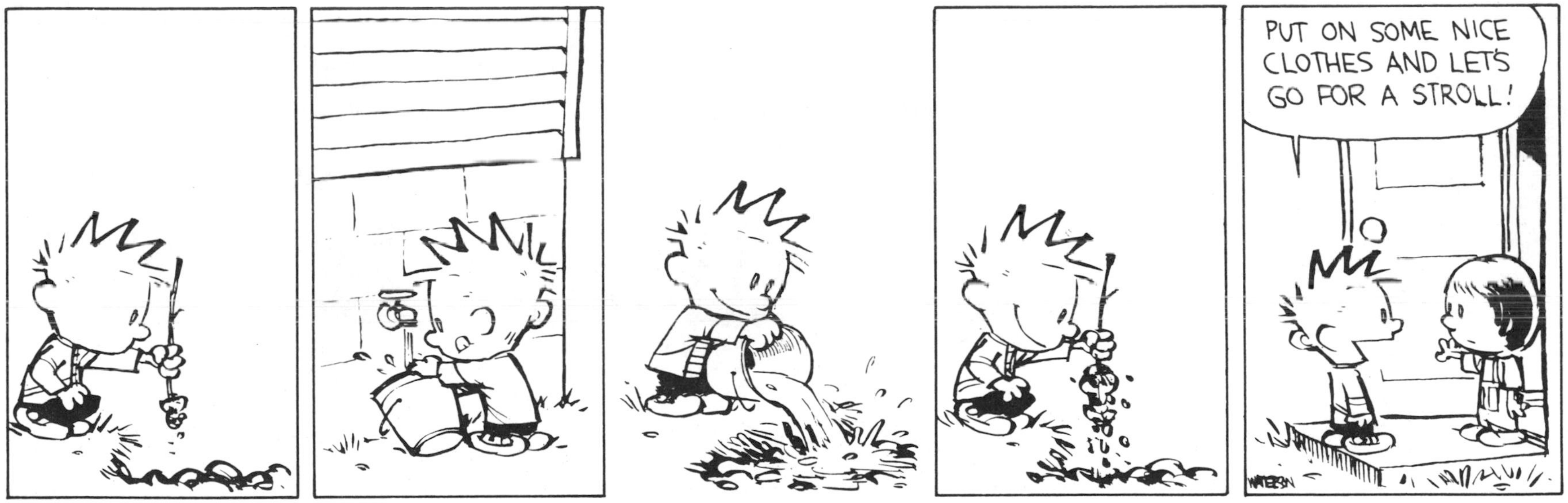
PUT ON SOME NICE CLOTHES AND LET'S GO FOR A STROLL!
WATTERSON

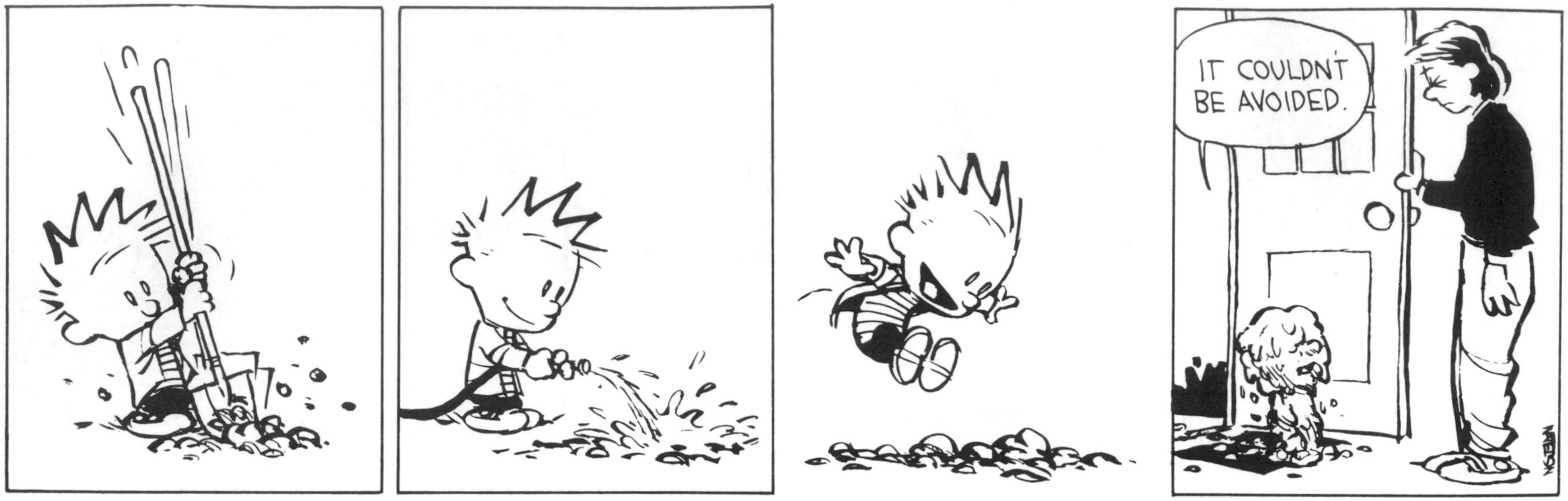
IT COULDN'T BE AVOIDED.

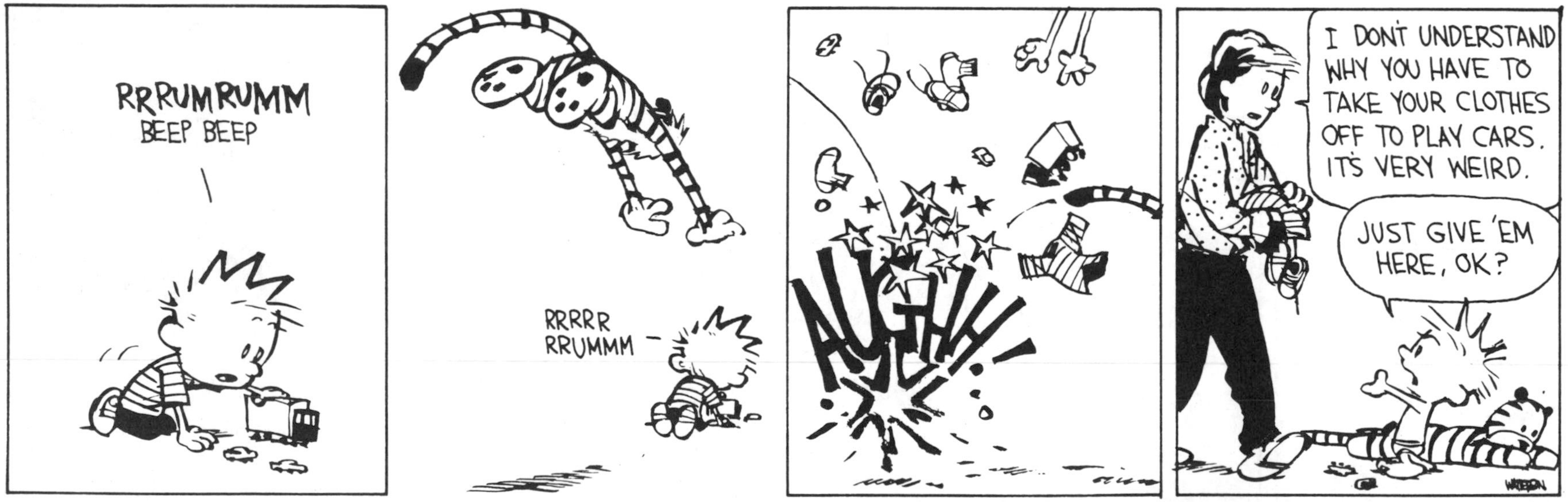
RRRUMRUMM
BEEP BEEP
RRRRR RRUMMM
AUGHH!
I DON'T UNDERSTAND WHY YOU HAVE TO TAKE YOUR CLOTHES OFF TO PLAY CARS. IT'S VERY WEIRD.
JUST GIVE 'EM HERE, OK?

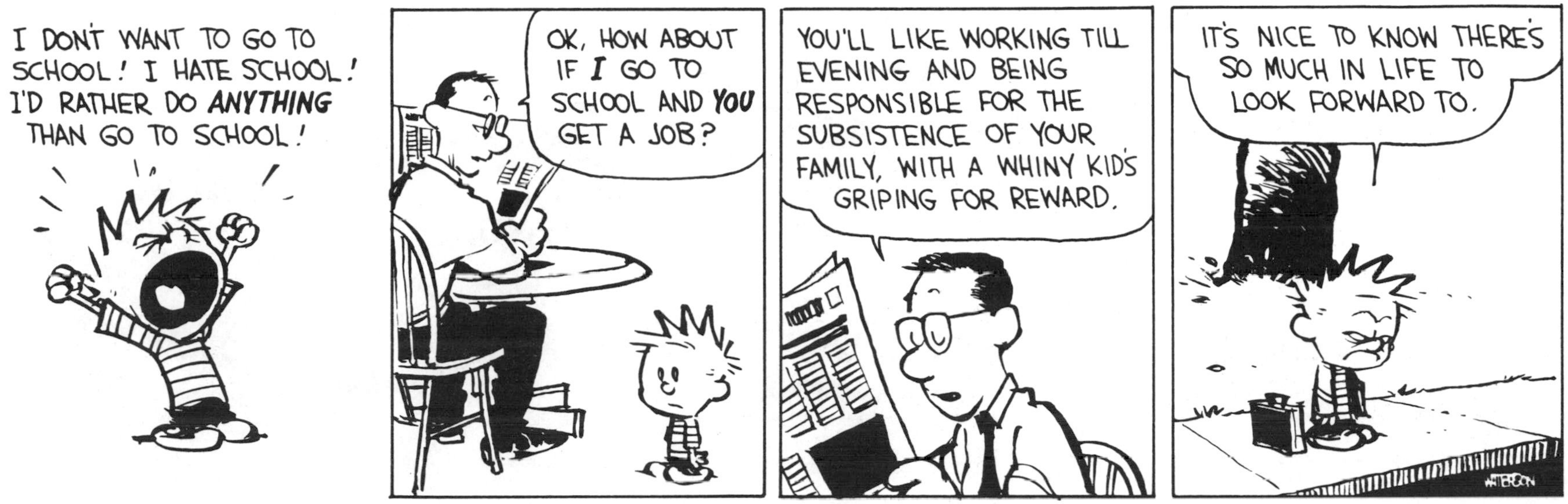
I DON'T WANT TO GO TO SCHOOL! I HATE SCHOOL! I'D RATHER DO **ANYTHING** THAN GO TO SCHOOL!
OK, HOW ABOUT IF ***I*** GO TO SCHOOL AND ***YOU*** GET A JOB?
YOU'LL LIKE WORKING TILL EVENING AND BEING RESPONSIBLE FOR THE SUBSISTENCE OF YOUR FAMILY, WITH A WHINY KID'S GRIPING FOR REWARD.
IT'S NICE TO KNOW THERE'S SO MUCH IN LIFE TO LOOK FORWARD TO.

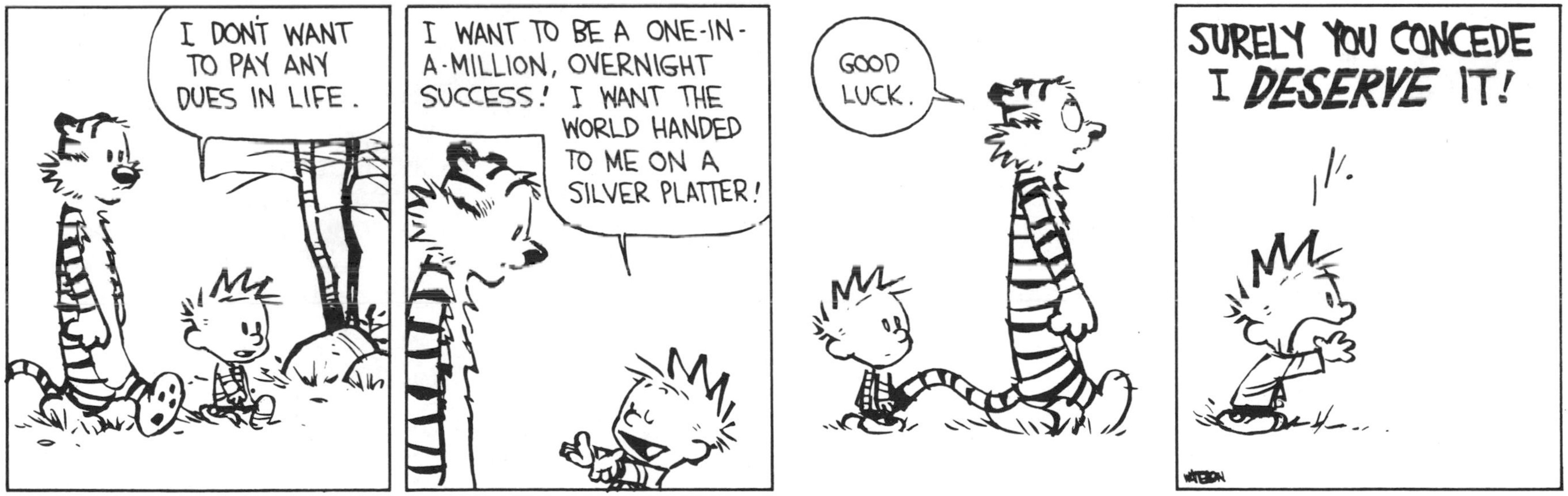
I DON'T WANT TO PAY ANY DUES IN LIFE.
I WANT TO BE A ONE-IN-A-MILLION, OVERNIGHT SUCCESS! I WANT THE WORLD HANDED TO ME ON A SILVER PLATTER!
GOOD LUCK.
SURELY YOU CONCEDE I ***DESERVE*** IT!

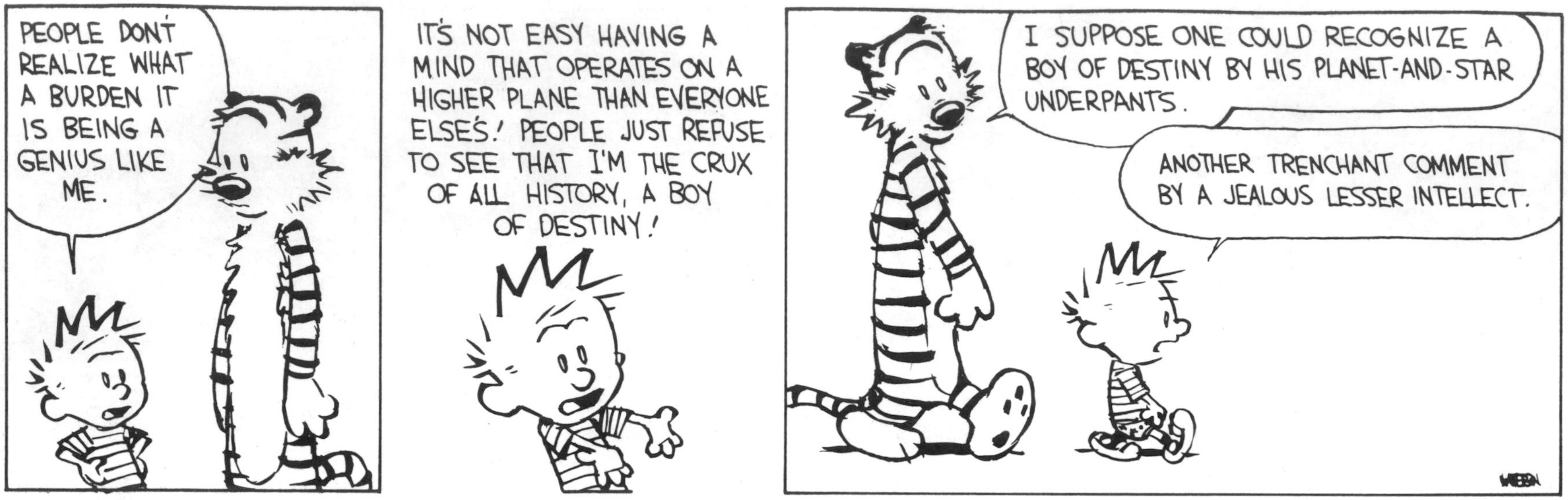
PEOPLE DON'T REALIZE WHAT A BURDEN IT IS BEING A GENIUS LIKE ME.
IT'S NOT EASY HAVING A MIND THAT OPERATES ON A HIGHER PLANE THAN EVERYONE ELSE'S! PEOPLE JUST REFUSE TO SEE THAT I'M THE CRUX OF ALL HISTORY, A BOY OF DESTINY!
I SUPPOSE ONE COULD RECOGNIZE A BOY OF DESTINY BY HIS PLANET-AND-STAR UNDERPANTS.
ANOTHER TRENCHANT COMMENT BY A JEALOUS LESSER INTELLECT.
WATERSON

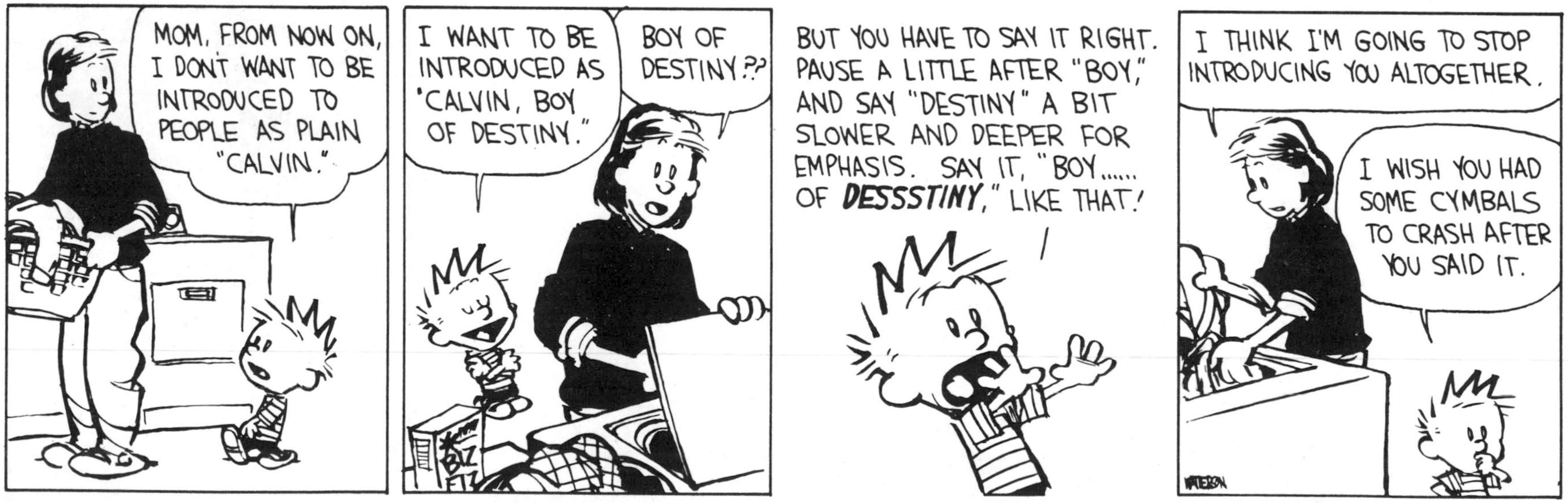
MOM, FROM NOW ON, I DON'T WANT TO BE INTRODUCED TO PEOPLE AS PLAIN "CALVIN."
I WANT TO BE INTRODUCED AS "CALVIN, BOY OF DESTINY."
BOY OF DESTINY ??
BUT YOU HAVE TO SAY IT RIGHT. PAUSE A LITTLE AFTER "BOY," AND SAY "DESTINY" A BIT SLOWER AND DEEPER FOR EMPHASIS. SAY IT, "BOY...... OF **DESSSTINY**," LIKE THAT!
I THINK I'M GOING TO STOP INTRODUCING YOU ALTOGETHER.
I WISH YOU HAD SOME CYMBALS TO CRASH AFTER YOU SAID IT.
WATERSON

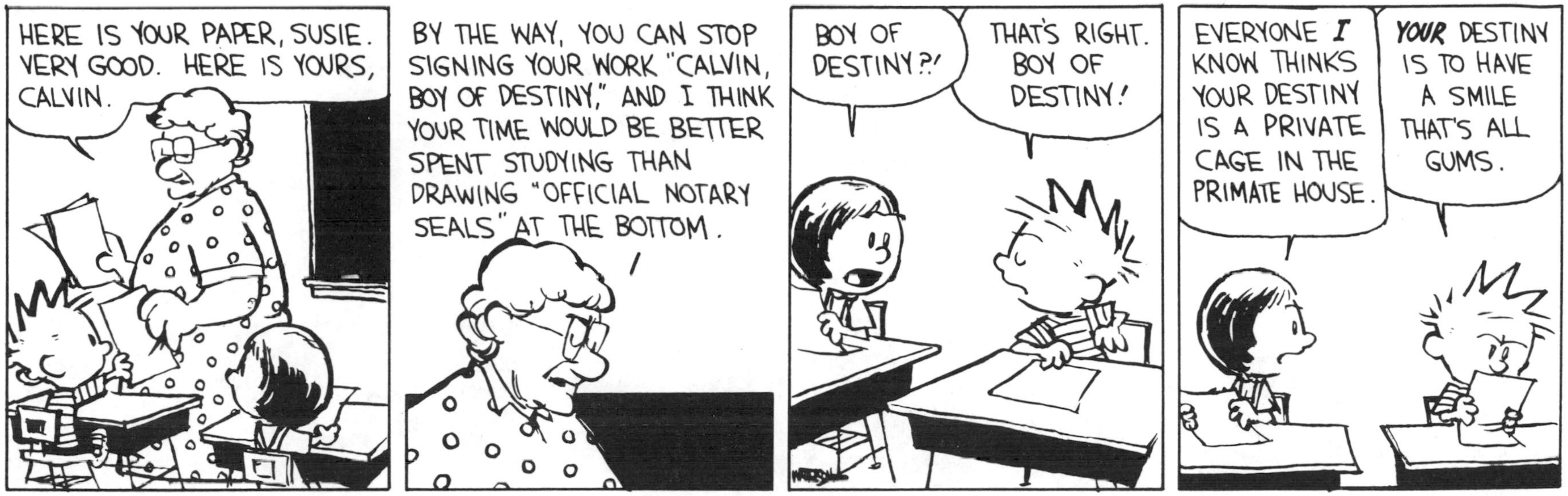
HERE IS YOUR PAPER, SUSIE. VERY GOOD. HERE IS YOURS, CALVIN.
BY THE WAY, YOU CAN STOP SIGNING YOUR WORK "CALVIN, BOY OF DESTINY," AND I THINK YOUR TIME WOULD BE BETTER SPENT STUDYING THAN DRAWING "OFFICIAL NOTARY SEALS" AT THE BOTTOM.
BOY OF DESTINY ?!
THAT'S RIGHT. BOY OF DESTINY!
EVERYONE *I* KNOW THINKS YOUR DESTINY IS A PRIVATE CAGE IN THE PRIMATE HOUSE.
YOUR DESTINY IS TO HAVE A SMILE THAT'S ALL GUMS.

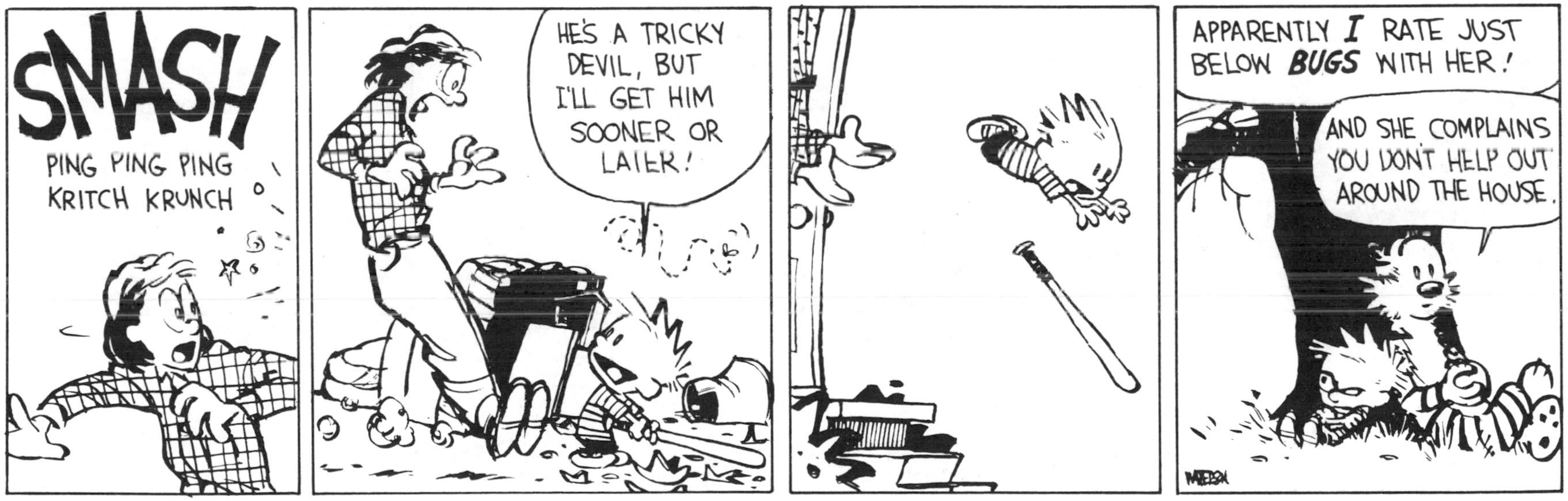
SMASH
PING PING PING
KRITCH KRUNCH
HE'S A TRICKY DEVIL, BUT I'LL GET HIM SOONER OR LATER!
APPARENTLY *I* RATE JUST BELOW **BUGS** WITH HER!
AND SHE COMPLAINS YOU DON'T HELP OUT AROUND THE HOUSE.

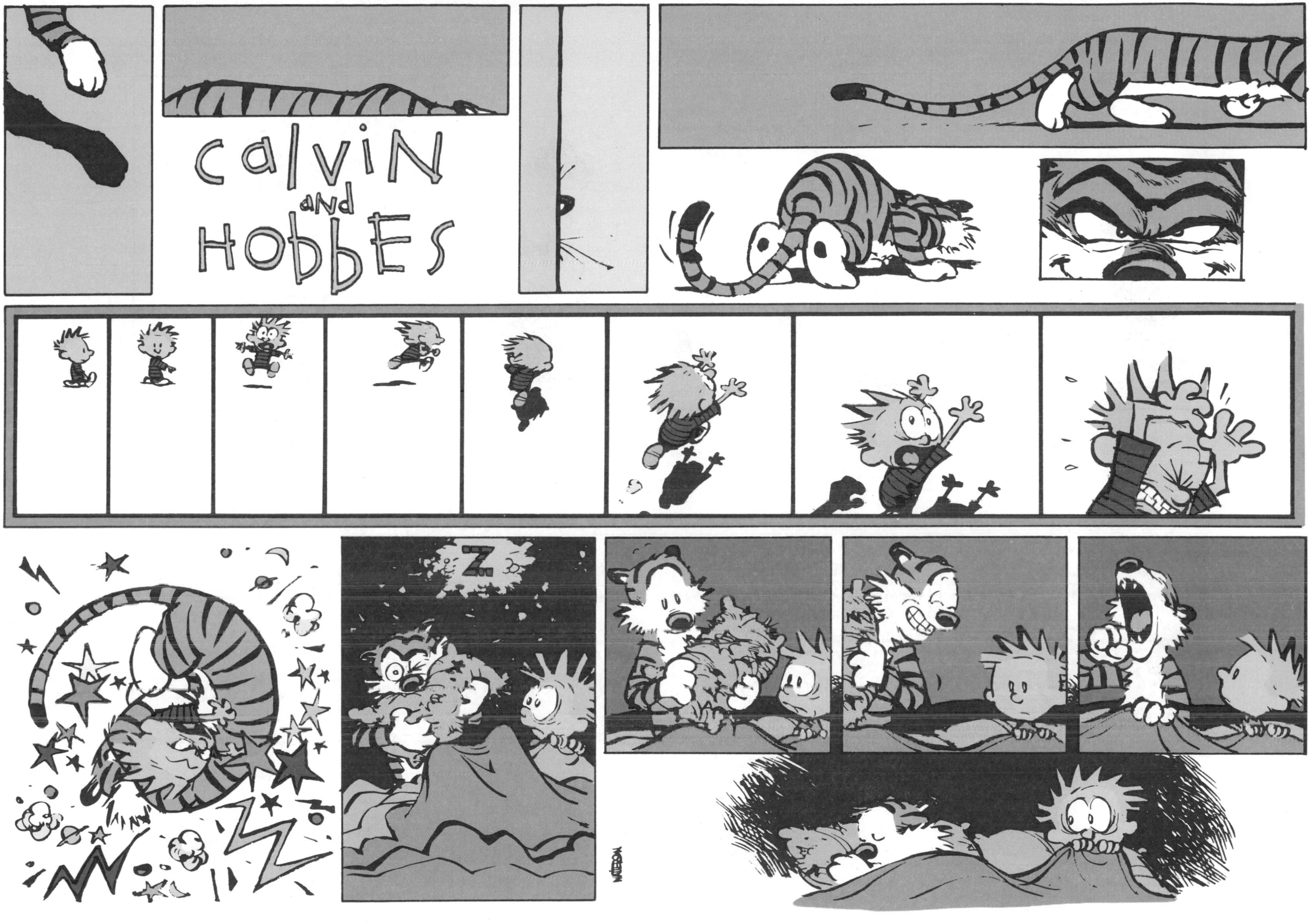
Calvin and Hobbes
Z

Wimp!
OH.... OH YEAH!??
WHAT REALLY BUGS ME IS KNOWING I'LL PROBABLY COME UP WITH A MUCH SHARPER RETORT SOMETIME TONIGHT.

CALVIN, CAN YOU TELL US WHAT LEWIS AND CLARK DID?
NO, BUT I CAN RECITE THE SECRET SUPERHERO ORIGIN OF EACH MEMBER OF CAPTAIN NAPALM'S THERMO-NUCLEAR LEAGUE OF LIBERTY.
SEE ME AFTER CLASS, CALVIN.
I'M NOT DUMB. I JUST HAVE A COMMAND OF THOROUGHLY USELESS INFORMATION.

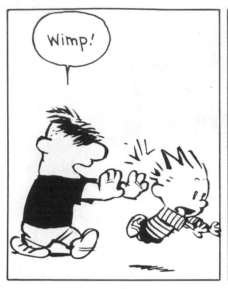

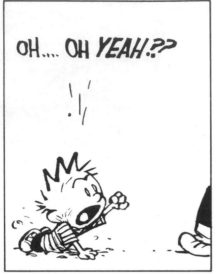

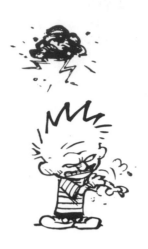

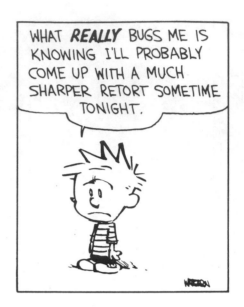

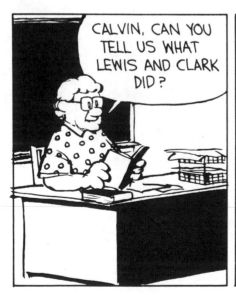

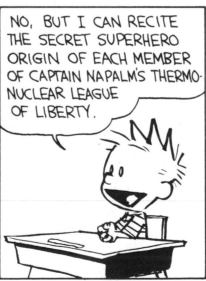

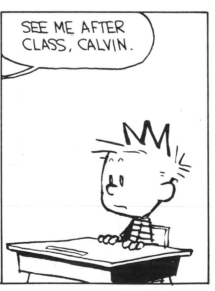

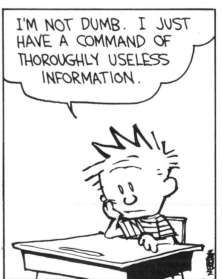

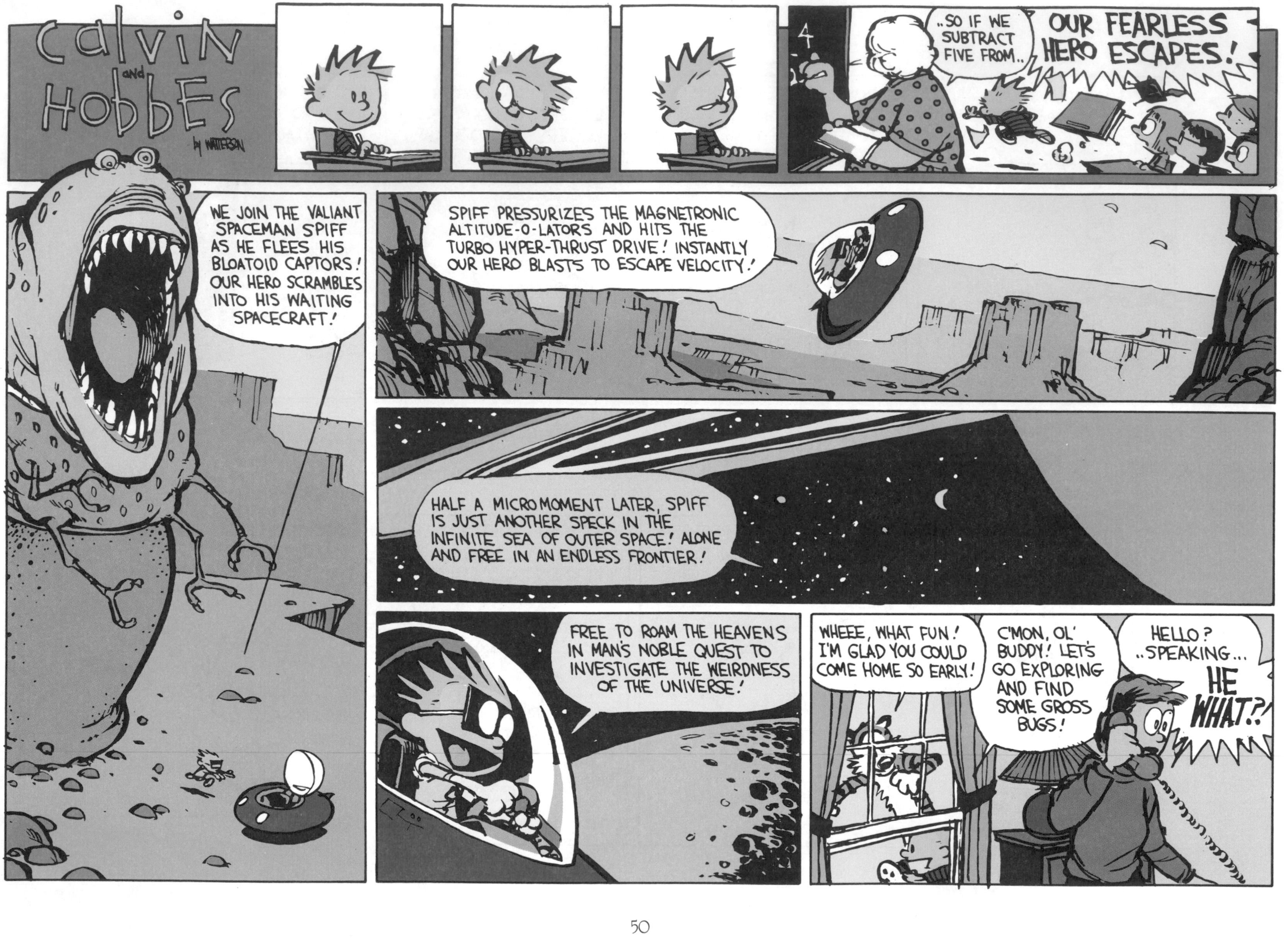
Calvin and Hobbes
by WATTERSON
..SO IF WE SUBTRACT FIVE FROM..
OUR FEARLESS HERO ESCAPES!
WE JOIN THE VALIANT SPACEMAN SPIFF AS HE FLEES HIS BLOATOID CAPTORS! OUR HERO SCRAMBLES INTO HIS WAITING SPACECRAFT!
SPIFF PRESSURIZES THE MAGNETRONIC ALTITUDE-O-LATORS AND HITS THE TURBO HYPER-THRUST DRIVE! INSTANTLY OUR HERO BLASTS TO ESCAPE VELOCITY!
HALF A MICROMOMENT LATER, SPIFF IS JUST ANOTHER SPECK IN THE INFINITE SEA OF OUTER SPACE! ALONE AND FREE IN AN ENDLESS FRONTIER!
FREE TO ROAM THE HEAVENS IN MAN'S NOBLE QUEST TO INVESTIGATE THE WEIRDNESS OF THE UNIVERSE!
WHEEE, WHAT FUN! I'M GLAD YOU COULD COME HOME SO EARLY!
C'MON, OL' BUDDY! LET'S GO EXPLORING AND FIND SOME GROSS BUGS!
HELLO? ..SPEAKING...
HE WHAT?!

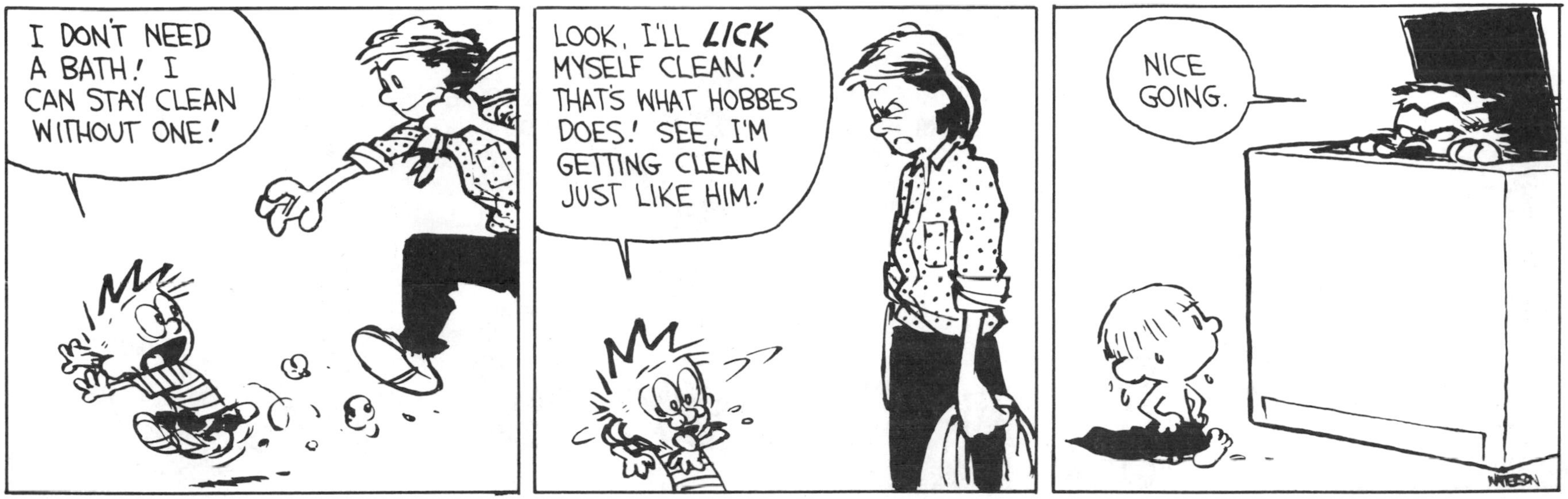
I DON'T NEED A BATH! I CAN STAY CLEAN WITHOUT ONE!
LOOK, I'LL LICK MYSELF CLEAN! THAT'S WHAT HOBBES DOES! SEE, I'M GETTING CLEAN JUST LIKE HIM!
NICE GOING.

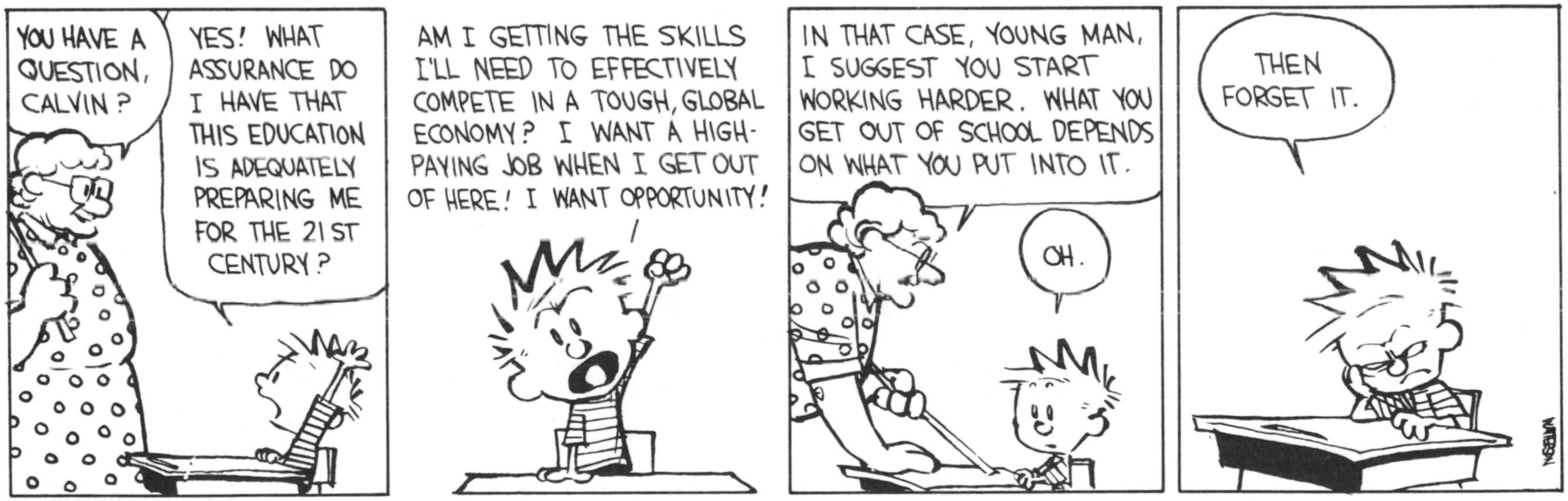
YOU HAVE A QUESTION, CALVIN?
YES! WHAT ASSURANCE DO I HAVE THAT THIS EDUCATION IS ADEQUATELY PREPARING ME FOR THE 21ST CENTURY?
AM I GETTING THE SKILLS I'LL NEED TO EFFECTIVELY COMPETE IN A TOUGH, GLOBAL ECONOMY? I WANT A HIGH-PAYING JOB WHEN I GET OUT OF HERE! I WANT OPPORTUNITY!
IN THAT CASE, YOUNG MAN, I SUGGEST YOU START WORKING HARDER. WHAT YOU GET OUT OF SCHOOL DEPENDS ON WHAT YOU PUT INTO IT.
OH.
THEN FORGET IT.

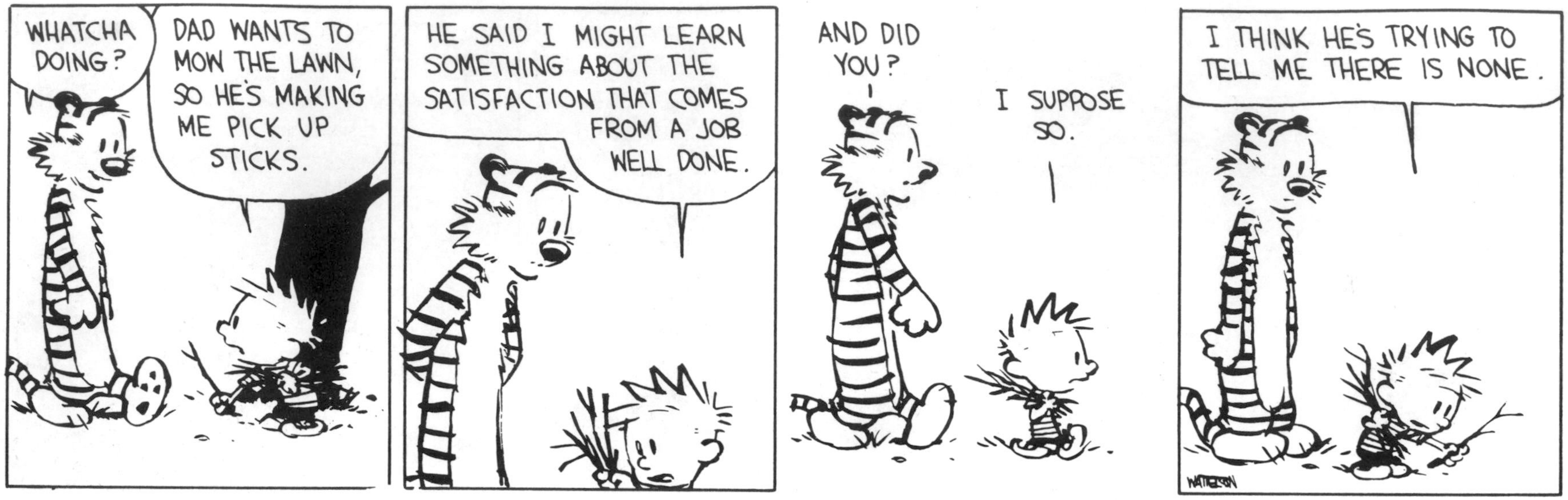
WHATCHA DOING?
DAD WANTS TO MOW THE LAWN, SO HE'S MAKING ME PICK UP STICKS.
HE SAID I MIGHT LEARN SOMETHING ABOUT THE SATISFACTION THAT COMES FROM A JOB WELL DONE.
AND DID YOU?
I SUPPOSE SO.
I THINK HE'S TRYING TO TELL ME THERE IS NONE.

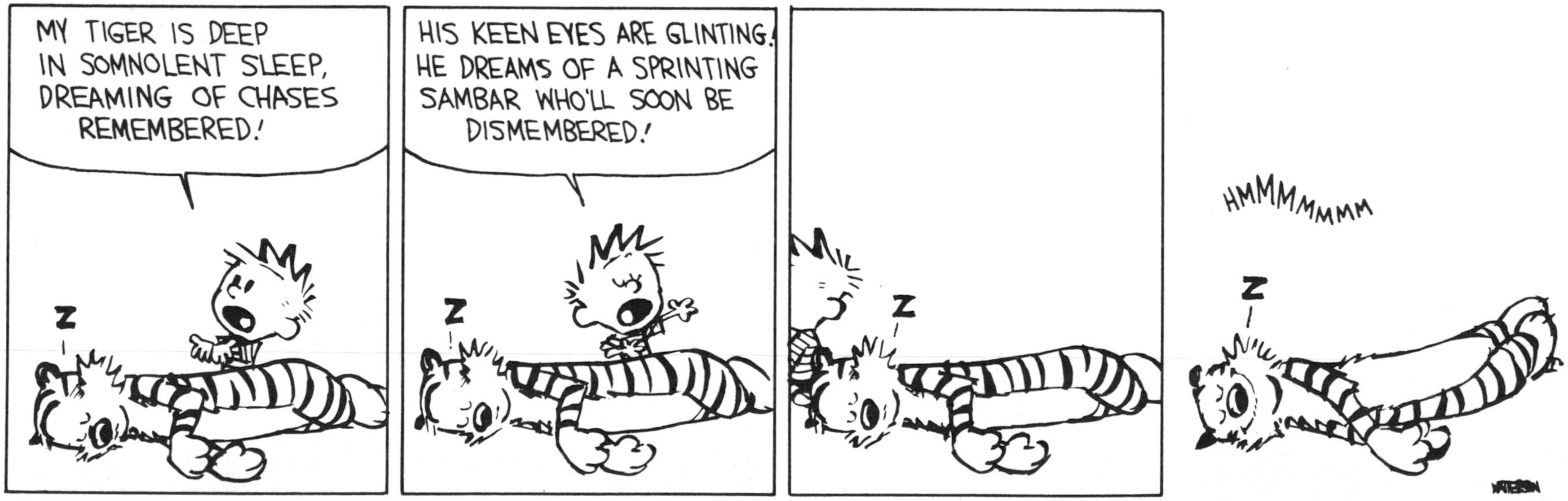
MY TIGER IS DEEP IN SOMNOLENT SLEEP, DREAMING OF CHASES REMEMBERED!
Z
HIS KEEN EYES ARE GLINTING! HE DREAMS OF A SPRINTING SAMBAR WHO'LL SOON BE DISMEMBERED!
Z
Z
HMMMMMMM
Z

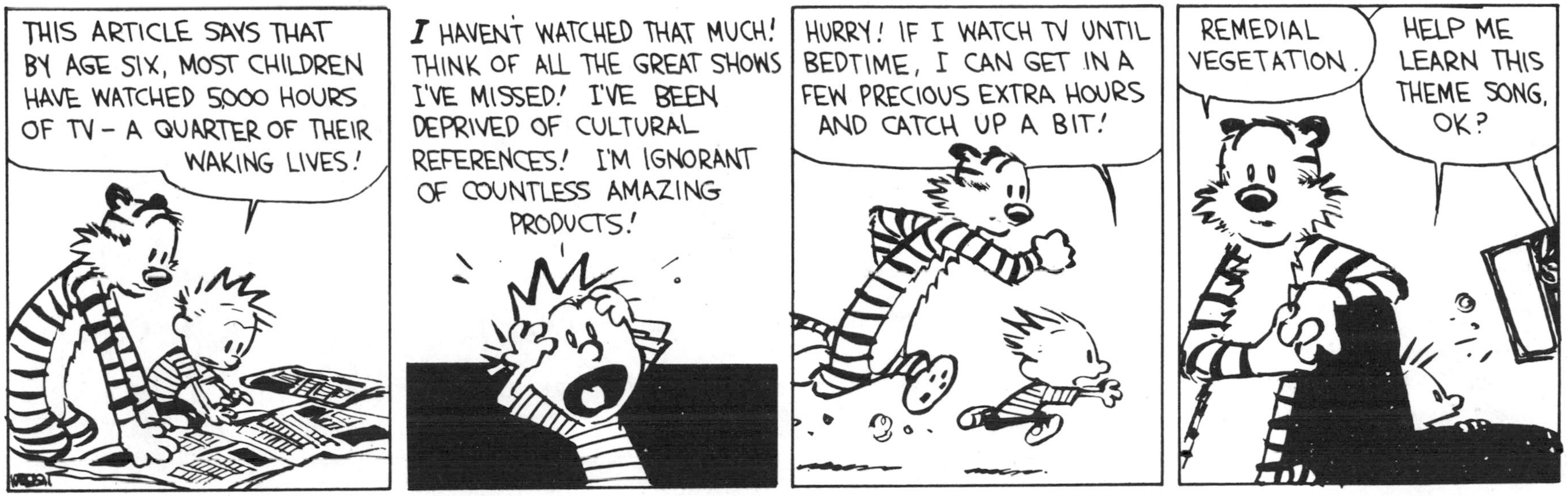
THIS ARTICLE SAYS THAT BY AGE SIX, MOST CHILDREN HAVE WATCHED 5,000 HOURS OF TV – A QUARTER OF THEIR WAKING LIVES!
I HAVEN'T WATCHED THAT MUCH! THINK OF ALL THE GREAT SHOWS I'VE MISSED! I'VE BEEN DEPRIVED OF CULTURAL REFERENCES! I'M IGNORANT OF COUNTLESS AMAZING PRODUCTS!
HURRY! IF I WATCH TV UNTIL BEDTIME, I CAN GET IN A FEW PRECIOUS EXTRA HOURS AND CATCH UP A BIT!
REMEDIAL VEGETATION.
HELP ME LEARN THIS THEME SONG, OK?

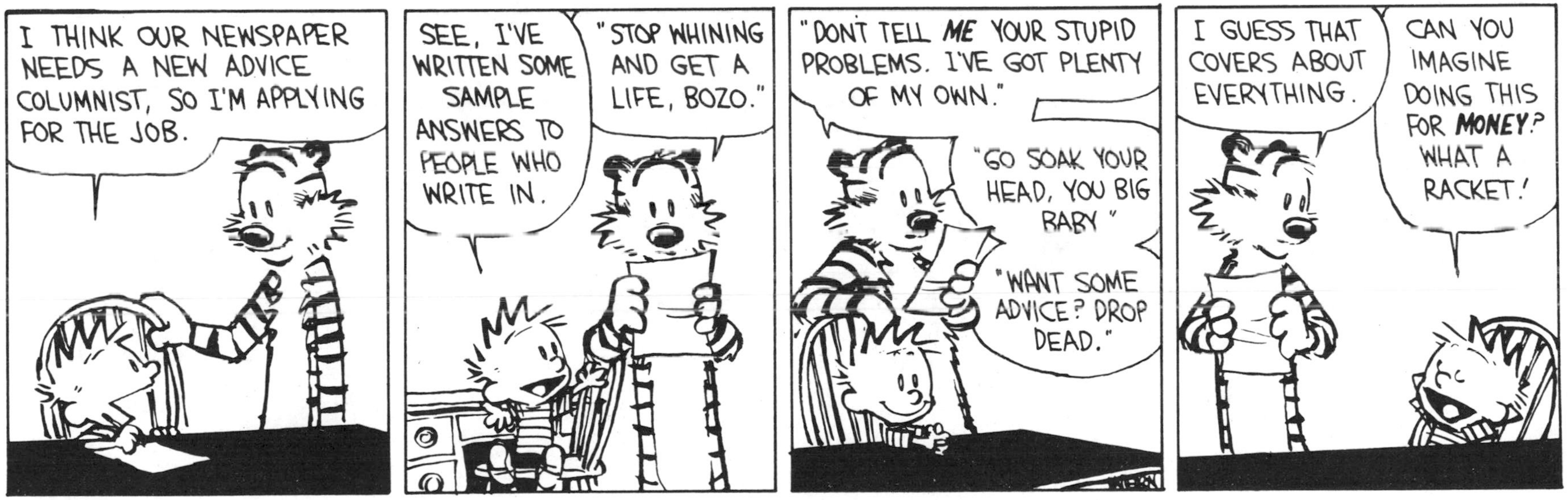
I THINK OUR NEWSPAPER NEEDS A NEW ADVICE COLUMNIST, SO I'M APPLYING FOR THE JOB.
SEE, I'VE WRITTEN SOME SAMPLE ANSWERS TO PEOPLE WHO WRITE IN.
"STOP WHINING AND GET A LIFE, BOZO."
"DON'T TELL ME YOUR STUPID PROBLEMS. I'VE GOT PLENTY OF MY OWN."
"GO SOAK YOUR HEAD, YOU BIG BABY."
"WANT SOME ADVICE? DROP DEAD."
I GUESS THAT COVERS ABOUT EVERYTHING.
CAN YOU IMAGINE DOING THIS FOR MONEY? WHAT A RACKET!

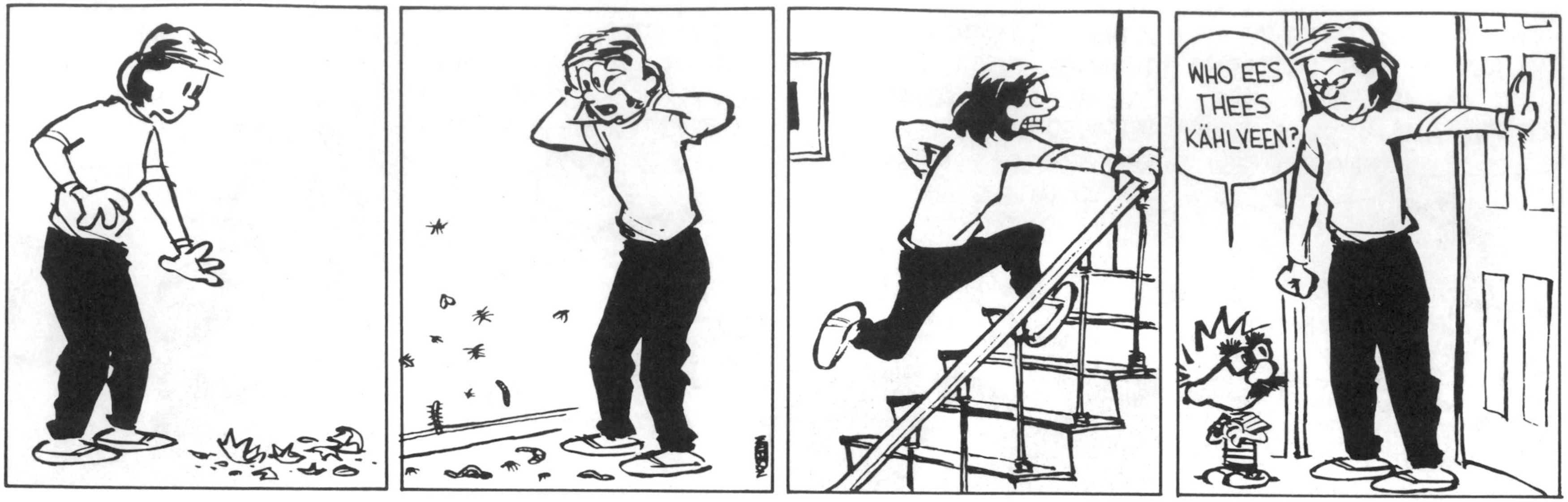
WHO EES THEES KÄHLYEEN?

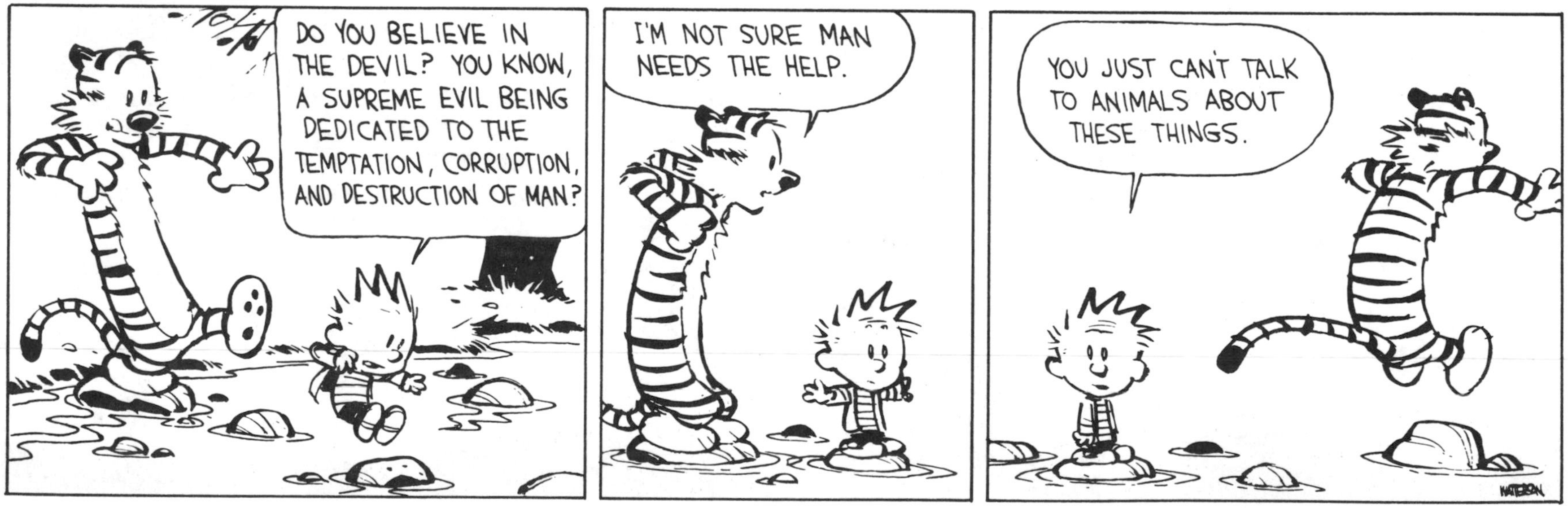
DO YOU BELIEVE IN THE DEVIL? YOU KNOW, A SUPREME EVIL BEING DEDICATED TO THE TEMPTATION, CORRUPTION, AND DESTRUCTION OF MAN?
I'M NOT SURE MAN NEEDS THE HELP.
YOU JUST CAN'T TALK TO ANIMALS ABOUT THESE THINGS.

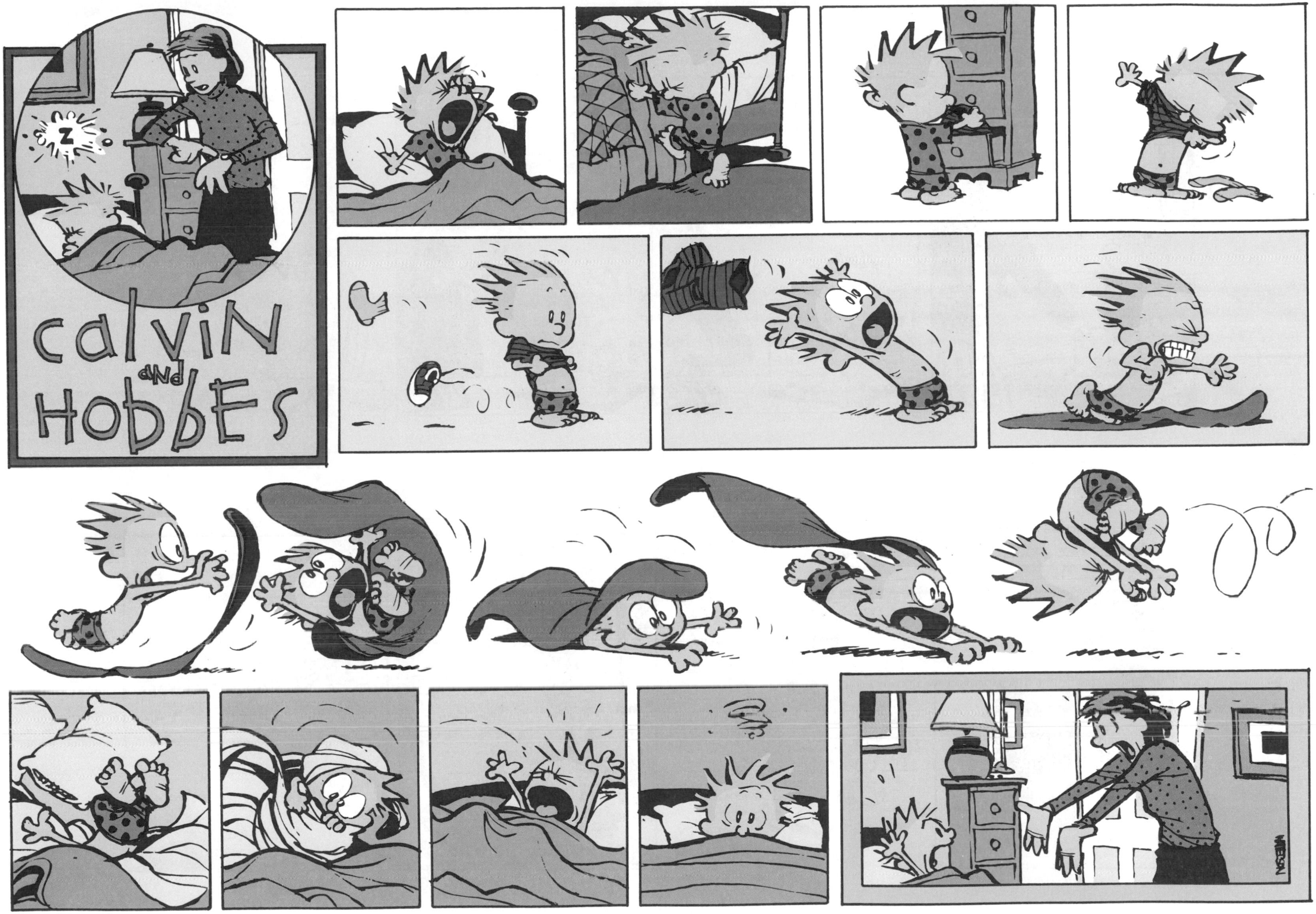
Z
calvin and HOBBES
WATTERSON

I'VE DECIDED I BELIEVE IN ASTROLOGY AND HOROSCOPES.

REALLY?

YOU BET. IT ONLY MAKES SENSE THAT EVERY FACET OF OUR DAILY LIVES SHOULD DEPEND UPON THE POSITION OF CELESTIAL BODIES HUNDREDS OF MILLIONS OF MILES AWAY.

LOOK HERE. TODAY I'LL HAVE "MANY KEY POLICIES IMPLEMENTED." I GET TO HAVE MY WAY!

OH THOSE MISCHIEVOUS PLANETS.

THE NEWSPAPER COULDN'T PRINT IT IF IT WEREN'T TRUE!

MY HOROSCOPE SAYS, "TURN-ABOUT MEANS CIRCUMSTANCES IN YOUR FAVOR. ASSERT VIEWS IN CONFIDENT MANNER. LUNAR CYCLE HIGH, MANY OF YOUR KEY POLICIES WILL BE IMPLEMENTED."

ISN'T THAT GREAT? TODAY I'M FATED TO GET MY WAY! THE HEAVENS DECREE IT!

SO WHAT ARE YOUR "KEY POLICIES"?

FIRST, OBVIOUSLY, IS "DON'T DO HOMEWORK." C'MON, LET'S GO OUT AND PLAY!

HERE COMES YOUR MOM AND IT LOOKS LIKE SHE HAS A BONE TO PICK WITH THE MOON.

HA! WATCH ME ASSERT MY VIEWS IN A CONFIDENT MANNER!

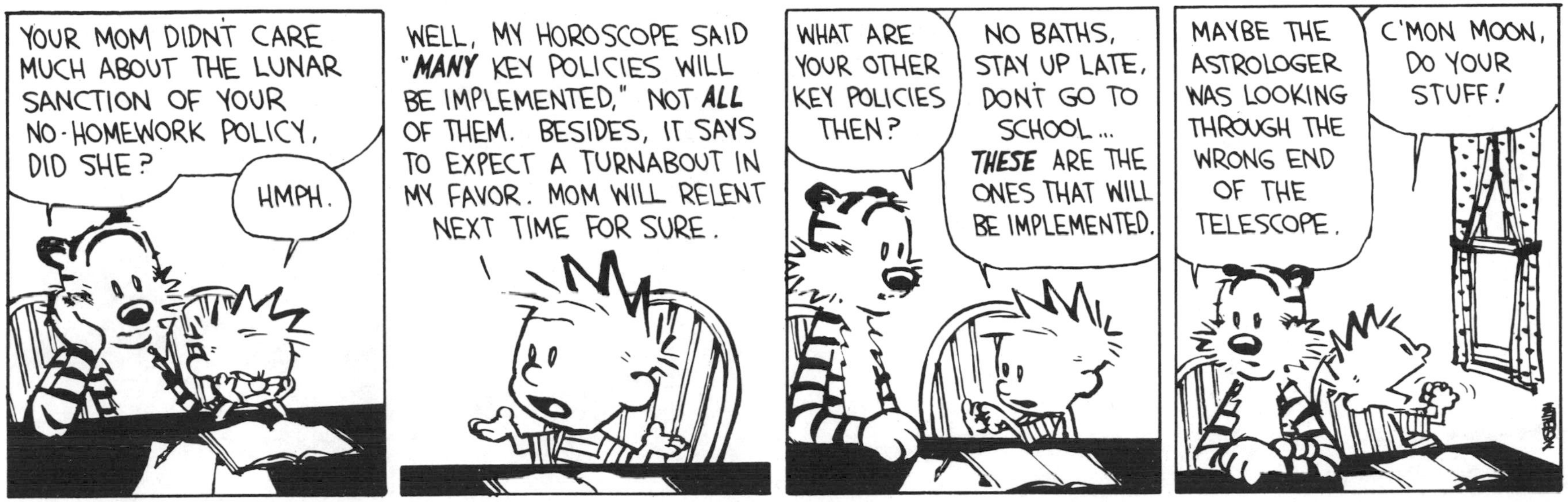
YOUR MOM DIDN'T CARE MUCH ABOUT THE LUNAR SANCTION OF YOUR NO-HOMEWORK POLICY, DID SHE?
HMPH.
WELL, MY HOROSCOPE SAID "MANY KEY POLICIES WILL BE IMPLEMENTED," NOT ALL OF THEM. BESIDES, IT SAYS TO EXPECT A TURNABOUT IN MY FAVOR. MOM WILL RELENT NEXT TIME FOR SURE.
WHAT ARE YOUR OTHER KEY POLICIES THEN?
NO BATHS, STAY UP LATE, DON'T GO TO SCHOOL... THESE ARE THE ONES THAT WILL BE IMPLEMENTED.
MAYBE THE ASTROLOGER WAS LOOKING THROUGH THE WRONG END OF THE TELESCOPE.
C'MON MOON, DO YOUR STUFF!

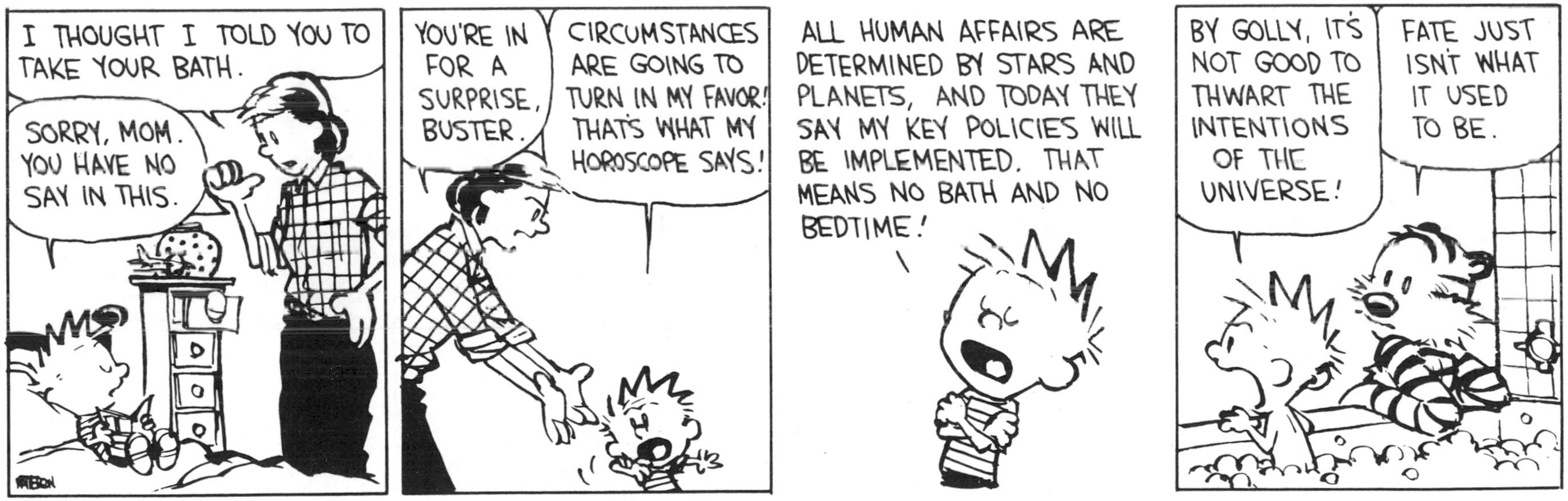
I THOUGHT I TOLD YOU TO TAKE YOUR BATH.
SORRY, MOM. YOU HAVE NO SAY IN THIS.
YOU'RE IN FOR A SURPRISE, BUSTER.
CIRCUMSTANCES ARE GOING TO TURN IN MY FAVOR! THAT'S WHAT MY HOROSCOPE SAYS!
ALL HUMAN AFFAIRS ARE DETERMINED BY STARS AND PLANETS, AND TODAY THEY SAY MY KEY POLICIES WILL BE IMPLEMENTED. THAT MEANS NO BATH AND NO BEDTIME!
BY GOLLY, IT'S NOT GOOD TO THWART THE INTENTIONS OF THE UNIVERSE!
FATE JUST ISN'T WHAT IT USED TO BE.

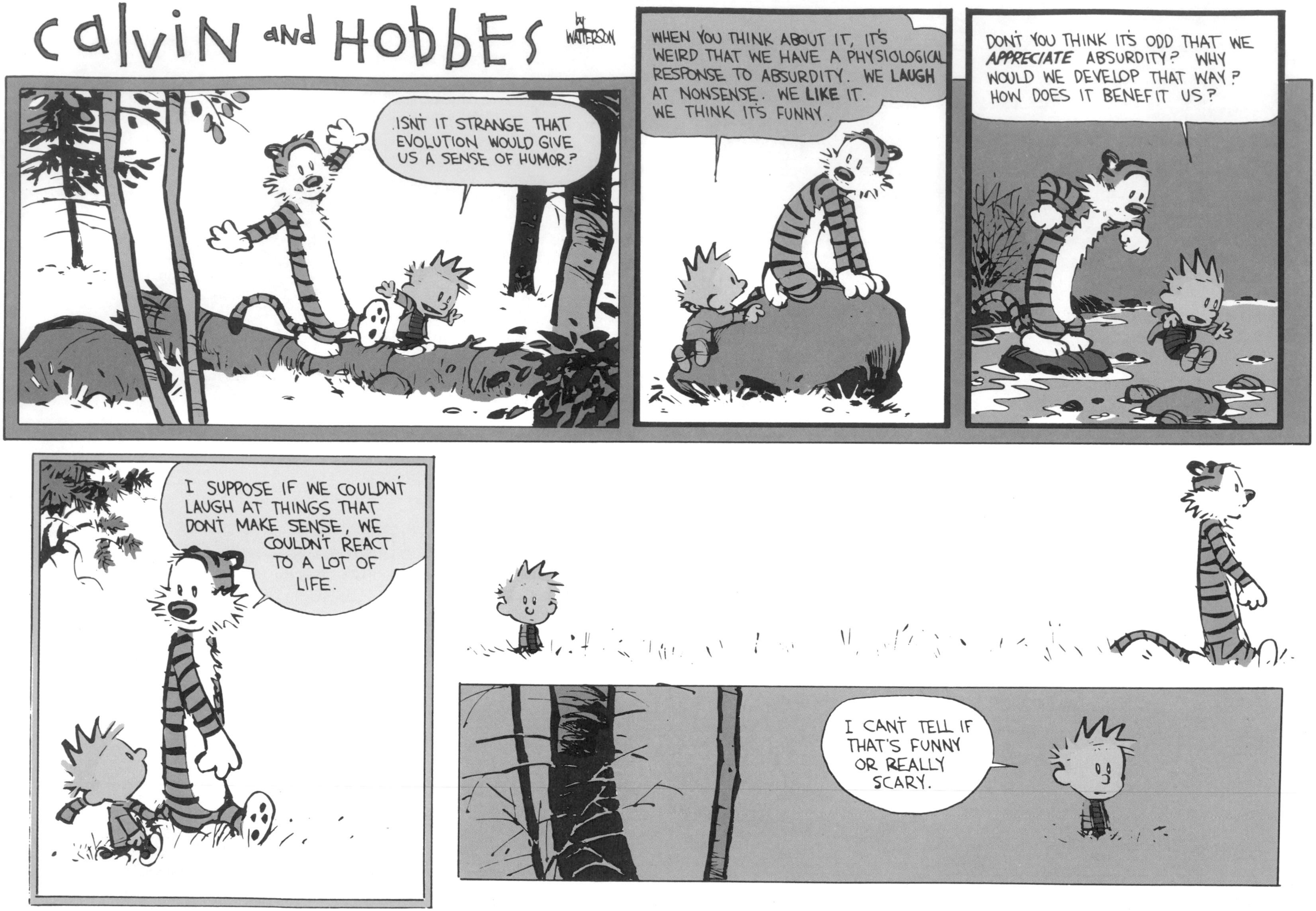
Calvin and HOBBES
by WATTERSON
ISN'T IT STRANGE THAT EVOLUTION WOULD GIVE US A SENSE OF HUMOR?
WHEN YOU THINK ABOUT IT, IT'S WEIRD THAT WE HAVE A PHYSIOLOGICAL RESPONSE TO ABSURDITY. WE LAUGH AT NONSENSE. WE LIKE IT. WE THINK IT'S FUNNY.
DON'T YOU THINK IT'S ODD THAT WE APPRECIATE ABSURDITY? WHY WOULD WE DEVELOP THAT WAY? HOW DOES IT BENEFIT US?
I SUPPOSE IF WE COULDN'T LAUGH AT THINGS THAT DON'T MAKE SENSE, WE COULDN'T REACT TO A LOT OF LIFE.
I CAN'T TELL IF THAT'S FUNNY OR REALLY SCARY.

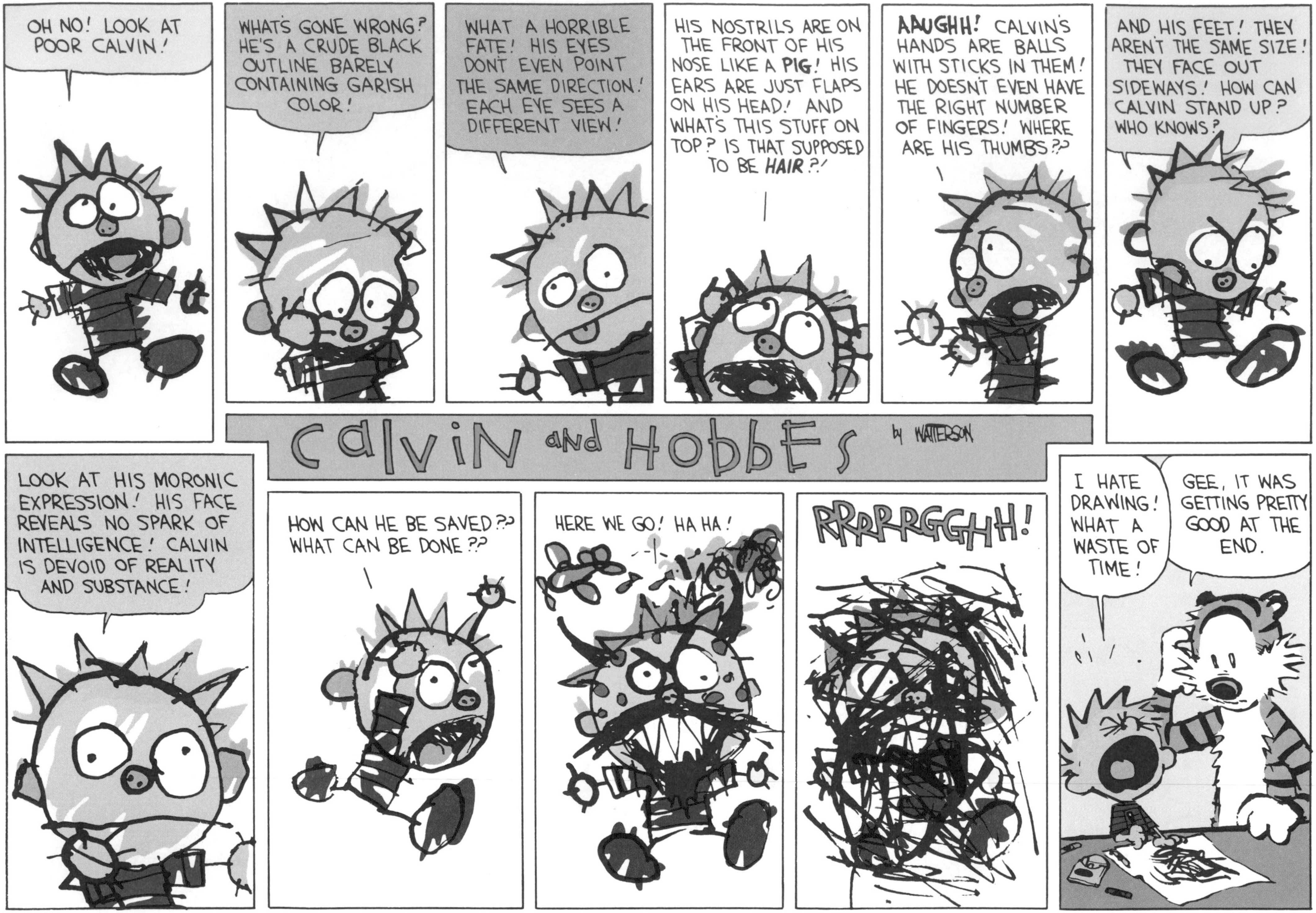
OH NO! LOOK AT POOR CALVIN!
WHAT'S GONE WRONG? HE'S A CRUDE BLACK OUTLINE BARELY CONTAINING GARISH COLOR!
WHAT A HORRIBLE FATE! HIS EYES DON'T EVEN POINT THE SAME DIRECTION! EACH EYE SEES A DIFFERENT VIEW!
HIS NOSTRILS ARE ON THE FRONT OF HIS NOSE LIKE A PIG! HIS EARS ARE JUST FLAPS ON HIS HEAD! AND WHAT'S THIS STUFF ON TOP? IS THAT SUPPOSED TO BE HAIR?!
AAUGHH! CALVIN'S HANDS ARE BALLS WITH STICKS IN THEM! HE DOESN'T EVEN HAVE THE RIGHT NUMBER OF FINGERS! WHERE ARE HIS THUMBS??
AND HIS FEET! THEY AREN'T THE SAME SIZE! THEY FACE OUT SIDEWAYS! HOW CAN CALVIN STAND UP? WHO KNOWS?
CALVIN and HOBBES
by WATTERSON
LOOK AT HIS MORONIC EXPRESSION! HIS FACE REVEALS NO SPARK OF INTELLIGENCE! CALVIN IS DEVOID OF REALITY AND SUBSTANCE!
HOW CAN HE BE SAVED?? WHAT CAN BE DONE??
HERE WE GO! HA HA!
RRRRRGGHH!
I HATE DRAWING! WHAT A WASTE OF TIME!
GEE, IT WAS GETTING PRETTY GOOD AT THE END.

70

OH BOY, THE NEW ISSUE OF "CHEWING"!

YOU GET A MAGAZINE?

WOW, THIS LOOKS GREAT! "SPECIAL SUGARLESS GUM ISSUE— CHOOSING AN ARTIFICIAL SWEETENER THAT'S RIGHT FOR *YOU* .... TONGUE EXERCISES FOR BIGGER BUBBLES .... RAD FASHION KNEEPADS FOR WALKING AND CHEWING .... *PLUS* AN INTERVIEW WITH BAZOOKA JOE!"

SEE, IT'S ALL TARGET MARKETING! ADVERTISERS DON'T WASTE THEIR TIME ON MASS AUDIENCES ANY MORE. THEY FIND YOUR SPECIAL INTEREST AND THEY NAIL YOU!

AS IF ADVERTISING WASN'T INTRUSIVE ENOUGH BEFORE.

OOH, THE '92 SPEARMINTS ARE OUT! I GOTTA GET TO A STORE!

I CAN'T BELIEVE THERE'S A MAGAZINE FOR GUM CHEWERS.

HECK, THERE MUST BE A *DOZEN* SUCH MAGAZINES.

EACH APPEALS TO A DIFFERENT FACTION. "CHEWING" IS HIGH-GLOSS, LITERATE AND SOPHISTICATED. "GUM ACTION" GOES FOR THE GONZO CHEWERS. "CHEWERS ILLUSTRATED" AIMS AT VINTAGE GUM COLLECTORS, AND SO ON!

EACH ONE ENCOURAGES YOU TO THINK YOU BELONG TO AN ELITE CLIQUE, SO ADVERTISERS CAN APPEAL TO YOUR EGO AND GET YOU TO CULTIVATE AN IMAGE THAT SETS YOU APART FROM THE CROWD. IT'S THE DIVIDE AND CONQUER TRICK.

I WONDER WHATEVER HAPPENED TO THE MELTING POT.

THERE'S NO MONEY IN IT.

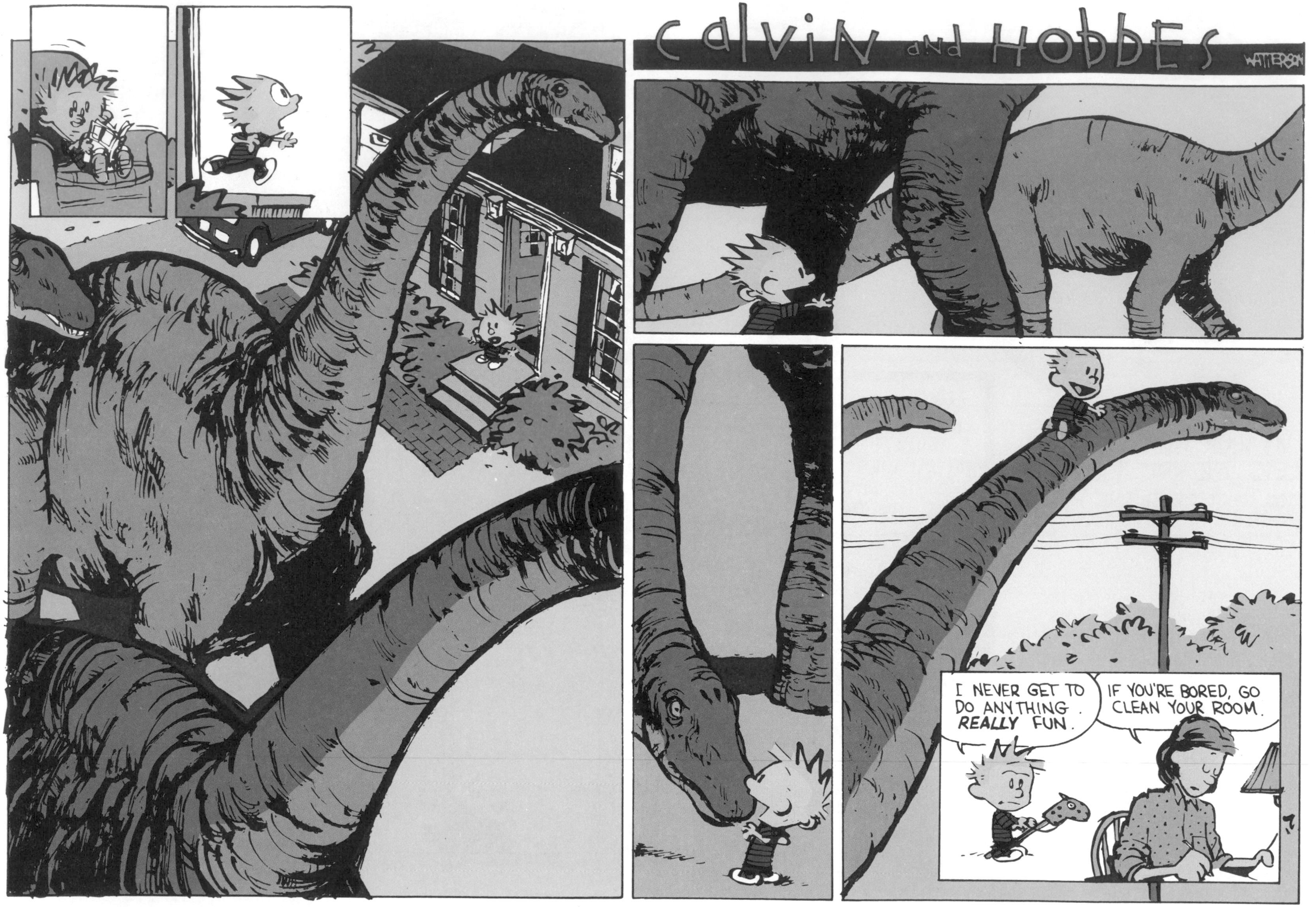

Calvin and HOBBES
WATTERSON
I NEVER GET TO DO ANYTHING. REALLY FUN.
IF YOU'RE BORED, GO CLEAN YOUR ROOM.

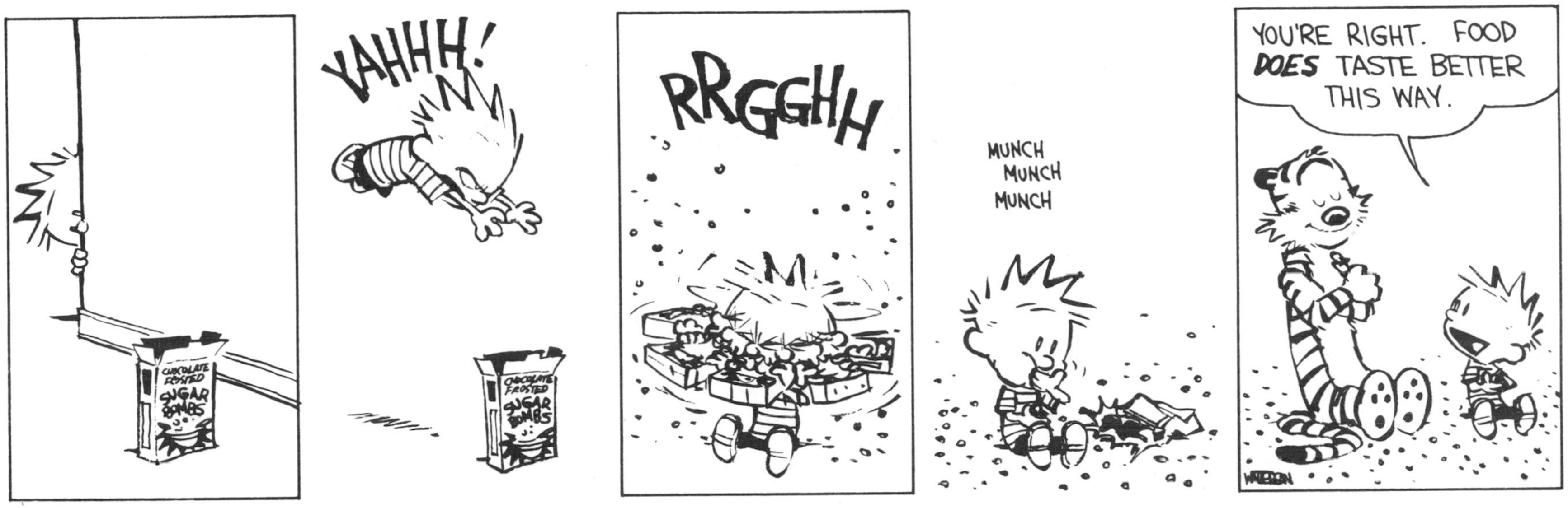
CHOCOLATE FROSTED SUGAR BOMBS
YAHHH!
CHOCOLATE FROSTED SUGAR BOMBS
RRGGHH
MUNCH MUNCH MUNCH
YOU'RE RIGHT. FOOD **DOES** TASTE BETTER THIS WAY.
WATTERSON

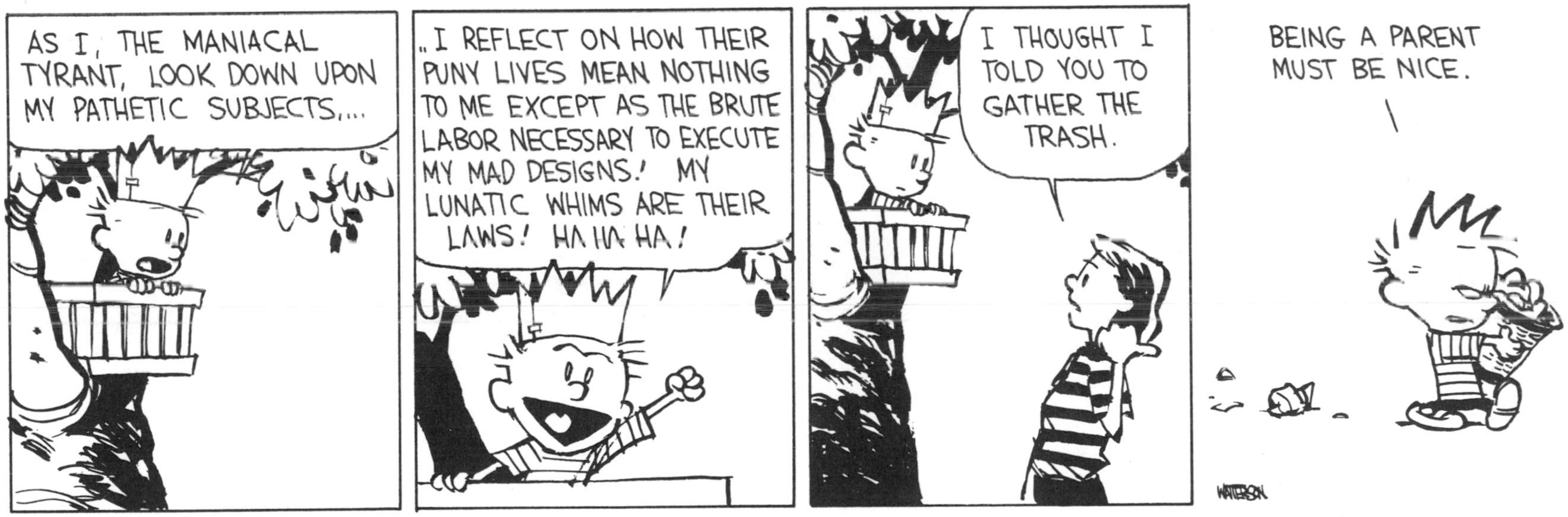
AS I, THE MANIACAL TYRANT, LOOK DOWN UPON MY PATHETIC SUBJECTS,...
..I REFLECT ON HOW THEIR PUNY LIVES MEAN NOTHING TO ME EXCEPT AS THE BRUTE LABOR NECESSARY TO EXECUTE MY MAD DESIGNS! MY LUNATIC WHIMS ARE THEIR LAWS! HA HA HA!
I THOUGHT I TOLD YOU TO GATHER THE TRASH.
BEING A PARENT MUST BE NICE.
WATTERSON

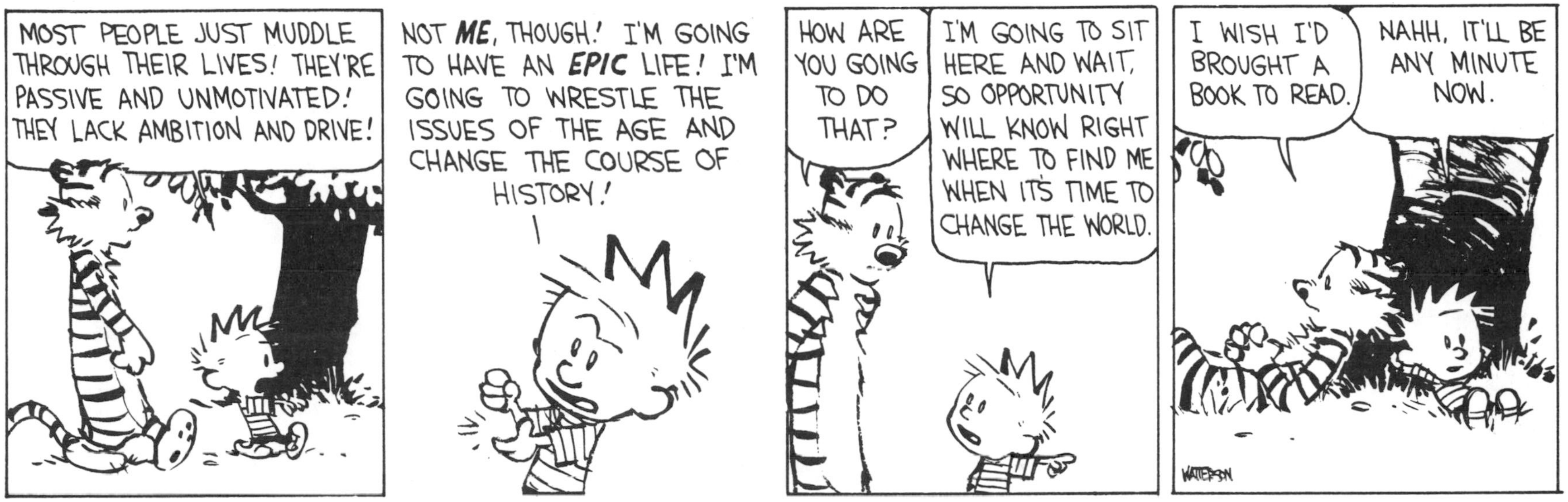
MOST PEOPLE JUST MUDDLE THROUGH THEIR LIVES! THEY'RE PASSIVE AND UNMOTIVATED! THEY LACK AMBITION AND DRIVE!
NOT ME, THOUGH! I'M GOING TO HAVE AN EPIC LIFE! I'M GOING TO WRESTLE THE ISSUES OF THE AGE AND CHANGE THE COURSE OF HISTORY!
HOW ARE YOU GOING TO DO THAT?
I'M GOING TO SIT HERE AND WAIT, SO OPPORTUNITY WILL KNOW RIGHT WHERE TO FIND ME WHEN IT'S TIME TO CHANGE THE WORLD.
I WISH I'D BROUGHT A BOOK TO READ.
NAHH, IT'LL BE ANY MINUTE NOW.
WATTERSON

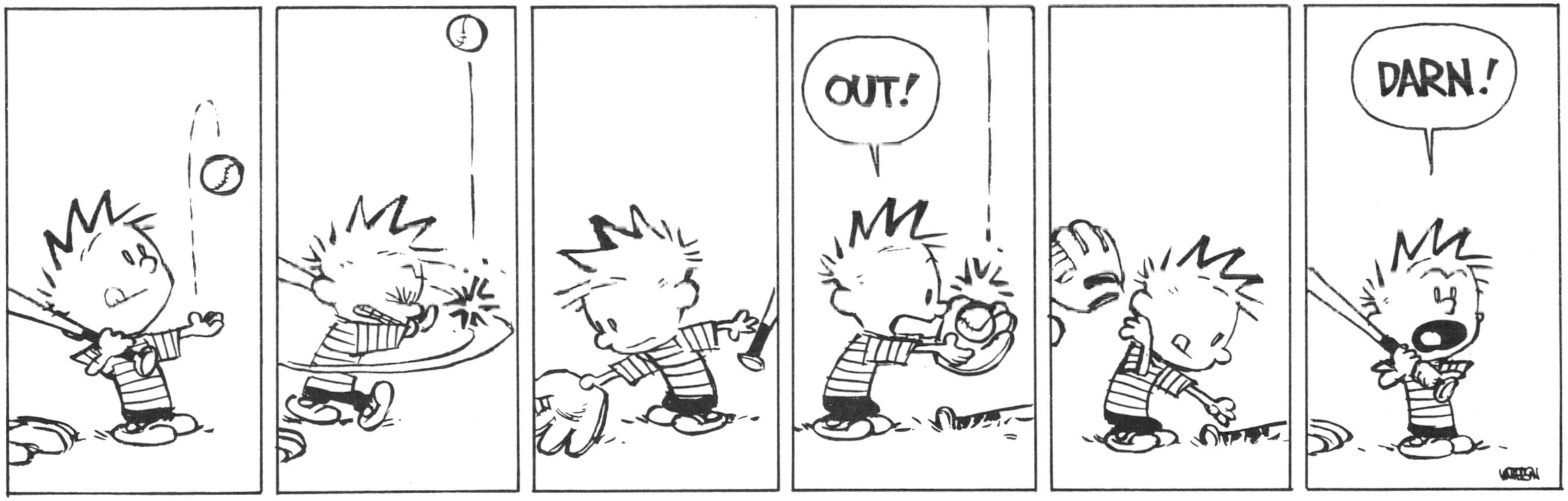
OUT!
DARN!
WATTERSON

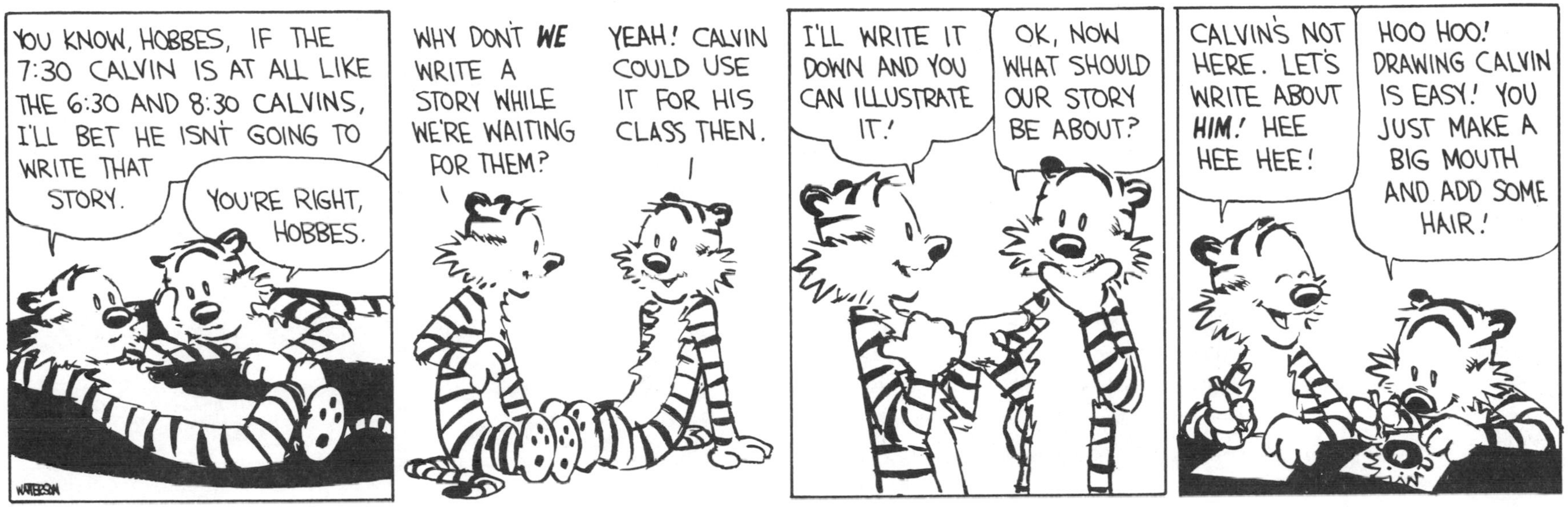
YOU KNOW, HOBBES, IF THE 7:30 CALVIN IS AT ALL LIKE THE 6:30 AND 8:30 CALVINS, I'LL BET HE ISN'T GOING TO WRITE THAT STORY.
YOU'RE RIGHT, HOBBES.
WHY DON'T **WE** WRITE A STORY WHILE WE'RE WAITING FOR THEM?
YEAH! CALVIN COULD USE IT FOR HIS CLASS THEN.
I'LL WRITE IT DOWN AND YOU CAN ILLUSTRATE IT!
OK, NOW WHAT SHOULD OUR STORY BE ABOUT?
CALVIN'S NOT HERE. LET'S WRITE ABOUT **HIM**! HEE HEE HEE!
HOO HOO! DRAWING CALVIN IS EASY! YOU JUST MAKE A BIG MOUTH AND ADD SOME HAIR!

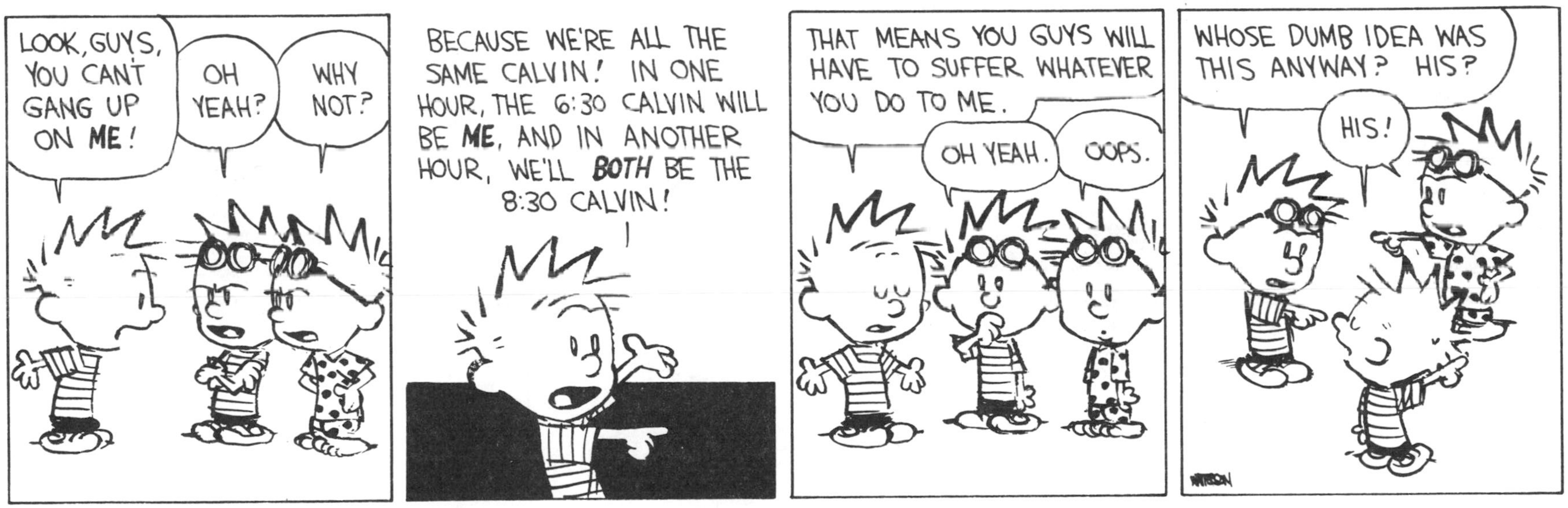
LOOK, GUYS, YOU CAN'T GANG UP ON **ME**!
OH YEAH?
WHY NOT?
BECAUSE WE'RE ALL THE SAME CALVIN! IN ONE HOUR, THE 6:30 CALVIN WILL BE **ME**, AND IN ANOTHER HOUR, WE'LL **BOTH** BE THE 8:30 CALVIN!
THAT MEANS YOU GUYS WILL HAVE TO SUFFER WHATEVER YOU DO TO ME.
OH YEAH.
OOPS.
WHOSE DUMB IDEA WAS THIS ANYWAY? HIS?
HIS!

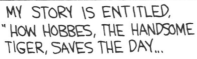

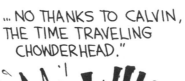

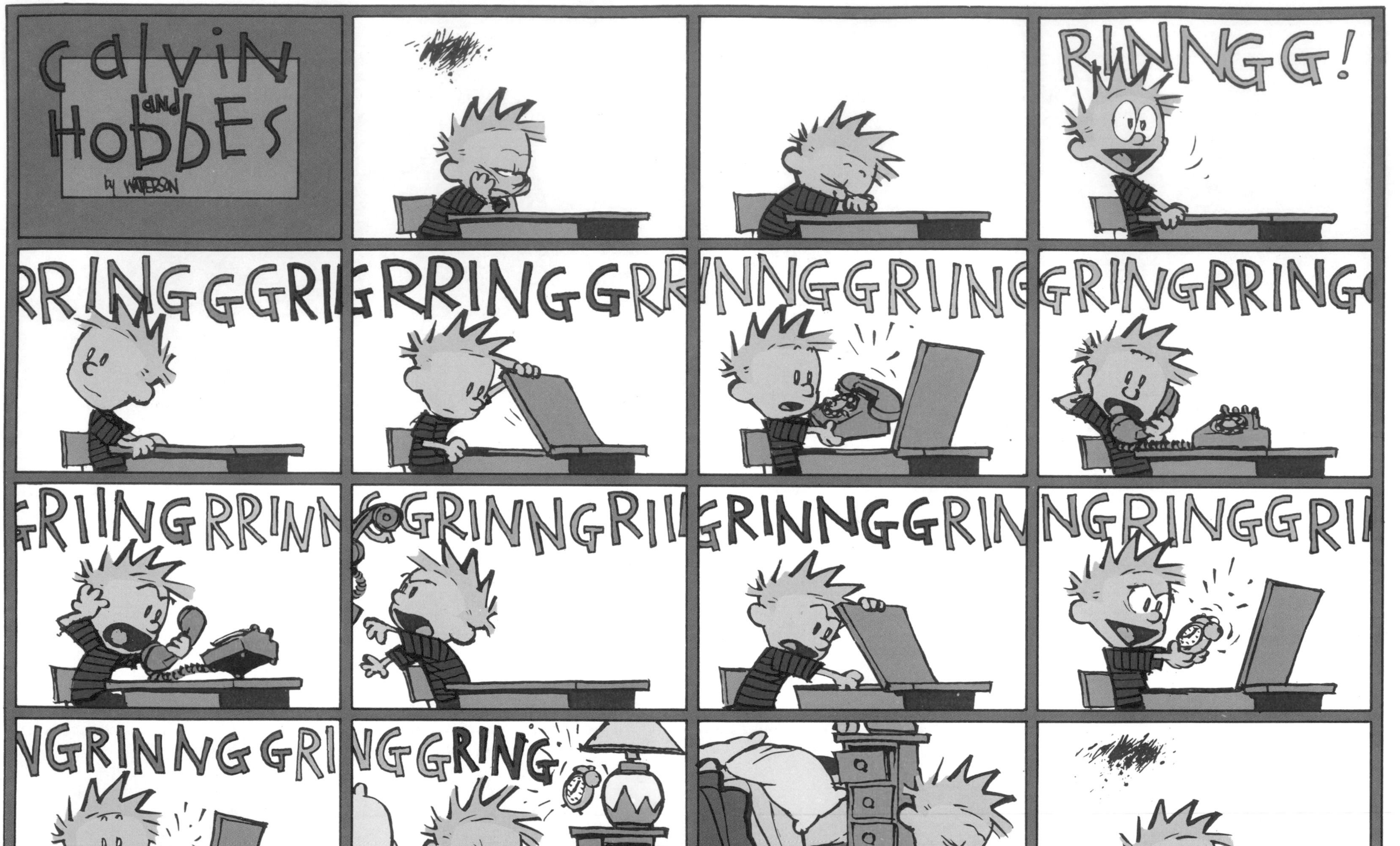
Calvin and Hobbes
by WATTERSON
RINNGG!
RRINGGGRI
GRRINGGRR
INNGGRIING
GRINGRRING
GRIINGRRINN
GGRINNGRII
GRINNGGRIN
NGRINGGRI
NGRINNGGRI
NGGRING

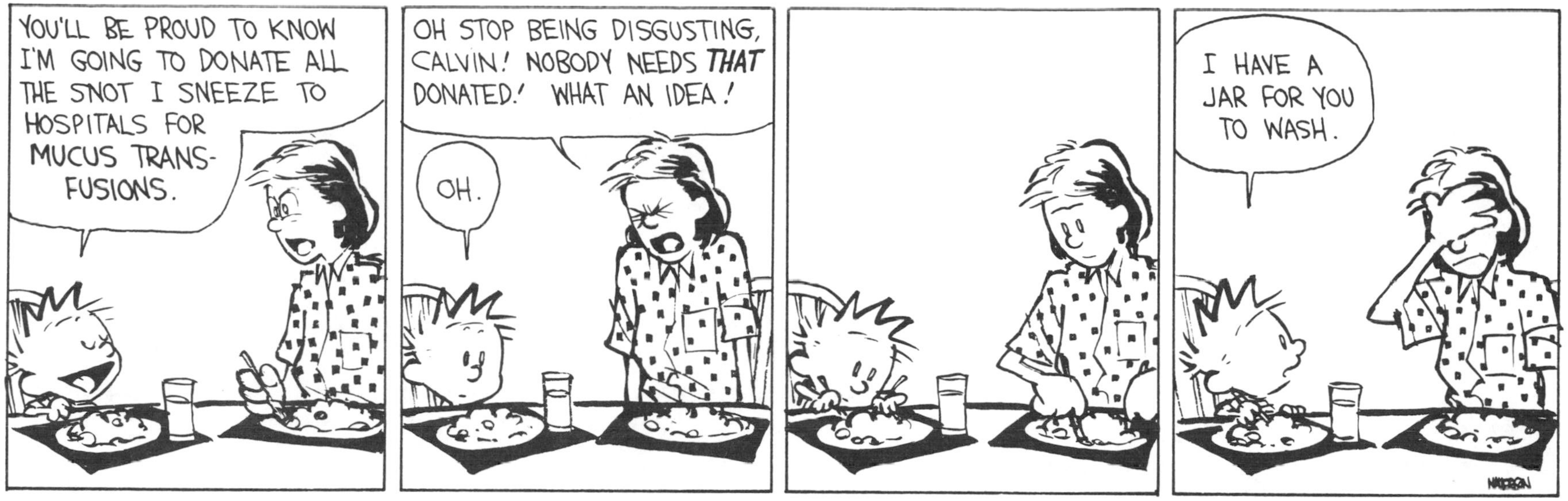
YOU'LL BE PROUD TO KNOW I'M GOING TO DONATE ALL THE SNOT I SNEEZE TO HOSPITALS FOR MUCUS TRANS-FUSIONS.
OH STOP BEING DISGUSTING, CALVIN! NOBODY NEEDS THAT DONATED! WHAT AN IDEA!
OH.
I HAVE A JAR FOR YOU TO WASH.

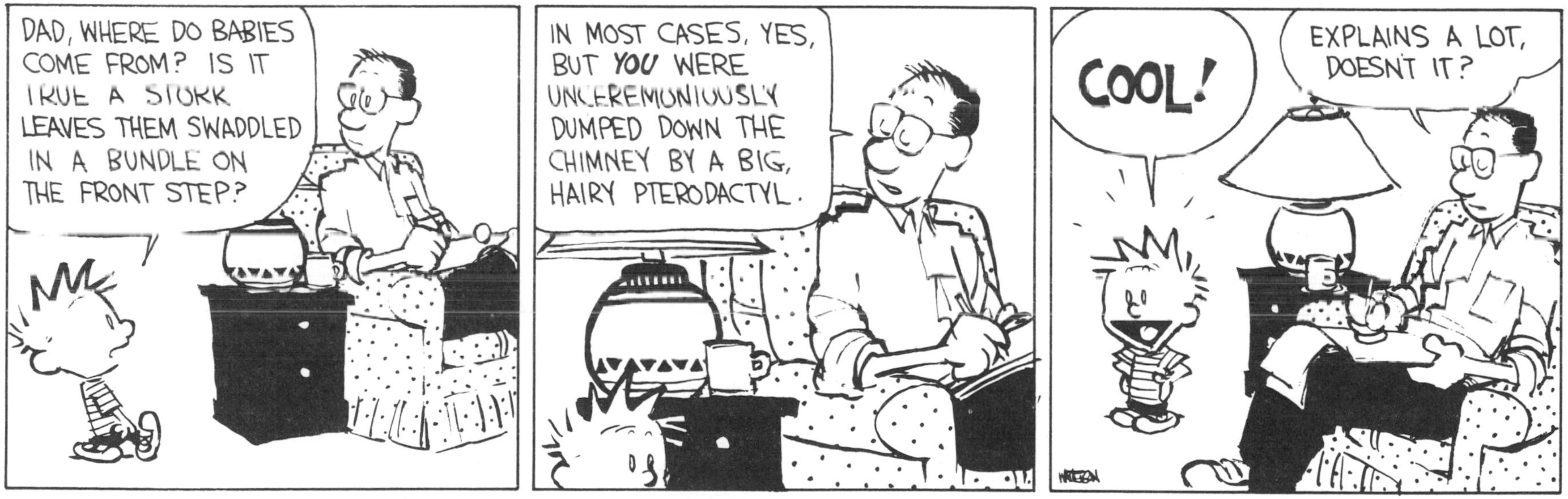
DAD, WHERE DO BABIES COME FROM? IS IT TRUE A STORK LEAVES THEM SWADDLED IN A BUNDLE ON THE FRONT STEP?
IN MOST CASES, YES, BUT YOU WERE UNCEREMONIOUSLY DUMPED DOWN THE CHIMNEY BY A BIG, HAIRY PTERODACTYL.
COOL!
EXPLAINS A LOT, DOESN'T IT?

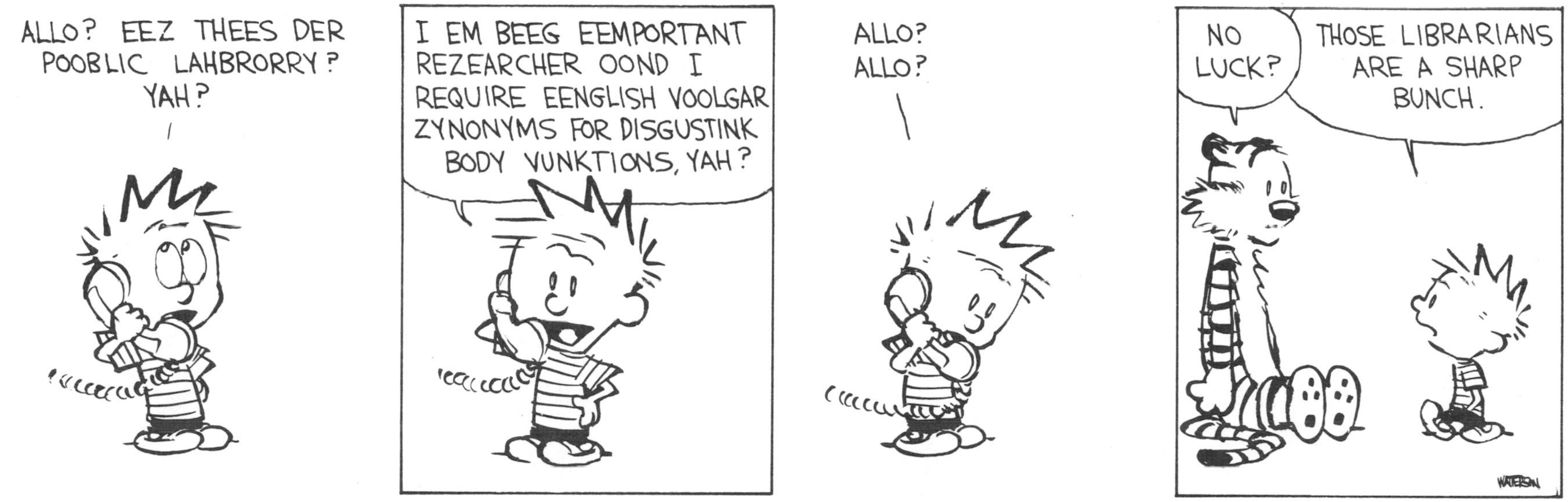
ALLO? EEZ THEES DER POOBLIC LAHBRORRY? YAH?
I EM BEEG EEMPORTANT REZEARCHER OOND I REQUIRE EENGLISH VOOLGAR ZYNONYMS FOR DISGUSTINK BODY VUNKTIONS, YAH?
ALLO? ALLO?
NO LUCK?
THOSE LIBRARIANS ARE A SHARP BUNCH.
WATTERSON

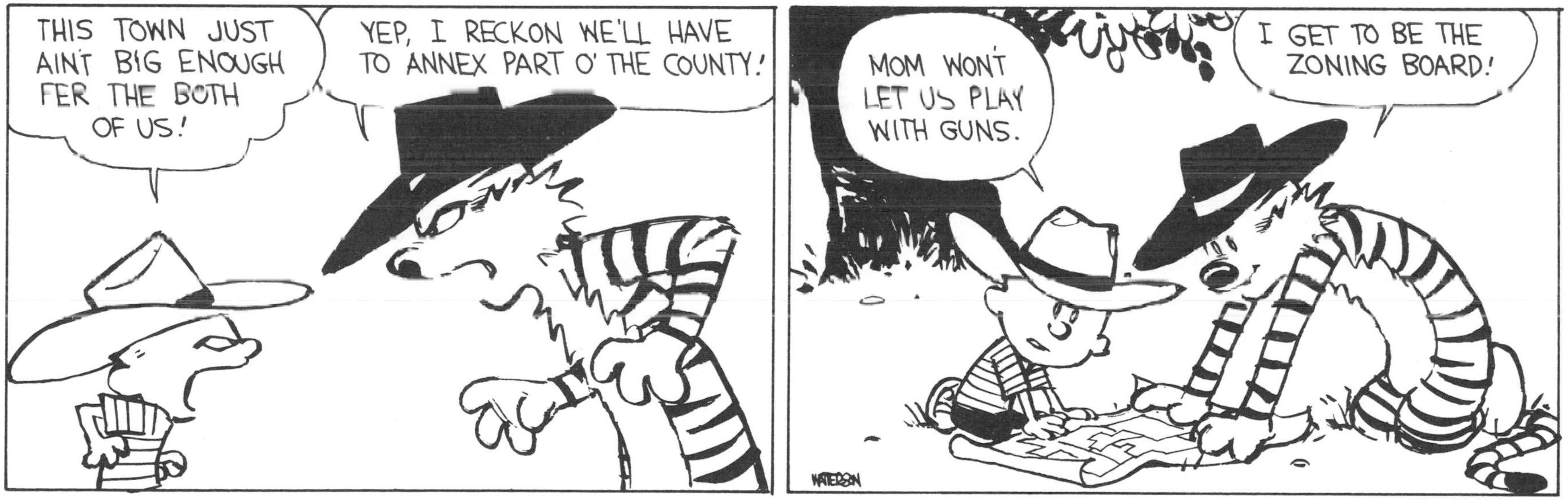
THIS TOWN JUST AIN'T BIG ENOUGH FER THE BOTH OF US!
YEP, I RECKON WE'LL HAVE TO ANNEX PART O' THE COUNTY!
MOM WON'T LET US PLAY WITH GUNS.
I GET TO BE THE ZONING BOARD!
WATTERSON

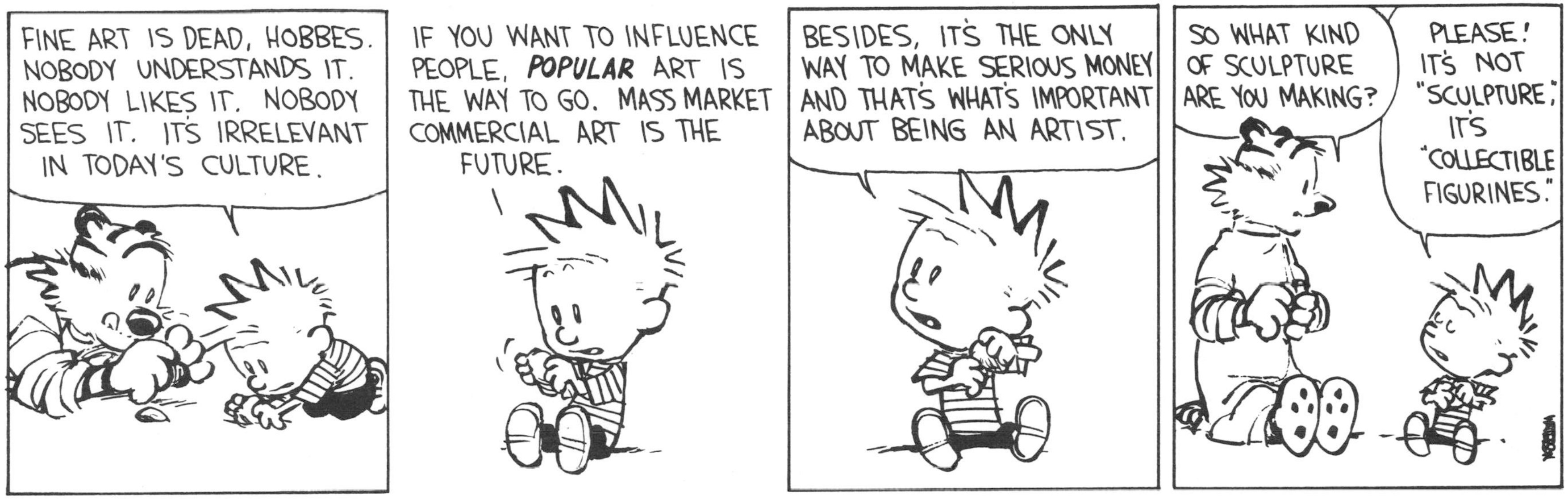
FINE ART IS DEAD, HOBBES. NOBODY UNDERSTANDS IT. NOBODY LIKES IT. NOBODY SEES IT. IT'S IRRELEVANT IN TODAY'S CULTURE.
IF YOU WANT TO INFLUENCE PEOPLE, POPULAR ART IS THE WAY TO GO. MASS MARKET COMMERCIAL ART IS THE FUTURE.
BESIDES, IT'S THE ONLY WAY TO MAKE SERIOUS MONEY AND THAT'S WHAT'S IMPORTANT ABOUT BEING AN ARTIST.
SO WHAT KIND OF SCULPTURE ARE YOU MAKING?
PLEASE! IT'S NOT "SCULPTURE," IT'S "COLLECTIBLE FIGURINES."

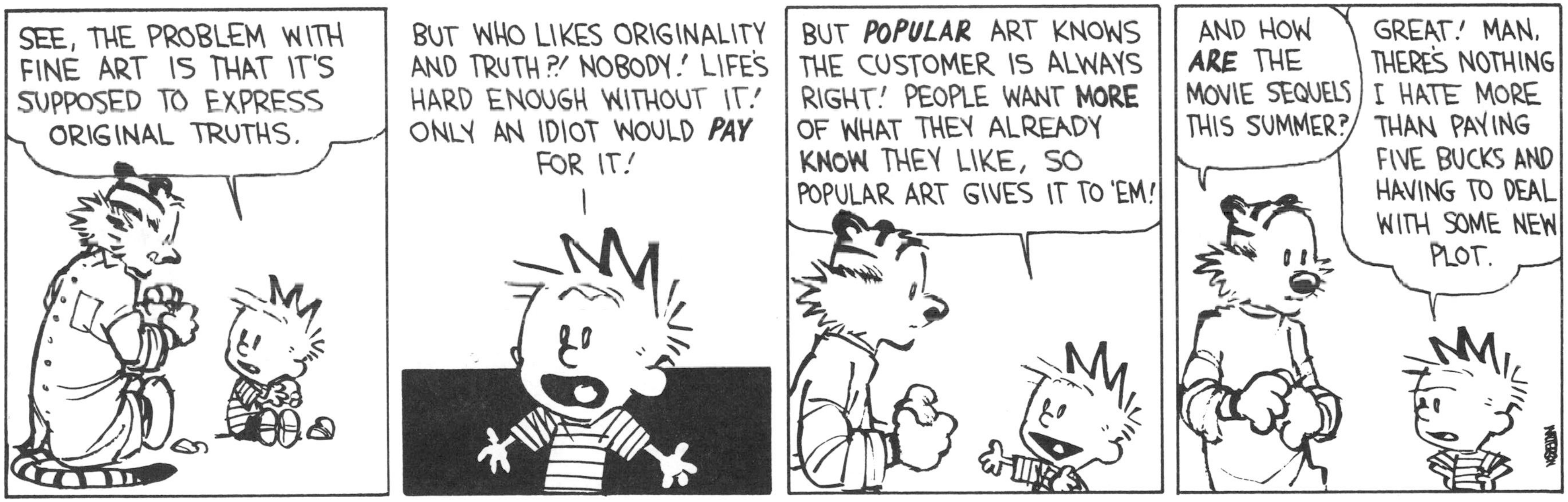
SEE, THE PROBLEM WITH FINE ART IS THAT IT'S SUPPOSED TO EXPRESS ORIGINAL TRUTHS.
BUT WHO LIKES ORIGINALITY AND TRUTH?! NOBODY! LIFE'S HARD ENOUGH WITHOUT IT! ONLY AN IDIOT WOULD PAY FOR IT!
BUT POPULAR ART KNOWS THE CUSTOMER IS ALWAYS RIGHT! PEOPLE WANT MORE OF WHAT THEY ALREADY KNOW THEY LIKE, SO POPULAR ART GIVES IT TO 'EM!
AND HOW ARE THE MOVIE SEQUELS THIS SUMMER?
GREAT! MAN, THERE'S NOTHING I HATE MORE THAN PAYING FIVE BUCKS AND HAVING TO DEAL WITH SOME NEW PLOT.

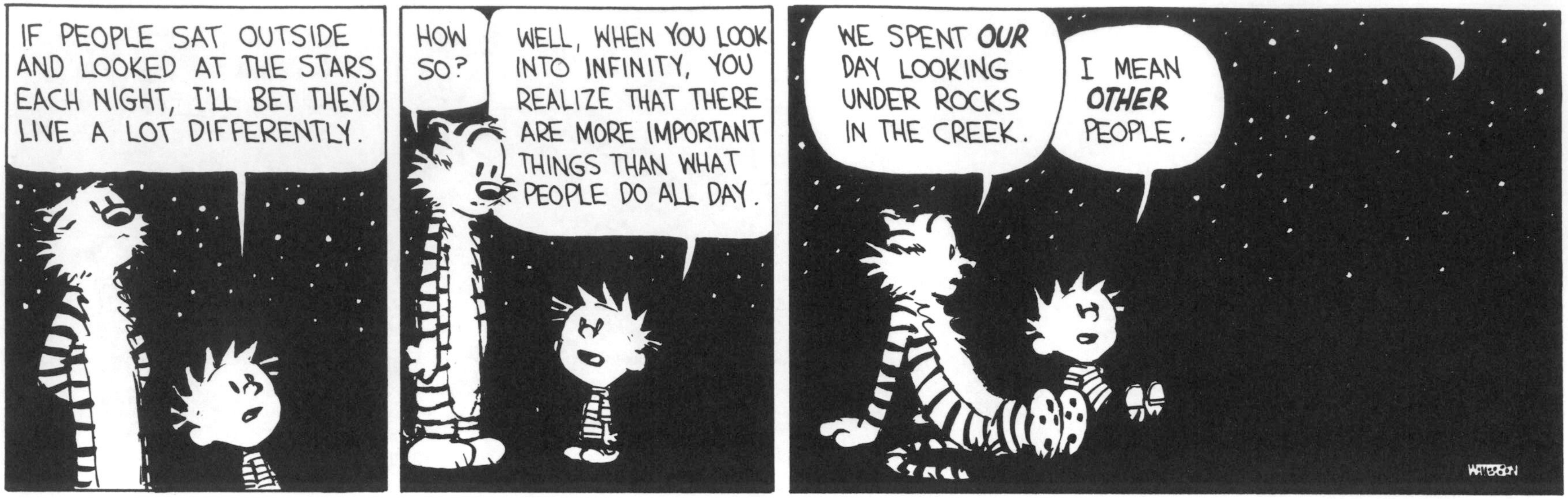
IF PEOPLE SAT OUTSIDE AND LOOKED AT THE STARS EACH NIGHT, I'LL BET THEY'D LIVE A LOT DIFFERENTLY.
HOW SO?
WELL, WHEN YOU LOOK INTO INFINITY, YOU REALIZE THAT THERE ARE MORE IMPORTANT THINGS THAN WHAT PEOPLE DO ALL DAY.
WE SPENT **OUR** DAY LOOKING UNDER ROCKS IN THE CREEK.
I MEAN **OTHER** PEOPLE.
WATTERSON

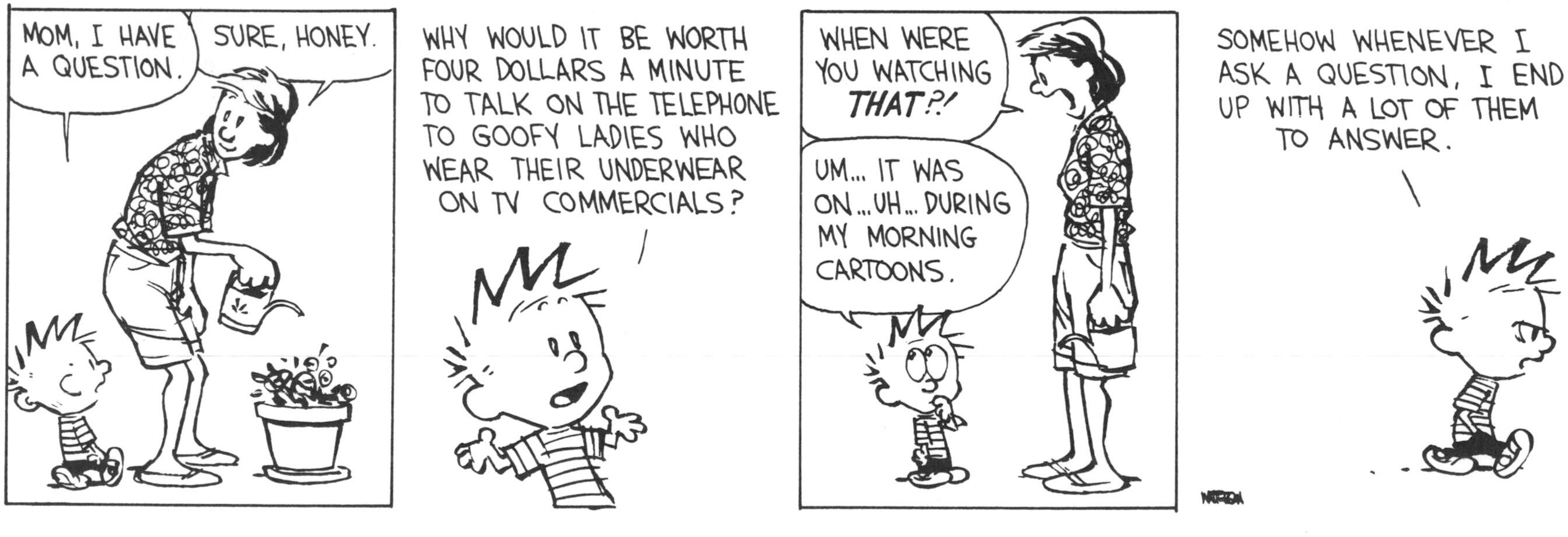
MOM, I HAVE A QUESTION.
SURE, HONEY.
WHY WOULD IT BE WORTH FOUR DOLLARS A MINUTE TO TALK ON THE TELEPHONE TO GOOFY LADIES WHO WEAR THEIR UNDERWEAR ON TV COMMERCIALS?
WHEN WERE YOU WATCHING ***THAT***?!
UM... IT WAS ON...UH... DURING MY MORNING CARTOONS.
SOMEHOW WHENEVER I ASK A QUESTION, I END UP WITH A LOT OF THEM TO ANSWER.
WATTERSON

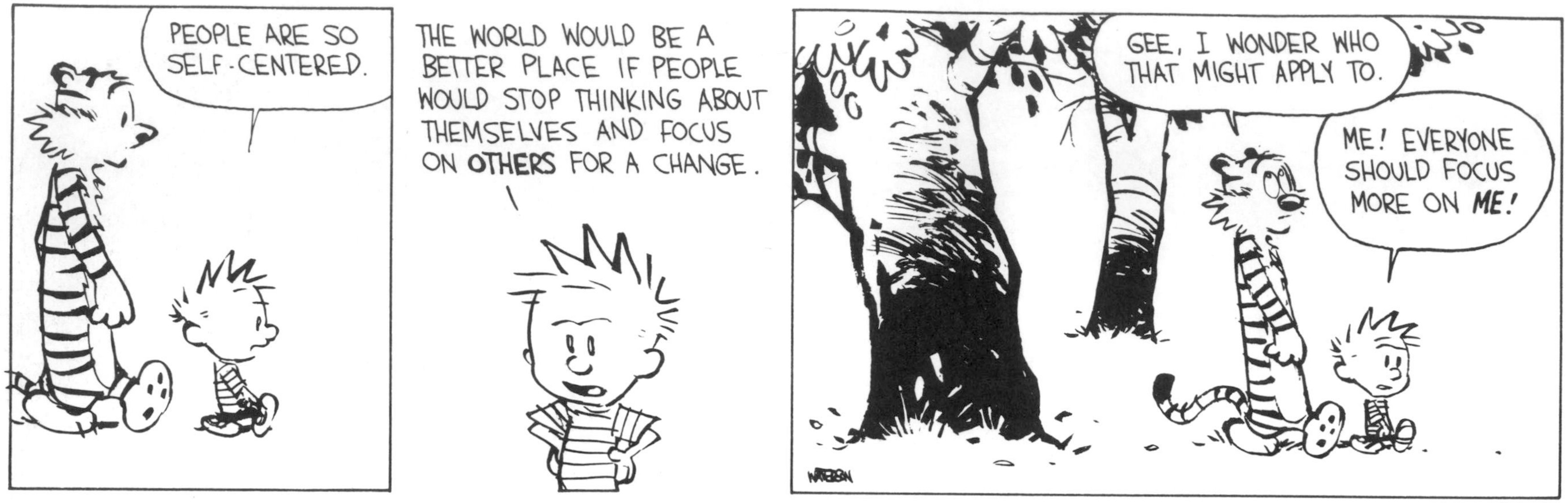
PEOPLE ARE SO SELF-CENTERED.
THE WORLD WOULD BE A BETTER PLACE IF PEOPLE WOULD STOP THINKING ABOUT THEMSELVES AND FOCUS ON **OTHERS** FOR A CHANGE.
GEE, I WONDER WHO THAT MIGHT APPLY TO.
ME! EVERYONE SHOULD FOCUS MORE ON **ME!**

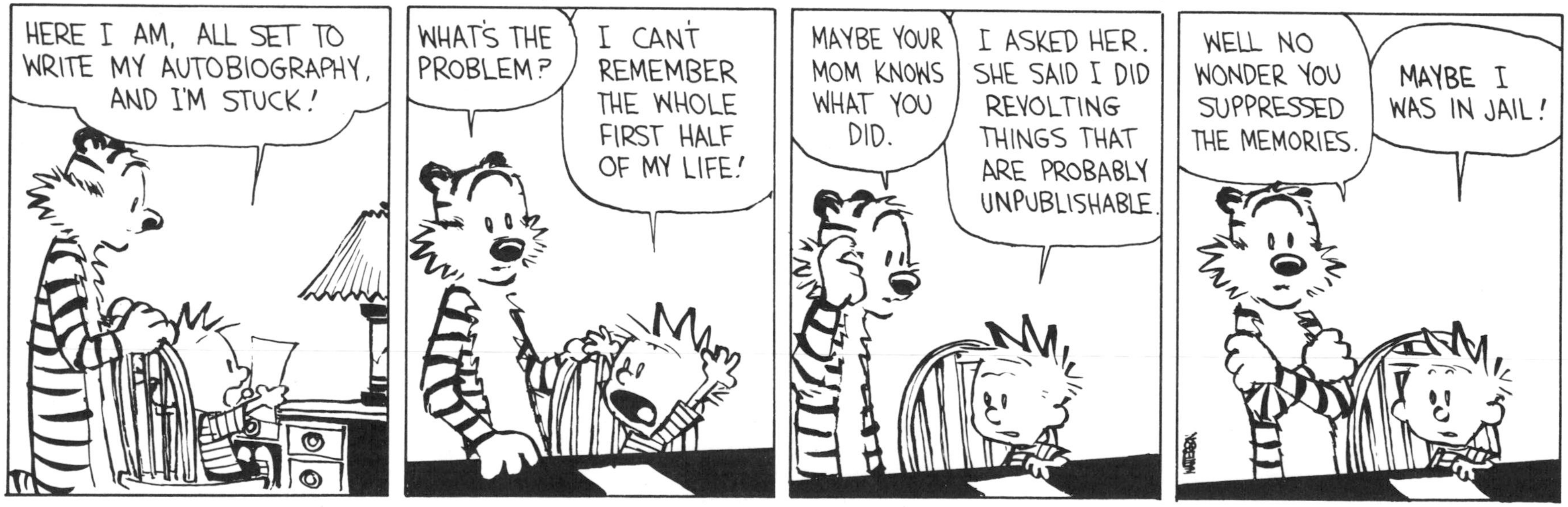
HERE I AM, ALL SET TO WRITE MY AUTOBIOGRAPHY, AND I'M STUCK!
WHAT'S THE PROBLEM?
I CAN'T REMEMBER THE WHOLE FIRST HALF OF MY LIFE!
MAYBE YOUR MOM KNOWS WHAT YOU DID.
I ASKED HER. SHE SAID I DID REVOLTING THINGS THAT ARE PROBABLY UNPUBLISHABLE.
WELL NO WONDER YOU SUPPRESSED THE MEMORIES.
MAYBE I WAS IN JAIL!

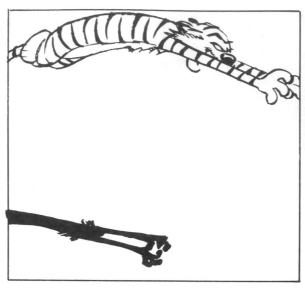

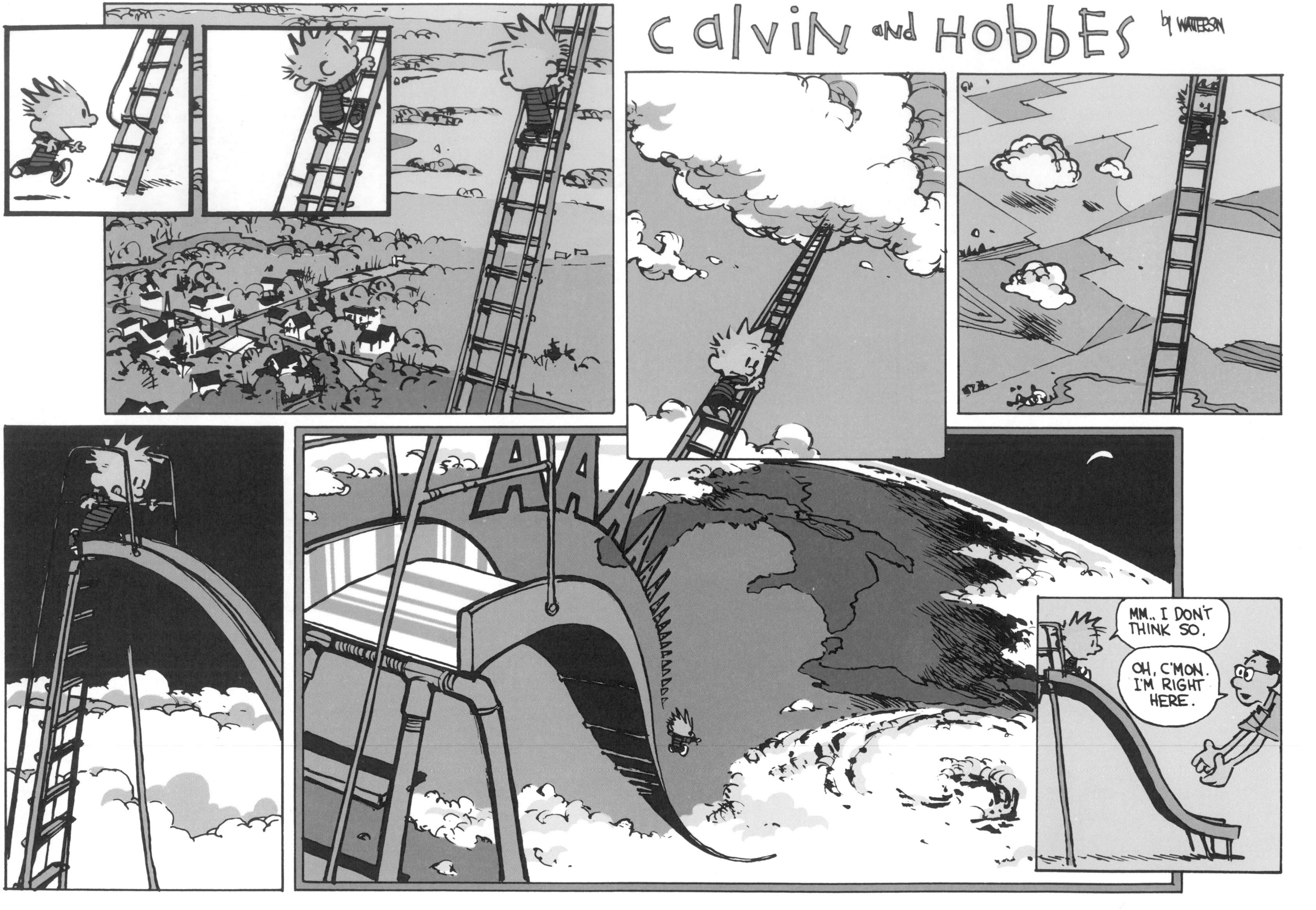
Calvin and HOBBES
by WATTERSON
AAAAAAAAAAAAAAA
MM.. I DON'T THINK SO.
OH, C'MON. I'M RIGHT HERE.

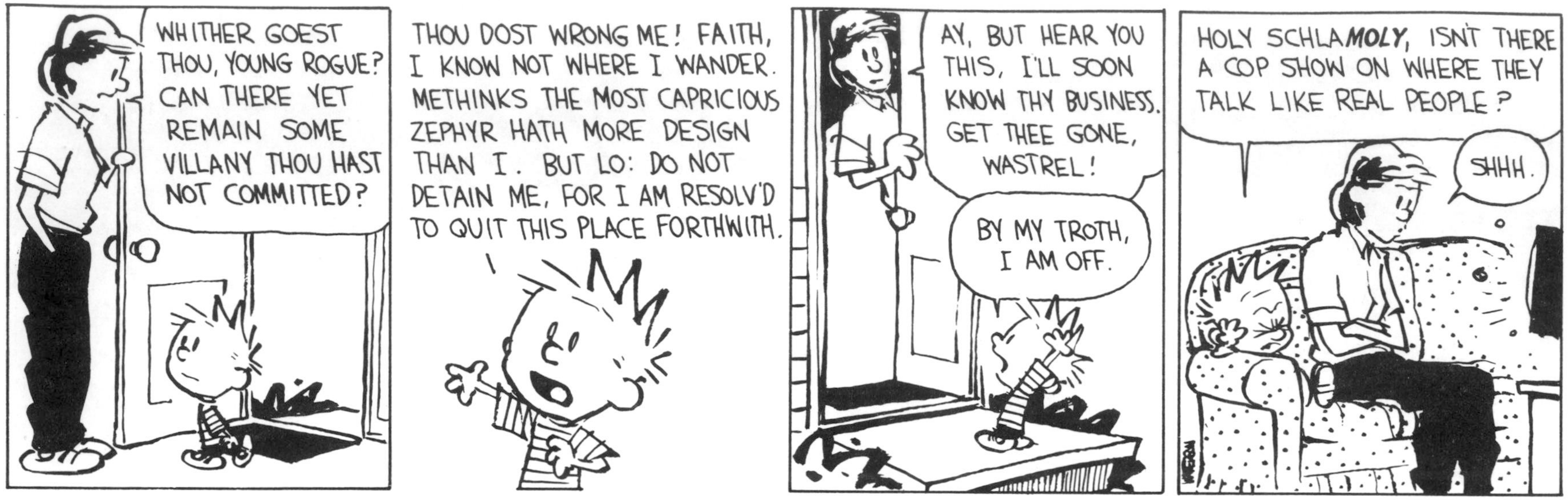
WHITHER GOEST THOU, YOUNG ROGUE? CAN THERE YET REMAIN SOME VILLANY THOU HAST NOT COMMITTED?
THOU DOST WRONG ME! FAITH, I KNOW NOT WHERE I WANDER. METHINKS THE MOST CAPRICIOUS ZEPHYR HATH MORE DESIGN THAN I. BUT LO: DO NOT DETAIN ME, FOR I AM RESOLV'D TO QUIT THIS PLACE FORTHWITH.
AY, BUT HEAR YOU THIS, I'LL SOON KNOW THY BUSINESS. GET THEE GONE, WASTREL!
BY MY TROTH, I AM OFF.
HOLY SCHLA**MOLY**, ISN'T THERE A COP SHOW ON WHERE THEY TALK LIKE REAL PEOPLE?
SHHH.

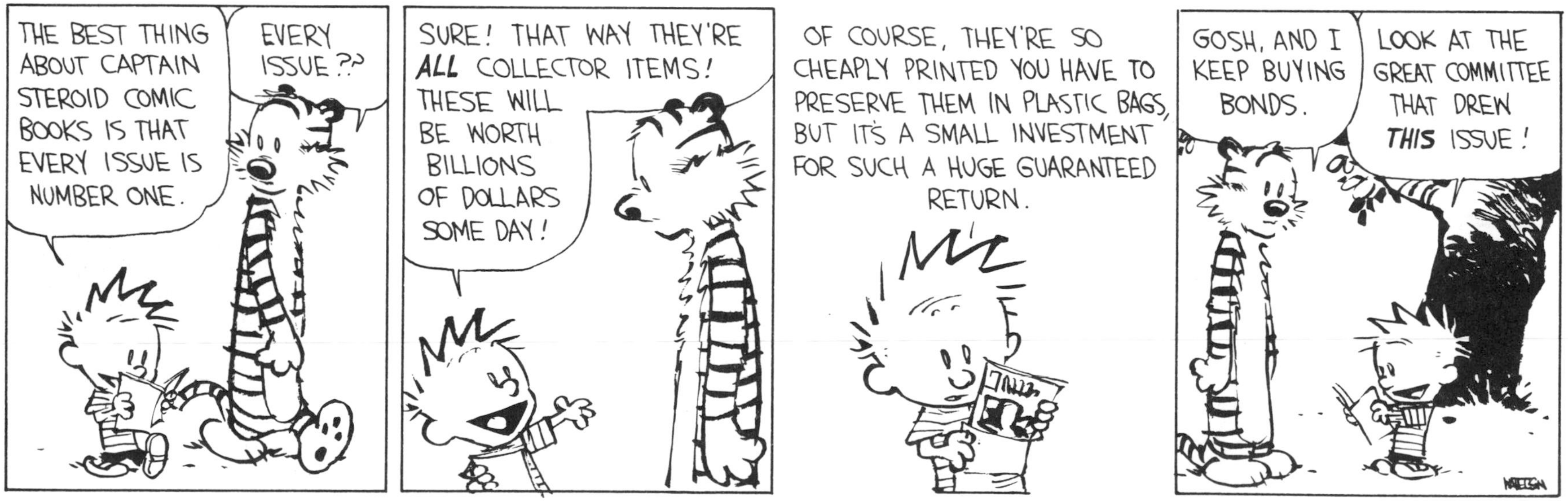
THE BEST THING ABOUT CAPTAIN STEROID COMIC BOOKS IS THAT EVERY ISSUE IS NUMBER ONE.
EVERY ISSUE??
SURE! THAT WAY THEY'RE **ALL** COLLECTOR ITEMS!
THESE WILL BE WORTH BILLIONS OF DOLLARS SOME DAY!
OF COURSE, THEY'RE SO CHEAPLY PRINTED YOU HAVE TO PRESERVE THEM IN PLASTIC BAGS, BUT IT'S A SMALL INVESTMENT FOR SUCH A HUGE GUARANTEED RETURN.
GOSH, AND I KEEP BUYING BONDS.
LOOK AT THE GREAT COMMITTEE THAT DREW **THIS** ISSUE!

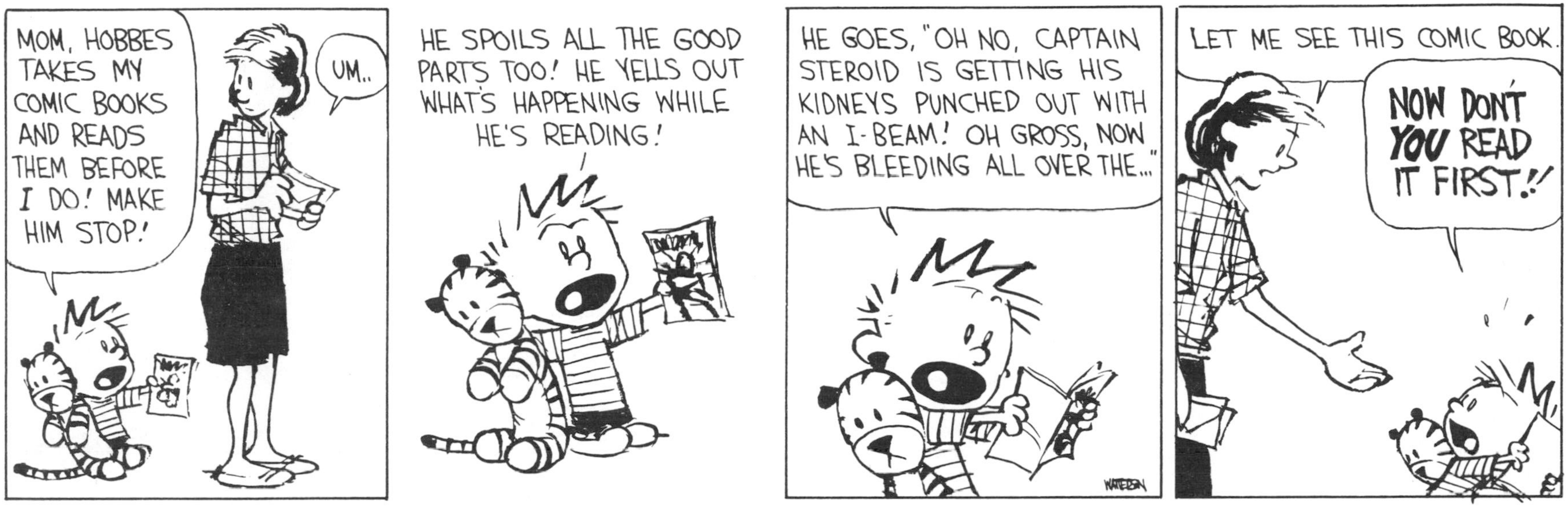

MOM, HOBBES TAKES MY COMIC BOOKS AND READS THEM BEFORE I DO! MAKE HIM STOP!
UM..
HE SPOILS ALL THE GOOD PARTS TOO! HE YELLS OUT WHAT'S HAPPENING WHILE HE'S READING!
HE GOES, "OH NO, CAPTAIN STEROID IS GETTING HIS KIDNEYS PUNCHED OUT WITH AN I-BEAM! OH GROSS, NOW HE'S BLEEDING ALL OVER THE..."
LET ME SEE THIS COMIC BOOK.
NOW DON'T YOU READ IT FIRST!!
WATTERSON

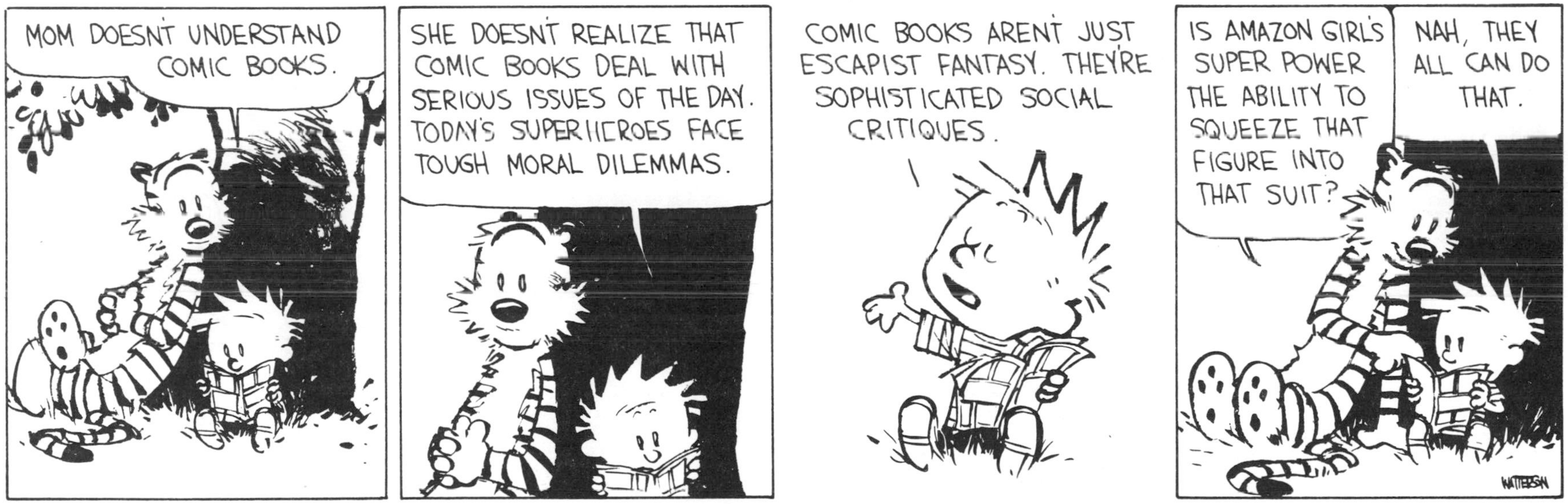

MOM DOESN'T UNDERSTAND COMIC BOOKS.
SHE DOESN'T REALIZE THAT COMIC BOOKS DEAL WITH SERIOUS ISSUES OF THE DAY. TODAY'S SUPERHEROES FACE TOUGH MORAL DILEMMAS.
COMIC BOOKS AREN'T JUST ESCAPIST FANTASY. THEY'RE SOPHISTICATED SOCIAL CRITIQUES.
IS AMAZON GIRL'S SUPER POWER THE ABILITY TO SQUEEZE THAT FIGURE INTO THAT SUIT?
NAH, THEY ALL CAN DO THAT.
WATTERSON

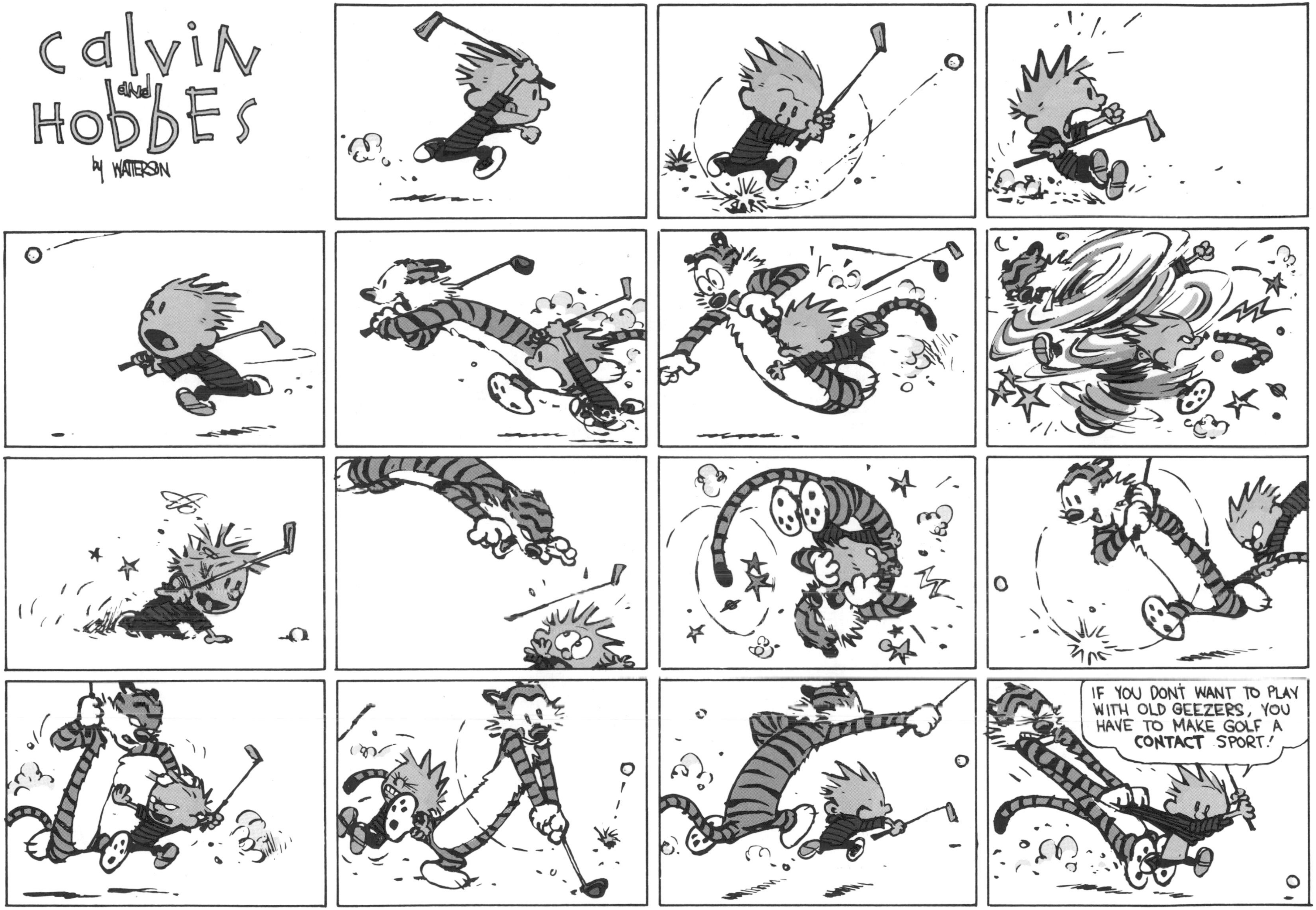
Calvin and Hobbes
by WATTERSON
IF YOU DON'T WANT TO PLAY WITH OLD GEEZERS, YOU HAVE TO MAKE GOLF A CONTACT SPORT!

FWOOSHH

IN ORDER TO DETERMINE IF THERE IS ANY UNIVERSAL MORAL LAW BEYOND HUMAN CONVENTION, I HAVE DEVISED THE FOLLOWING TEST.

I WILL THROW THIS WATER BALLOON AT SUSIE DERKINS UNLESS I RECEIVE SOME SIGN WITHIN THE NEXT 30 SECONDS THAT THIS IS WRONG.

IT IS IN THE UNIVERSE'S POWER TO STOP ME. I'LL ACCEPT ANY REMARKABLE PHYSICAL HAPPENSTANCE AS A SIGN THAT I SHOULDN'T DO THIS.

READY?... GO!

TUM TE TUM DOO DOO

...NOTHING'S HAPPENINNGG... FIVE SECONDS TO GO!

TIME'S UP! THAT PROVES IT! THERE'S NO MORAL LAW!

WHEEE!

HA HA!

Calvin and Hobbes

by WATTERSON

HEY SUSIE!!

SPLOOSH!

HELP! HELP! HE

WHY DOES THE UNIVERSE ALWAYS GIVE YOU THE SIGN *AFTER* YOU DO IT??

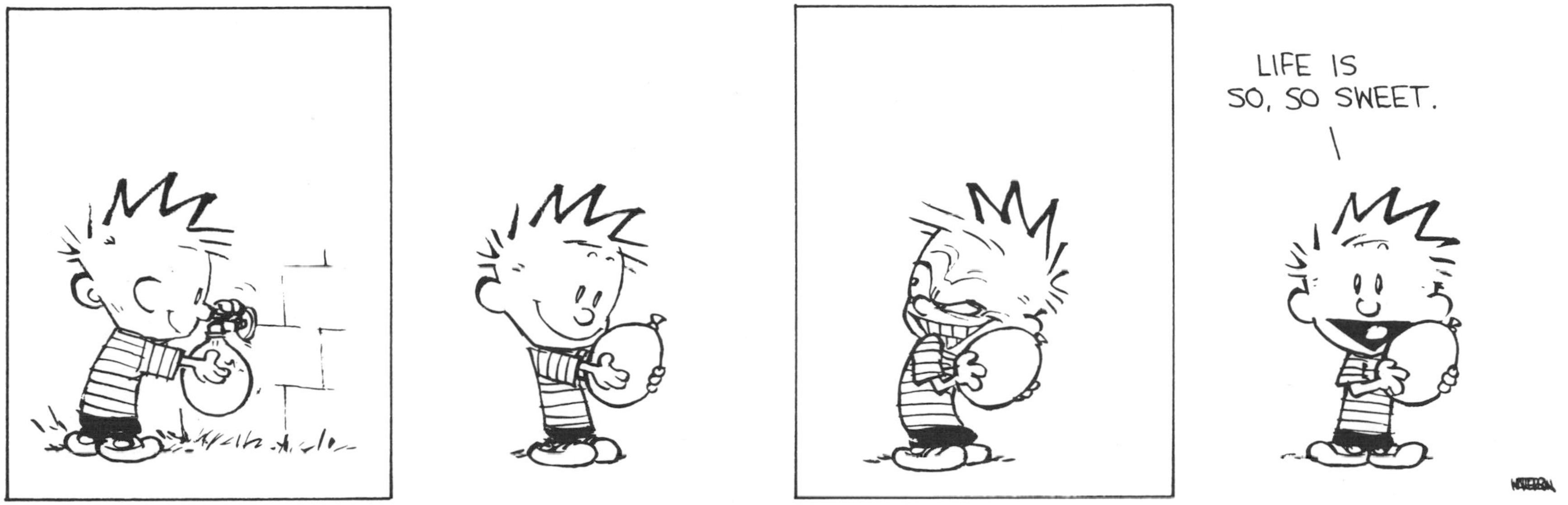
LIFE IS SO, SO SWEET.

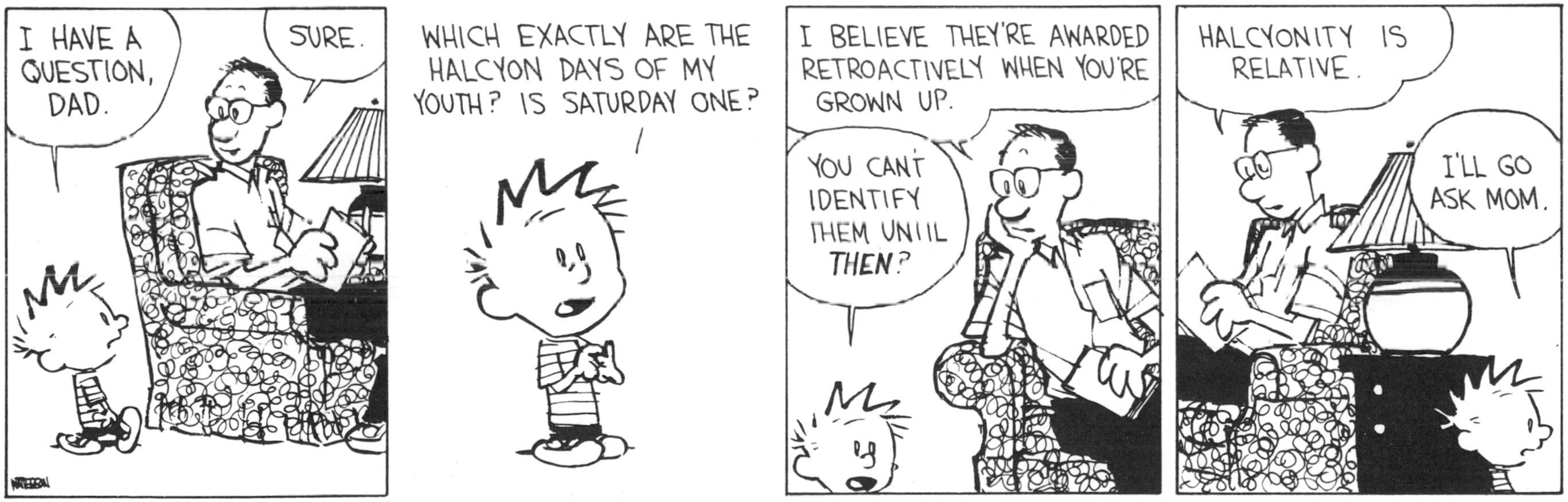
I HAVE A QUESTION, DAD.
SURE.
WHICH EXACTLY ARE THE HALCYON DAYS OF MY YOUTH? IS SATURDAY ONE?
I BELIEVE THEY'RE AWARDED RETROACTIVELY WHEN YOU'RE GROWN UP.
YOU CAN'T IDENTIFY THEM UNTIL *THEN*?
HALCYONITY IS RELATIVE.
I'LL GO ASK MOM.

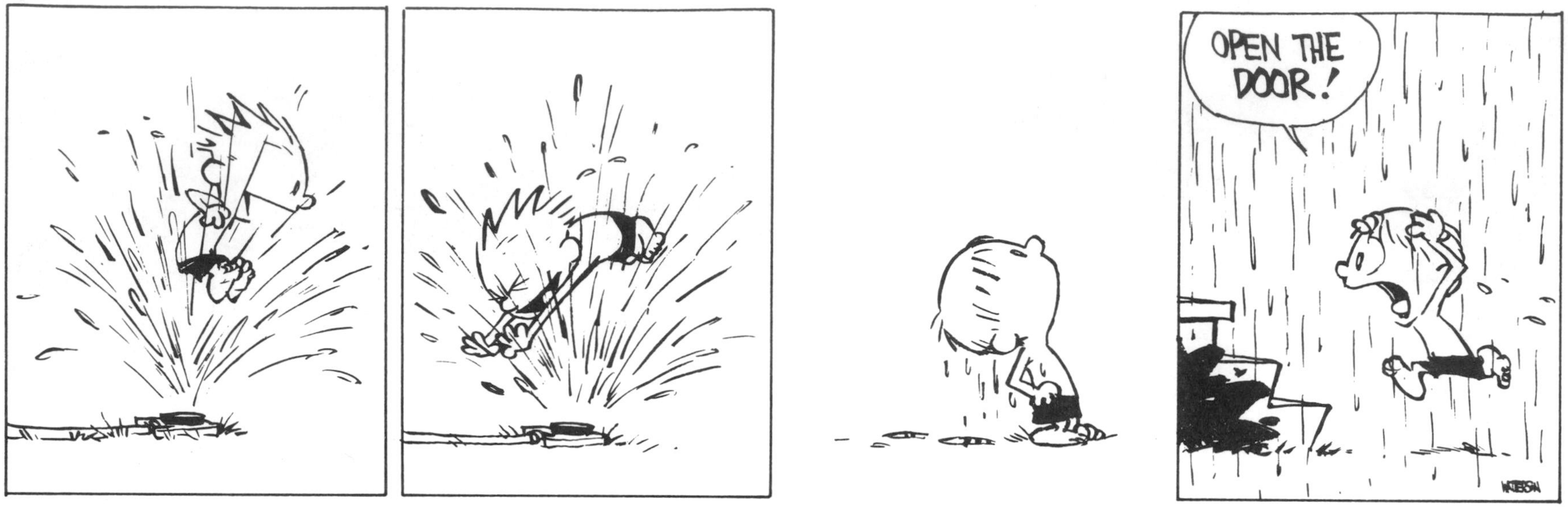
OPEN THE DOOR!

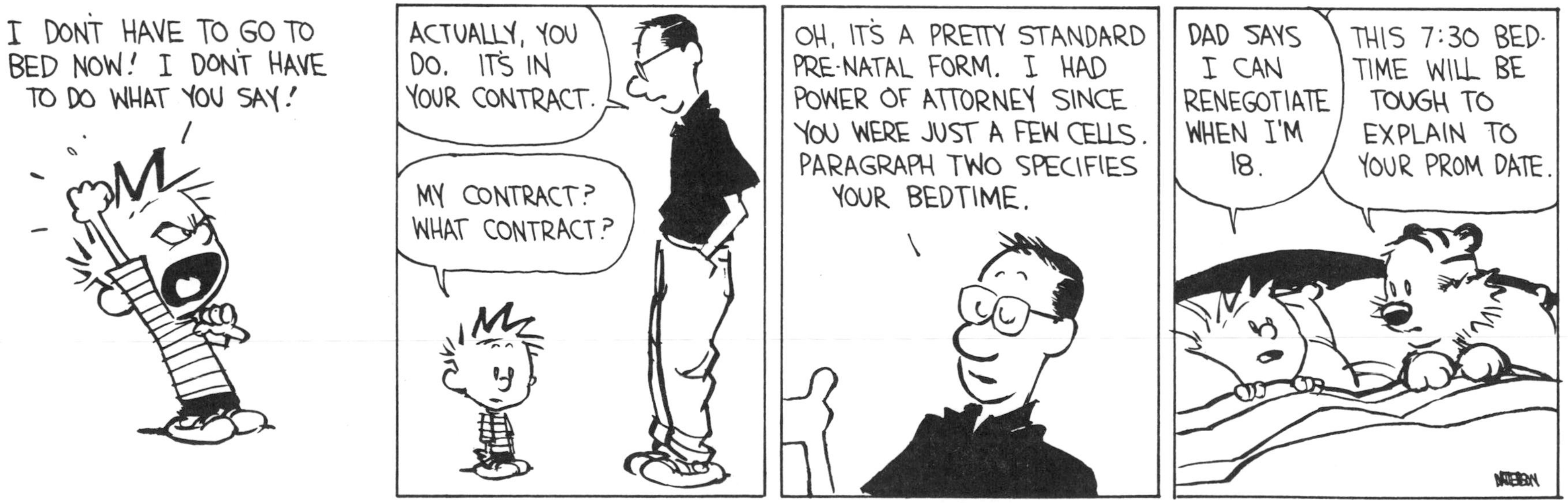
I DON'T HAVE TO GO TO BED NOW! I DON'T HAVE TO DO WHAT YOU SAY!
ACTUALLY, YOU DO. IT'S IN YOUR CONTRACT.
MY CONTRACT? WHAT CONTRACT?
OH, IT'S A PRETTY STANDARD PRE-NATAL FORM. I HAD POWER OF ATTORNEY SINCE YOU WERE JUST A FEW CELLS. PARAGRAPH TWO SPECIFIES YOUR BEDTIME.
DAD SAYS I CAN RENEGOTIATE WHEN I'M 18.
THIS 7:30 BED-TIME WILL BE TOUGH TO EXPLAIN TO YOUR PROM DATE.

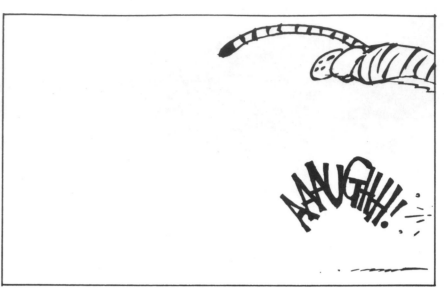

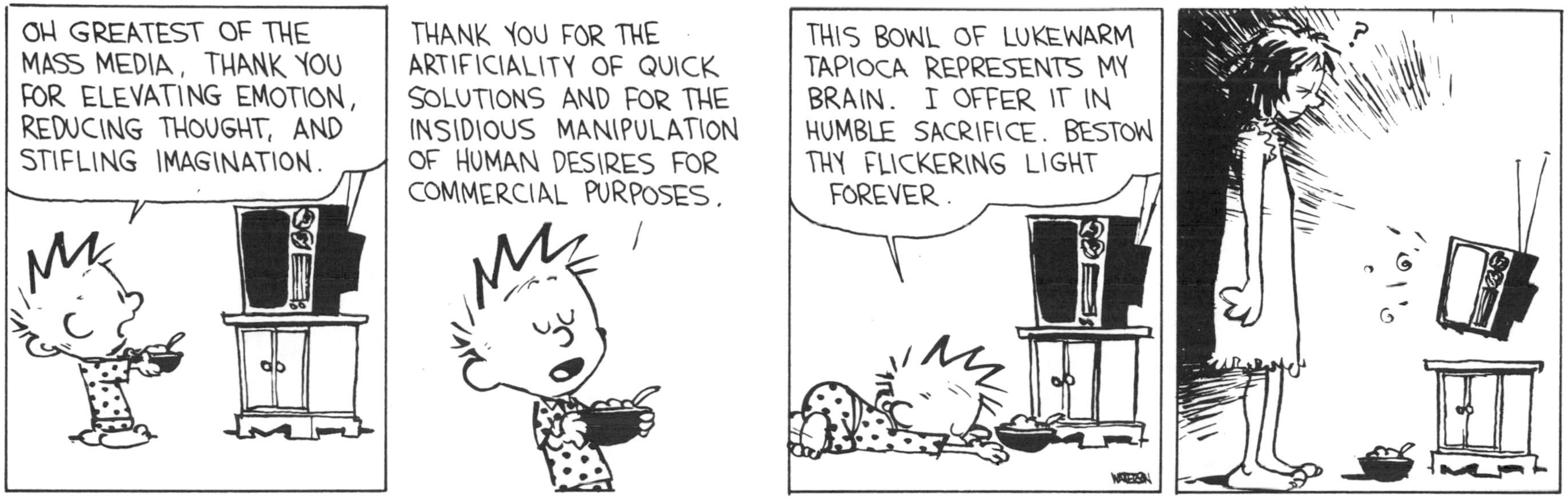
OH GREATEST OF THE MASS MEDIA, THANK YOU FOR ELEVATING EMOTION, REDUCING THOUGHT, AND STIFLING IMAGINATION.
THANK YOU FOR THE ARTIFICIALITY OF QUICK SOLUTIONS AND FOR THE INSIDIOUS MANIPULATION OF HUMAN DESIRES FOR COMMERCIAL PURPOSES.
THIS BOWL OF LUKEWARM TAPIOCA REPRESENTS MY BRAIN. I OFFER IT IN HUMBLE SACRIFICE. BESTOW THY FLICKERING LIGHT FOREVER.
?

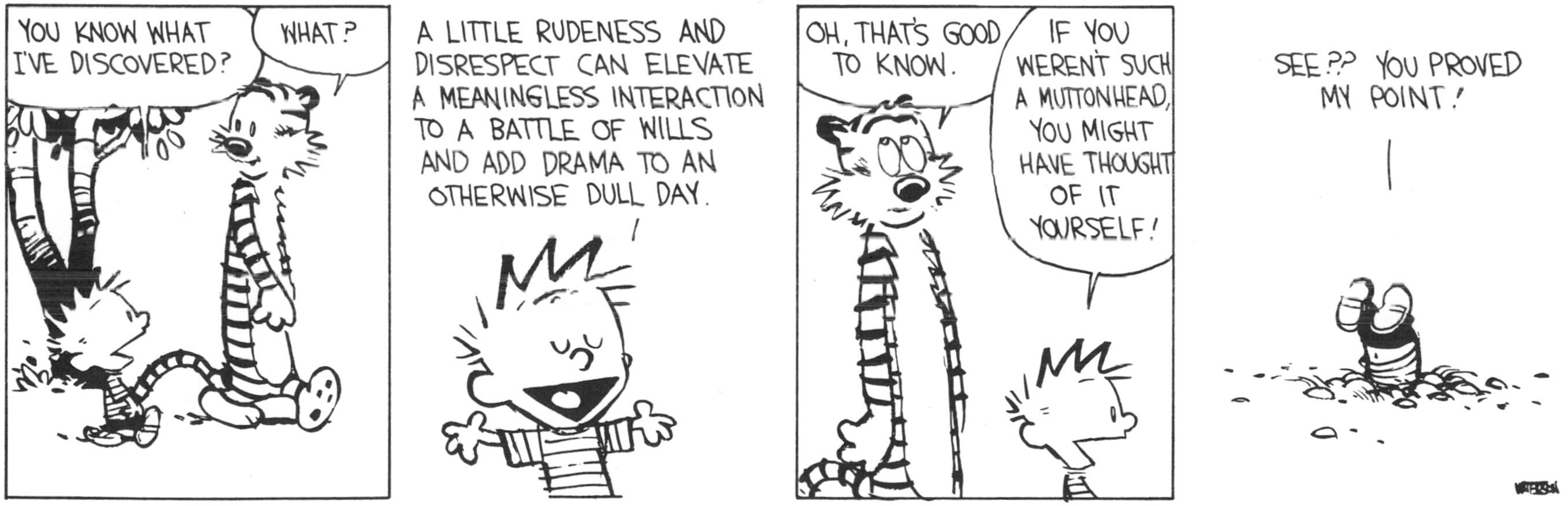
YOU KNOW WHAT I'VE DISCOVERED?
WHAT?
A LITTLE RUDENESS AND DISRESPECT CAN ELEVATE A MEANINGLESS INTERACTION TO A BATTLE OF WILLS AND ADD DRAMA TO AN OTHERWISE DULL DAY.
OH, THAT'S GOOD TO KNOW.
IF YOU WERENT SUCH A MUTTONHEAD, YOU MIGHT HAVE THOUGHT OF IT YOURSELF!
SEE?? YOU PROVED MY POINT!

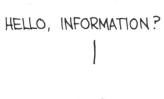

HELLO, INFORMATION?

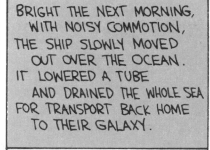

THE ALIENS CAME FROM A FAR DISTANT WORLD IN A LARGE YELLOW SHIP THAT BLINKED AS IT TWIRLED. IT ROUNDED THE MOON, AND ENTERED OUR SKY. WE KNEW THEY HAD COME BUT WE DIDN'T KNOW WHY.
BRIGHT THE NEXT MORNING, WITH NOISY COMMOTION, THE SHIP SLOWLY MOVED OUT OVER THE OCEAN. IT LOWERED A TUBE AND DRAINED THE WHOLE SEA FOR TRANSPORT BACK HOME TO THEIR GALAXY.
THE TUBE THEN SUCKED UP THE CLOUDS AND THE AIR, CAUSING NO SMALL AMOUNT OF EARTHLING DESPAIR. WITH NOTHING TO BREATHE, WE STARTED TO DIE. "HELP US! PLEASE STOP!" WAS THE PUBLIC OUTCRY.
A HATCH OPENED UP AND THE ALIENS SAID, "WE'RE SORRY TO LEARN THAT YOU SOON WILL BE DEAD, BUT THOUGH YOU MAY FIND THIS SLIGHTLY MACABRE, WE PREFER YOUR EXTINCTION TO THE LOSS OF OUR JOB."
Calvin and Hobbes
by WATTERSON
THAT'S MY SCIENCE FICTION STORY. THINK IT'S TOO FAR-FETCHED?
NOT ENOUGH, REALLY.

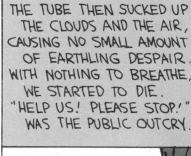

I'M SICK OF HEARING ABOUT PERSONAL RESPONSIBILITY! I'VE ALREADY DONE MY PART TO MAKE THE WORLD A BETTER PLACE TO LIVE.
REALLY?
SURE! I WAS BORN!
OH YES, I FORGOT TO THANK YOU.
JOIN THE CLUB!
WATTERSON

MAN, IT MUST BE 100 DEGREES TODAY!
ANIMALS SURE ARE DUMB TO HAVE ALL THAT FUR.
PEOPLE SURE ARE UGLY WITHOUT IT.
!
I'LL BET HE'S CRANKY BECAUSE HE'S SO HOT.
WATTERSON

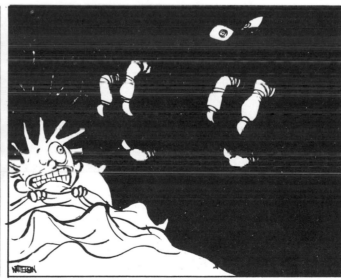

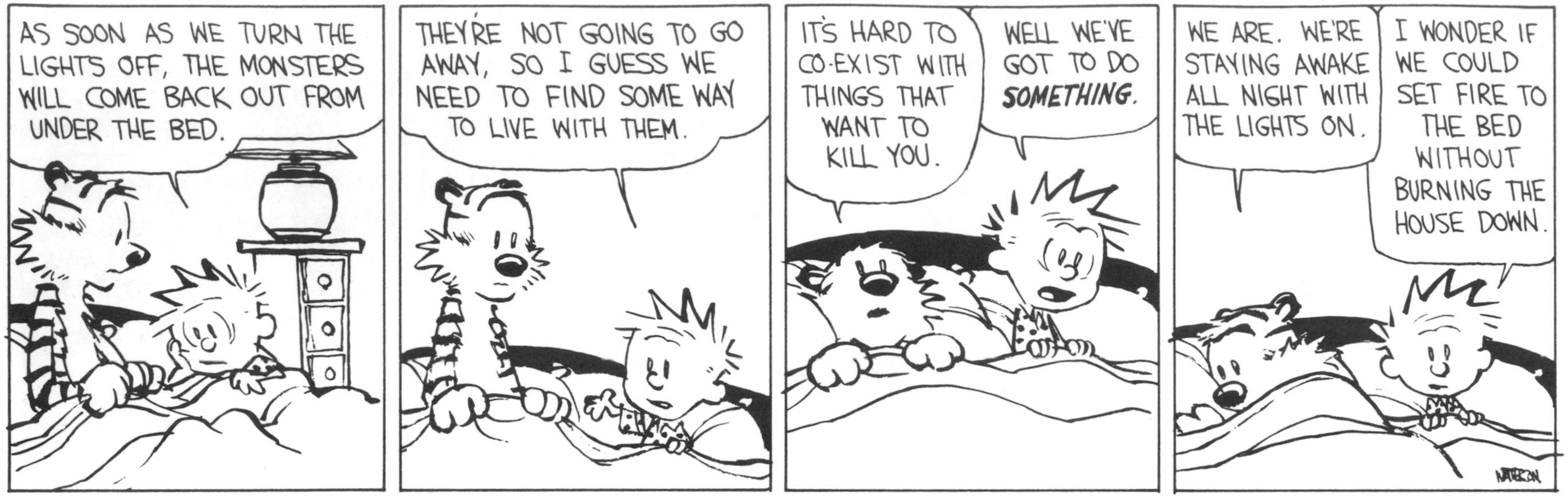
AS SOON AS WE TURN THE LIGHTS OFF, THE MONSTERS WILL COME BACK OUT FROM UNDER THE BED.
THEY'RE NOT GOING TO GO AWAY, SO I GUESS WE NEED TO FIND SOME WAY TO LIVE WITH THEM.
IT'S HARD TO CO-EXIST WITH THINGS THAT WANT TO KILL YOU.
WELL WE'VE GOT TO DO **SOMETHING**.
WE ARE. WE'RE STAYING AWAKE ALL NIGHT WITH THE LIGHTS ON.
I WONDER IF WE COULD SET FIRE TO THE BED WITHOUT BURNING THE HOUSE DOWN.

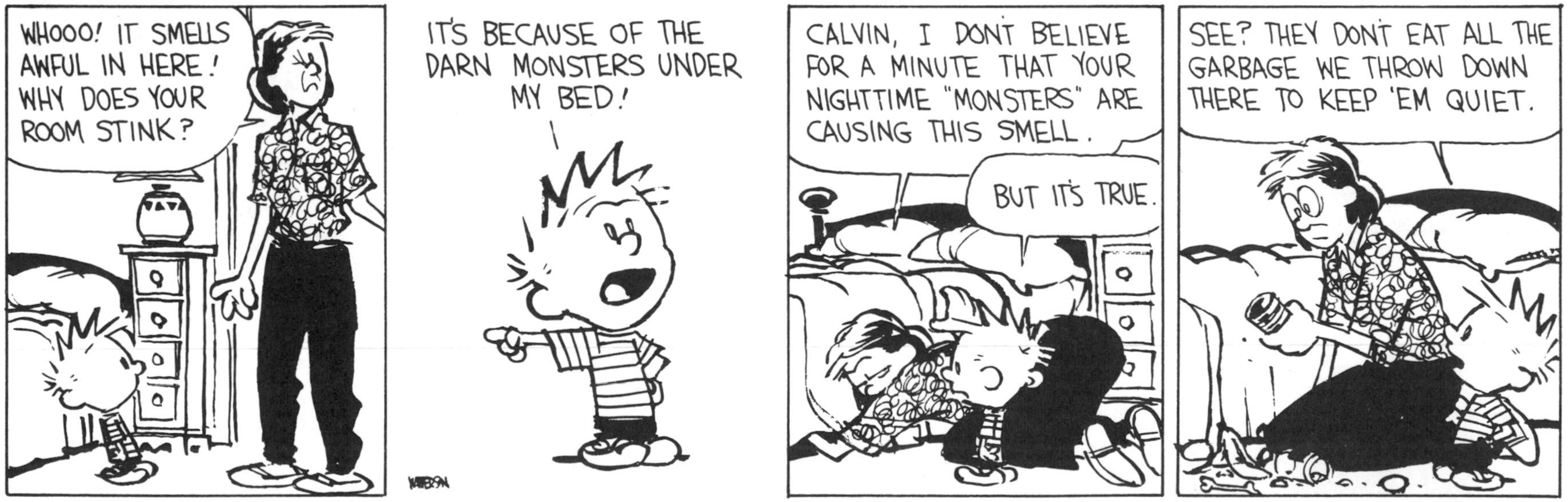
WHOOO! IT SMELLS AWFUL IN HERE! WHY DOES YOUR ROOM STINK?
IT'S BECAUSE OF THE DARN MONSTERS UNDER MY BED!
CALVIN, I DON'T BELIEVE FOR A MINUTE THAT YOUR NIGHTTIME "MONSTERS" ARE CAUSING THIS SMELL.
BUT IT'S TRUE.
SEE? THEY DON'T EAT ALL THE GARBAGE WE THROW DOWN THERE TO KEEP 'EM QUIET.

Calvin
and
Hobbes
by WATTERSON

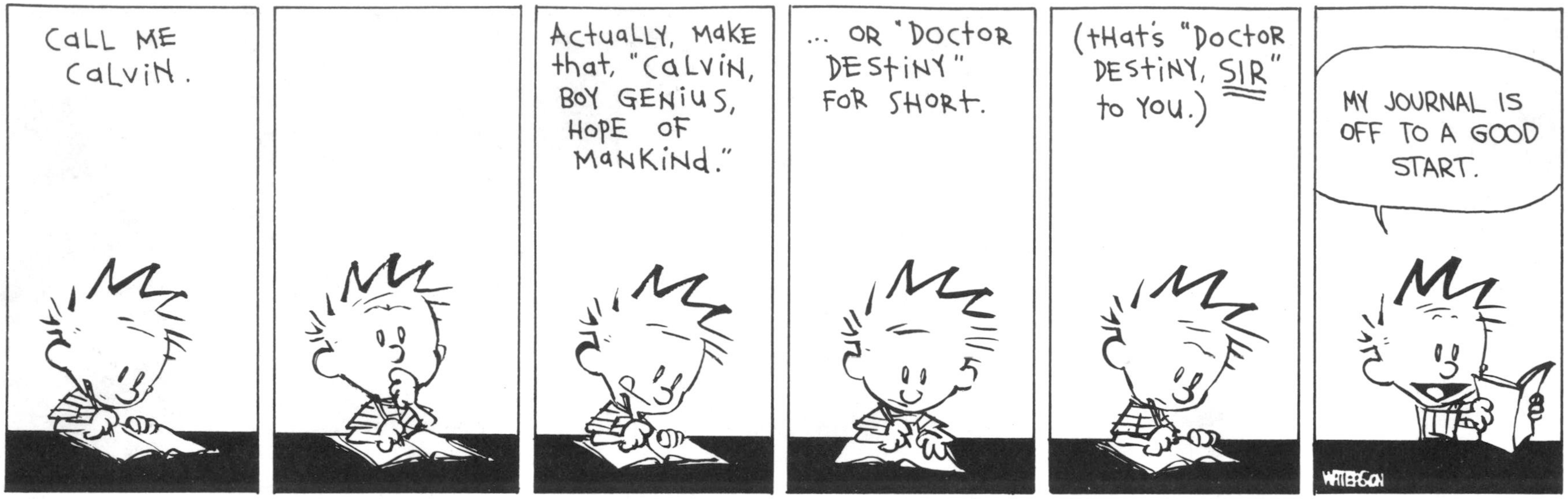
CALL ME CALVIN.
ACTUALLY, MAKE THAT, "CALVIN, BOY GENIUS, HOPE OF MANKIND."
... OR "DOCTOR DESTINY" FOR SHORT.
(THAT'S "DOCTOR DESTINY, SIR" TO YOU.)
MY JOURNAL IS OFF TO A GOOD START.
WATTERSON

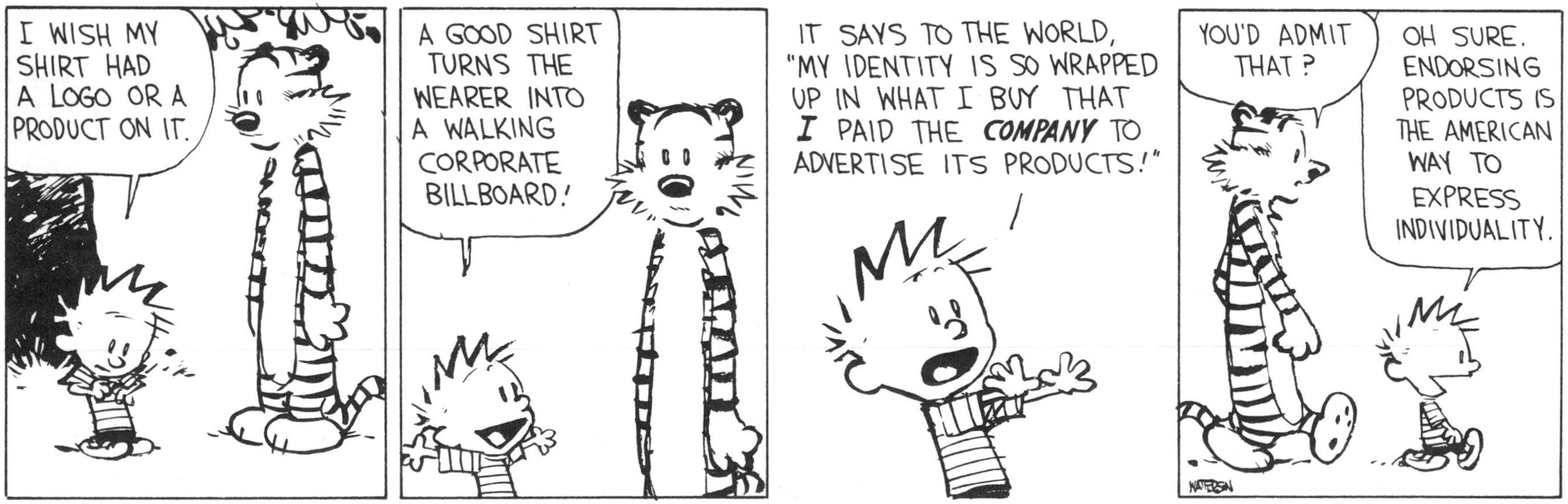
I WISH MY SHIRT HAD A LOGO OR A PRODUCT ON IT.
A GOOD SHIRT TURNS THE WEARER INTO A WALKING CORPORATE BILLBOARD!
IT SAYS TO THE WORLD, "MY IDENTITY IS SO WRAPPED UP IN WHAT I BUY THAT I PAID THE COMPANY TO ADVERTISE ITS PRODUCTS!"
YOU'D ADMIT THAT?
OH SURE. ENDORSING PRODUCTS IS THE AMERICAN WAY TO EXPRESS INDIVIDUALITY.
WATTERSON

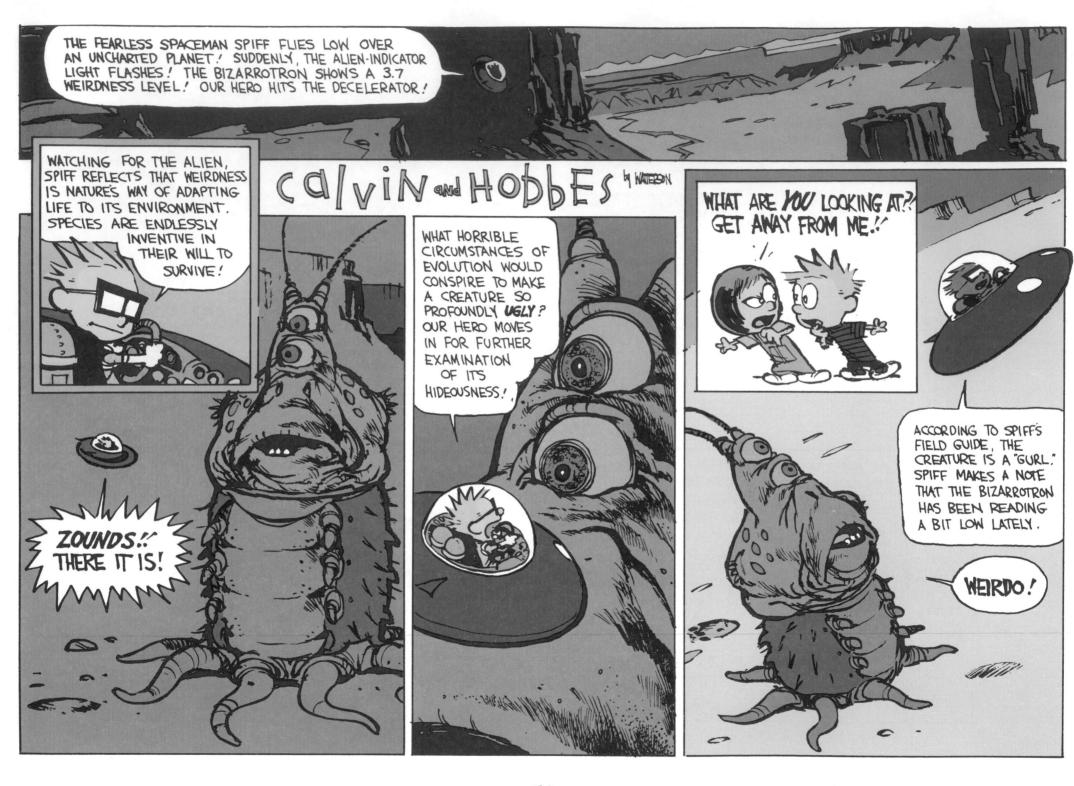

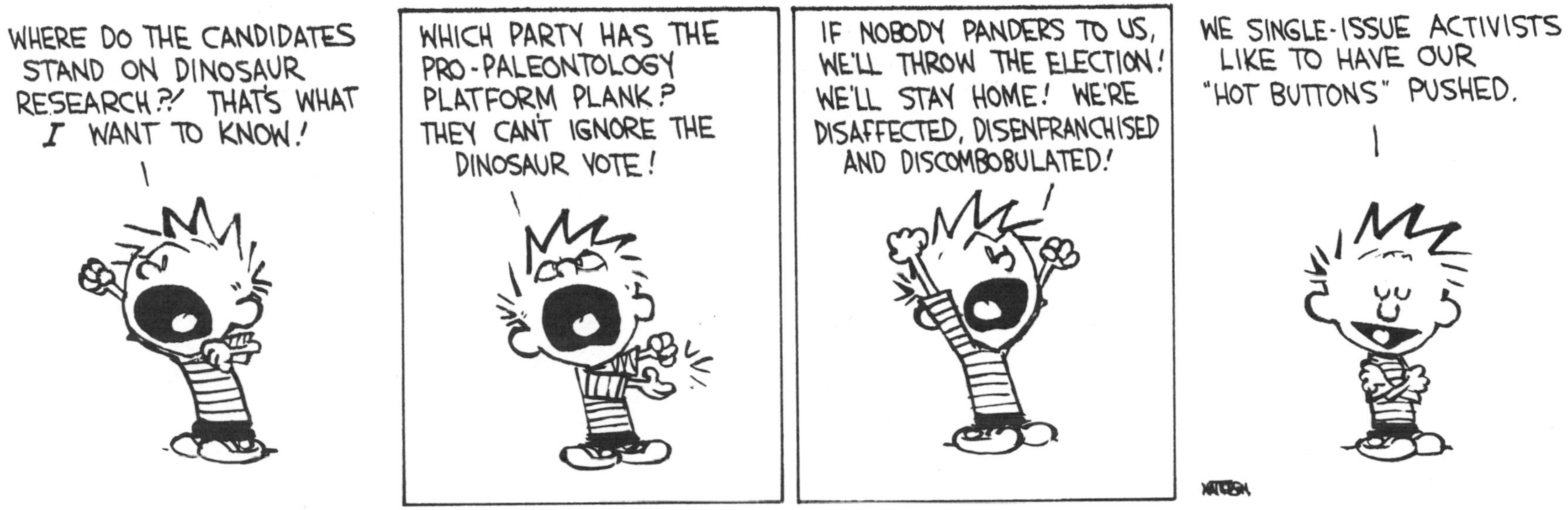
WHERE DO THE CANDIDATES STAND ON DINOSAUR RESEARCH?! THAT'S WHAT I WANT TO KNOW!
WHICH PARTY HAS THE PRO-PALEONTOLOGY PLATFORM PLANK? THEY CAN'T IGNORE THE DINOSAUR VOTE!
IF NOBODY PANDERS TO US, WE'LL THROW THE ELECTION! WE'LL STAY HOME! WE'RE DISAFFECTED, DISENFRANCHISED AND DISCOMBOBULATED!
WE SINGLE-ISSUE ACTIVISTS LIKE TO HAVE OUR "HOT BUTTONS" PUSHED.

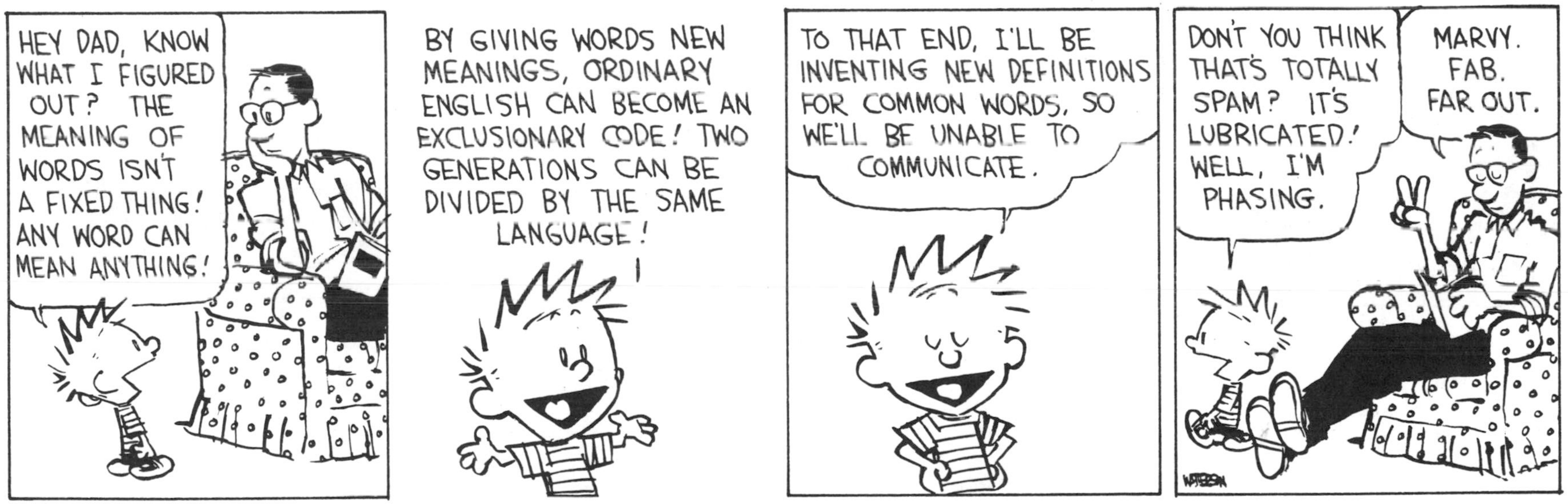
HEY DAD, KNOW WHAT I FIGURED OUT? THE MEANING OF WORDS ISN'T A FIXED THING! ANY WORD CAN MEAN ANYTHING!
BY GIVING WORDS NEW MEANINGS, ORDINARY ENGLISH CAN BECOME AN EXCLUSIONARY CODE! TWO GENERATIONS CAN BE DIVIDED BY THE SAME LANGUAGE!
TO THAT END, I'LL BE INVENTING NEW DEFINITIONS FOR COMMON WORDS, SO WE'LL BE UNABLE TO COMMUNICATE.
DON'T YOU THINK THAT'S TOTALLY SPAM? IT'S LUBRICATED! WELL, I'M PHASING.
MARVY. FAB. FAR OUT.

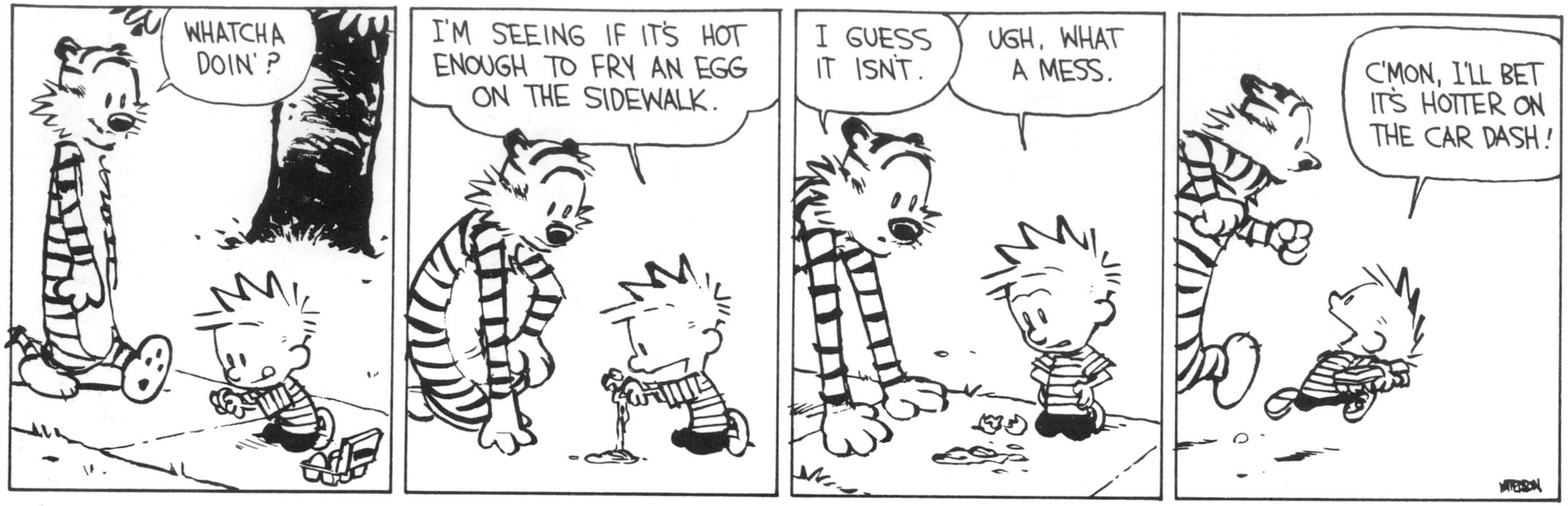
WHATCHA DOIN'?
I'M SEEING IF IT'S HOT ENOUGH TO FRY AN EGG ON THE SIDEWALK.
I GUESS IT ISN'T.
UGH, WHAT A MESS.
C'MON, I'LL BET IT'S HOTTER ON THE CAR DASH!

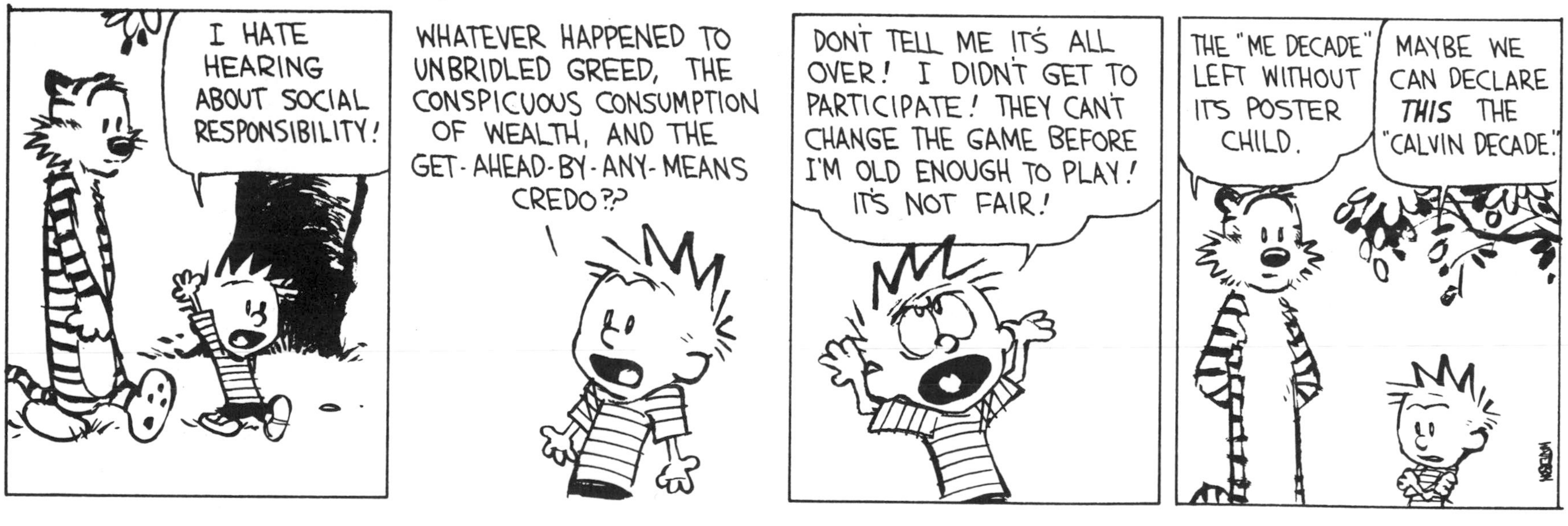
I HATE HEARING ABOUT SOCIAL RESPONSIBILITY!
WHATEVER HAPPENED TO UNBRIDLED GREED, THE CONSPICUOUS CONSUMPTION OF WEALTH, AND THE GET-AHEAD-BY-ANY-MEANS CREDO??
DON'T TELL ME IT'S ALL OVER! I DIDN'T GET TO PARTICIPATE! THEY CAN'T CHANGE THE GAME BEFORE I'M OLD ENOUGH TO PLAY! IT'S NOT FAIR!
THE "ME DECADE" LEFT WITHOUT ITS POSTER CHILD.
MAYBE WE CAN DECLARE **THIS** THE "CALVIN DECADE."

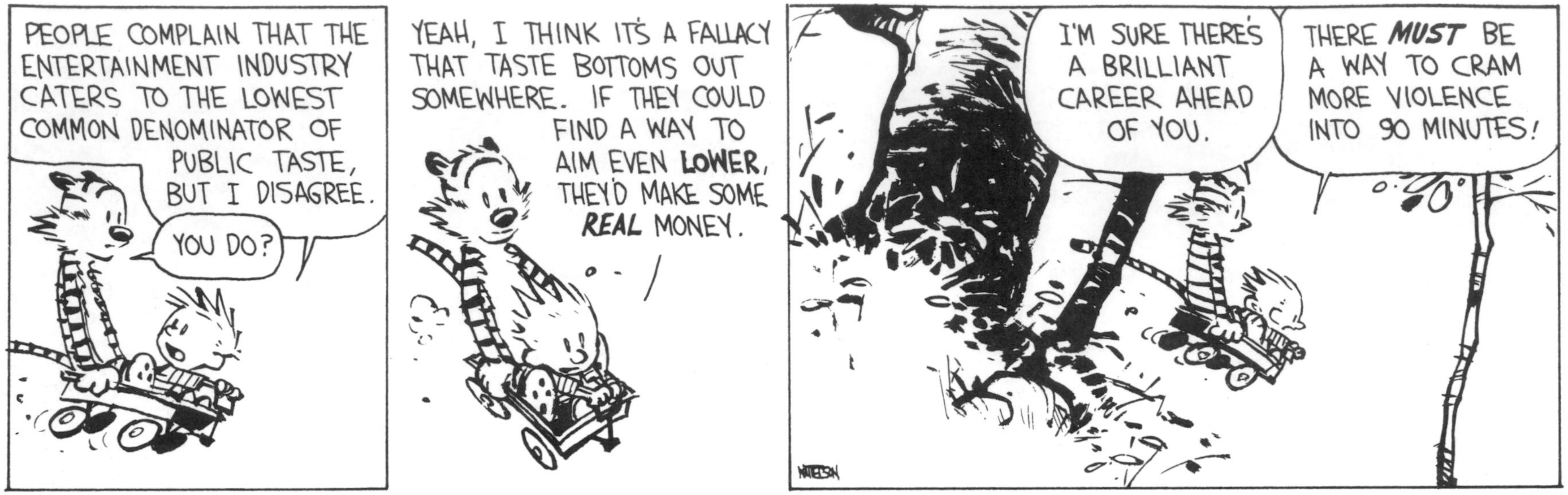
PEOPLE COMPLAIN THAT THE ENTERTAINMENT INDUSTRY CATERS TO THE LOWEST COMMON DENOMINATOR OF PUBLIC TASTE, BUT I DISAGREE.
YOU DO?
YEAH, I THINK IT'S A FALLACY THAT TASTE BOTTOMS OUT SOMEWHERE. IF THEY COULD FIND A WAY TO AIM EVEN **LOWER**, THEY'D MAKE SOME ***REAL*** MONEY.
I'M SURE THERE'S A BRILLIANT CAREER AHEAD OF YOU.
THERE ***MUST*** BE A WAY TO CRAM MORE VIOLENCE INTO 90 MINUTES!

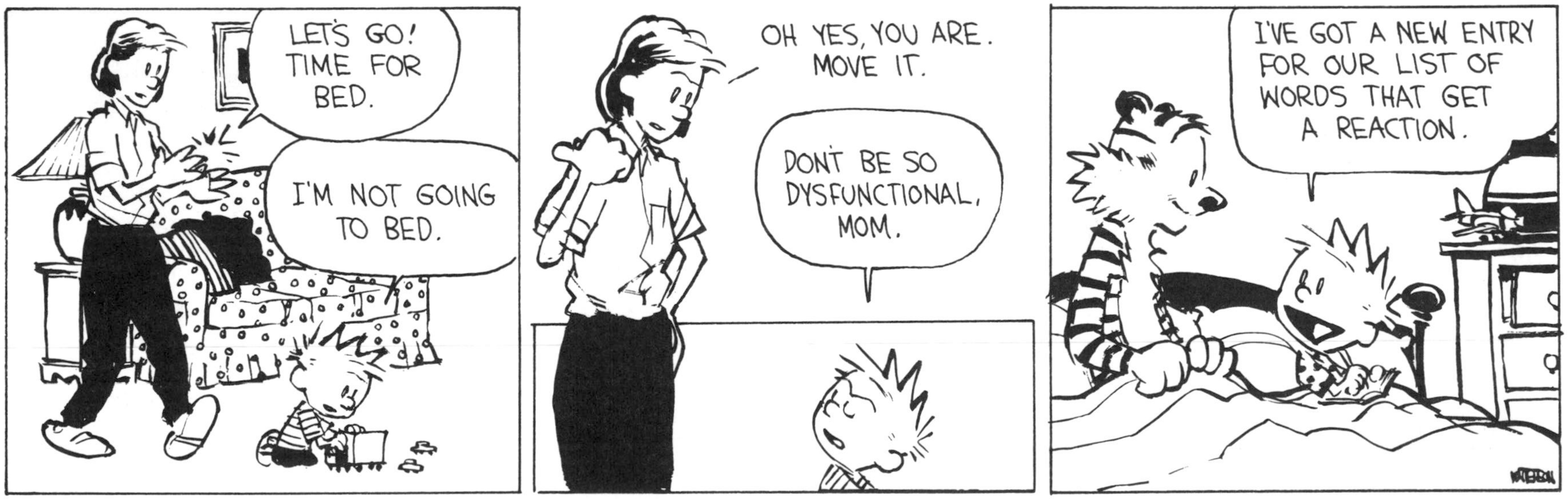
LET'S GO! TIME FOR BED.
I'M NOT GOING TO BED.
OH YES, YOU ARE. MOVE IT.
DON'T BE SO DYSFUNCTIONAL, MOM.
I'VE GOT A NEW ENTRY FOR OUR LIST OF WORDS THAT GET A REACTION.

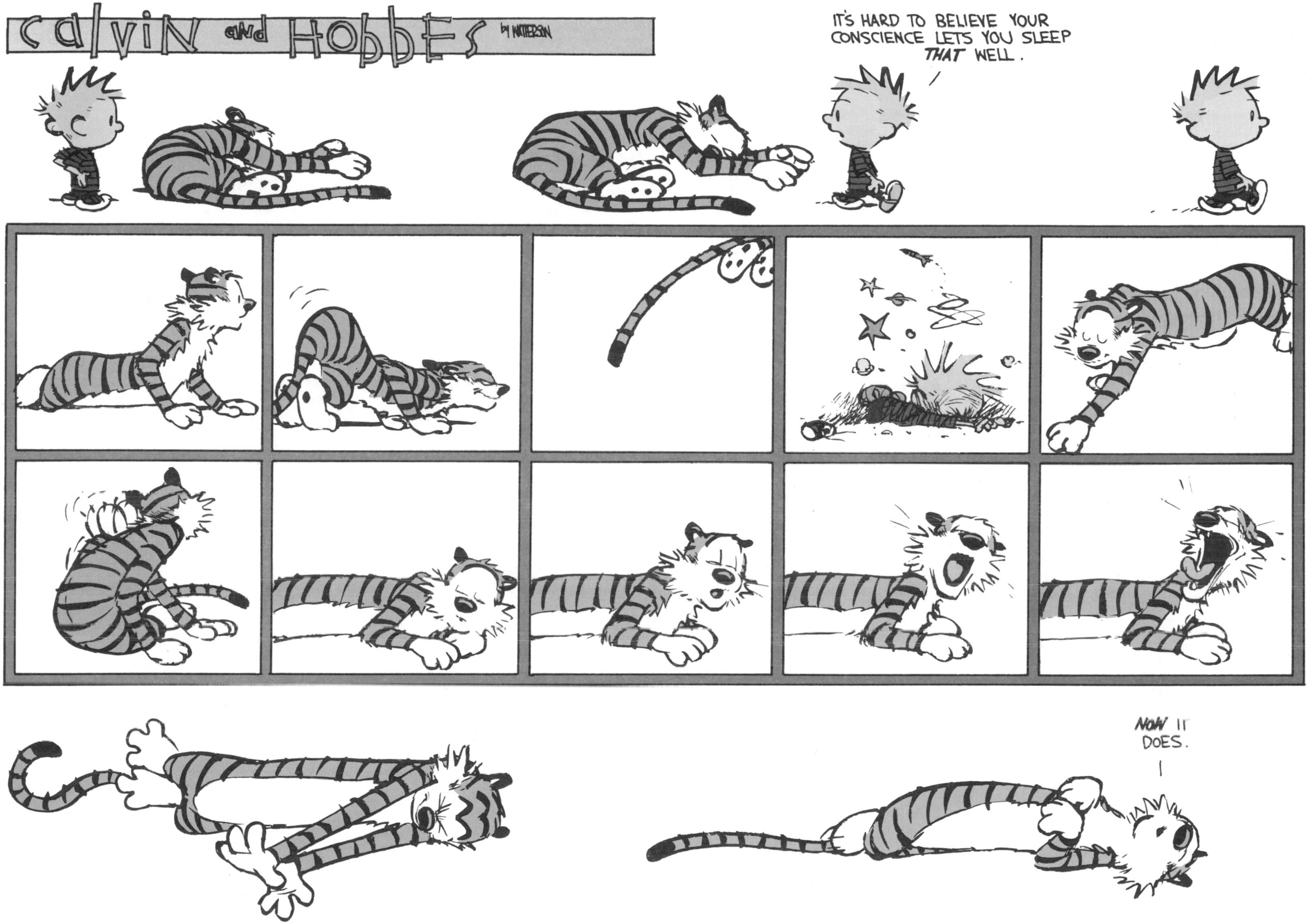
calvin and HOBBES by WATTERSON
IT'S HARD TO BELIEVE YOUR CONSCIENCE LETS YOU SLEEP THAT WELL.
NOW IT DOES.

I NEED TO MAKE FRIENDS WITH SOME LESS TERRITORIAL ANIMALS.

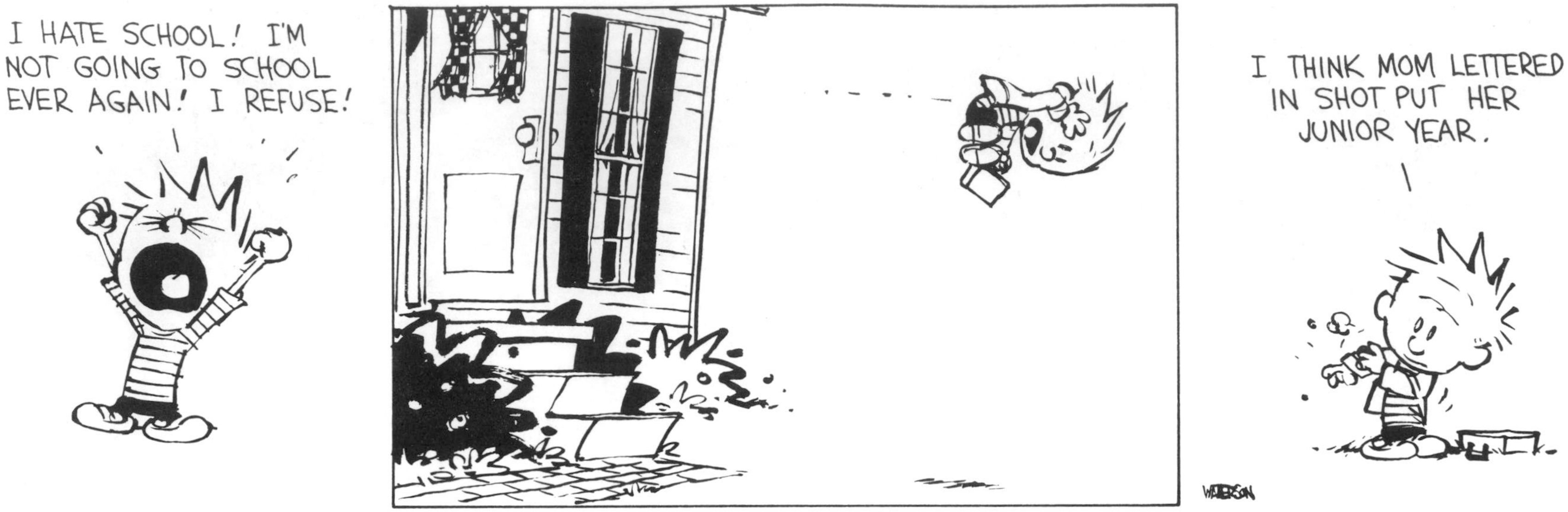
I HATE SCHOOL! I'M NOT GOING TO SCHOOL EVER AGAIN! I REFUSE!
I THINK MOM LETTERED IN SHOT PUT HER JUNIOR YEAR.
WATTERSON

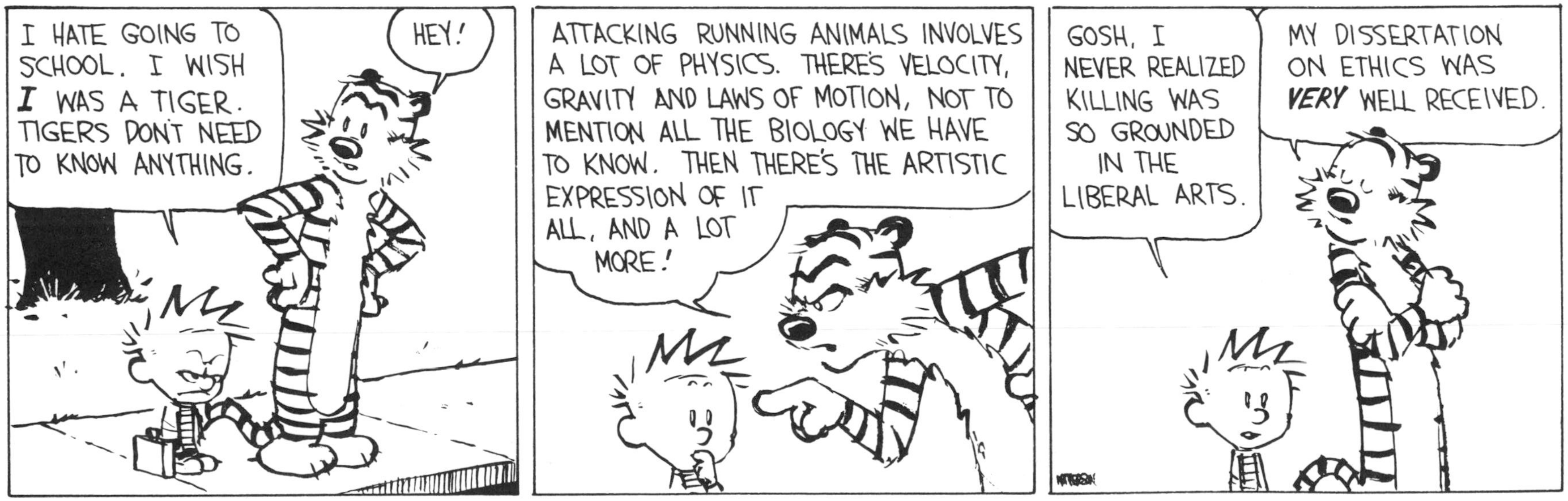
I HATE GOING TO SCHOOL. I WISH *I* WAS A TIGER. TIGERS DON'T NEED TO KNOW ANYTHING.
HEY!
ATTACKING RUNNING ANIMALS INVOLVES A LOT OF PHYSICS. THERE'S VELOCITY, GRAVITY AND LAWS OF MOTION, NOT TO MENTION ALL THE BIOLOGY WE HAVE TO KNOW. THEN THERE'S THE ARTISTIC EXPRESSION OF IT ALL, AND A LOT MORE!
GOSH, I NEVER REALIZED KILLING WAS SO GROUNDED IN THE LIBERAL ARTS.
MY DISSERTATION ON ETHICS WAS ***VERY*** WELL RECEIVED.

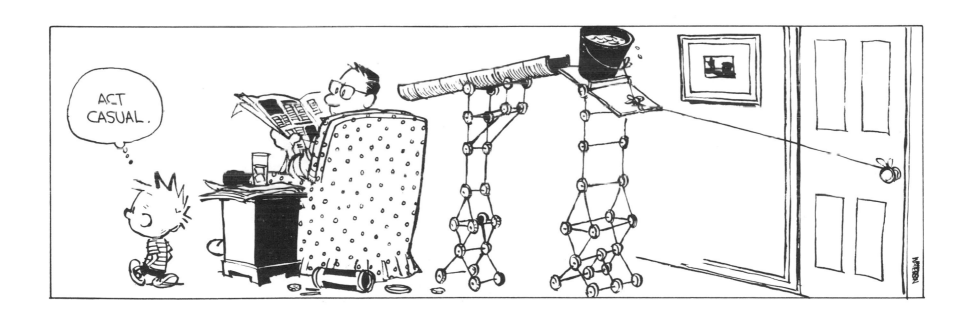

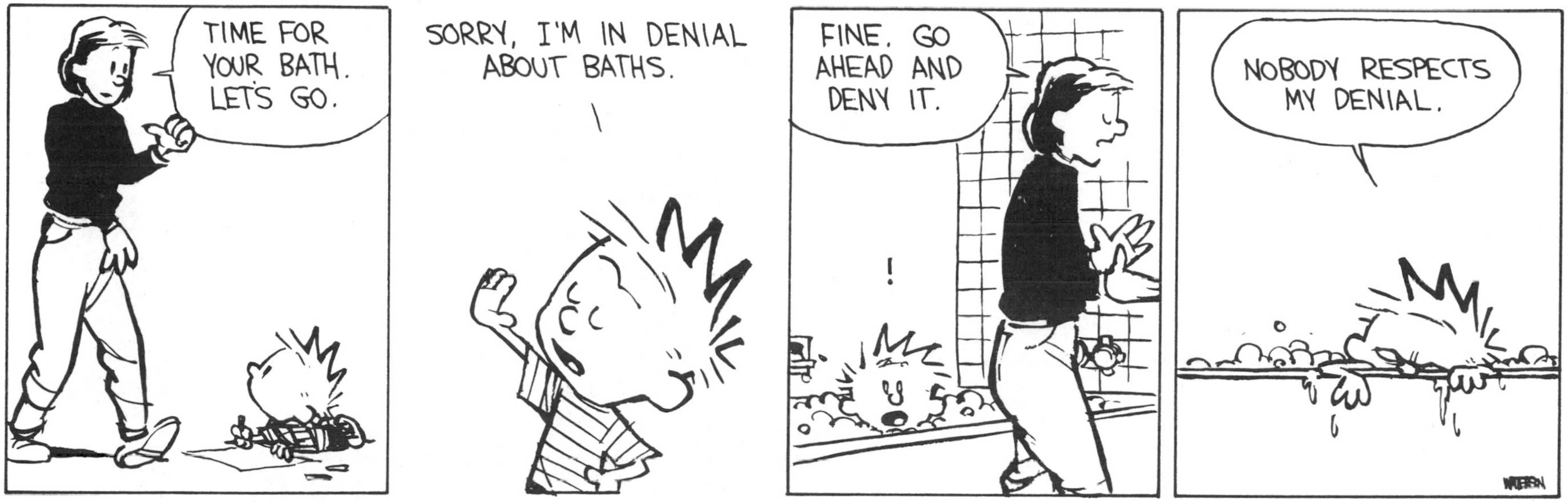
TIME FOR YOUR BATH. LET'S GO.
SORRY, I'M IN DENIAL ABOUT BATHS.
FINE. GO AHEAD AND DENY IT.
!
NOBODY RESPECTS MY DENIAL.

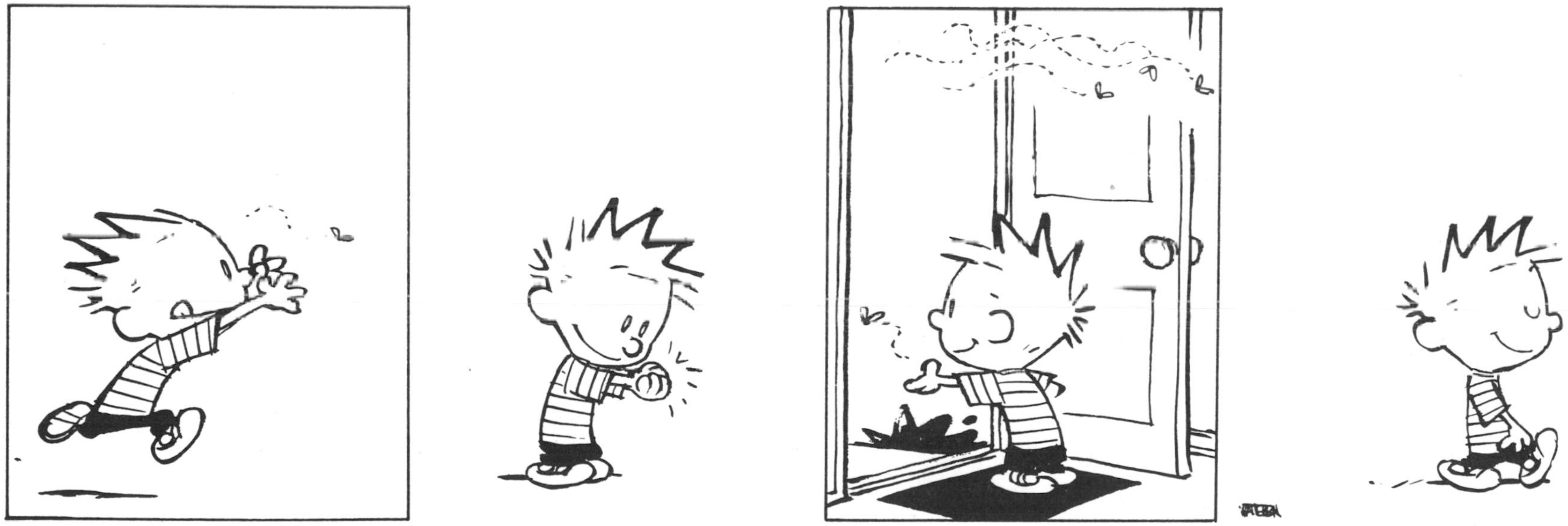

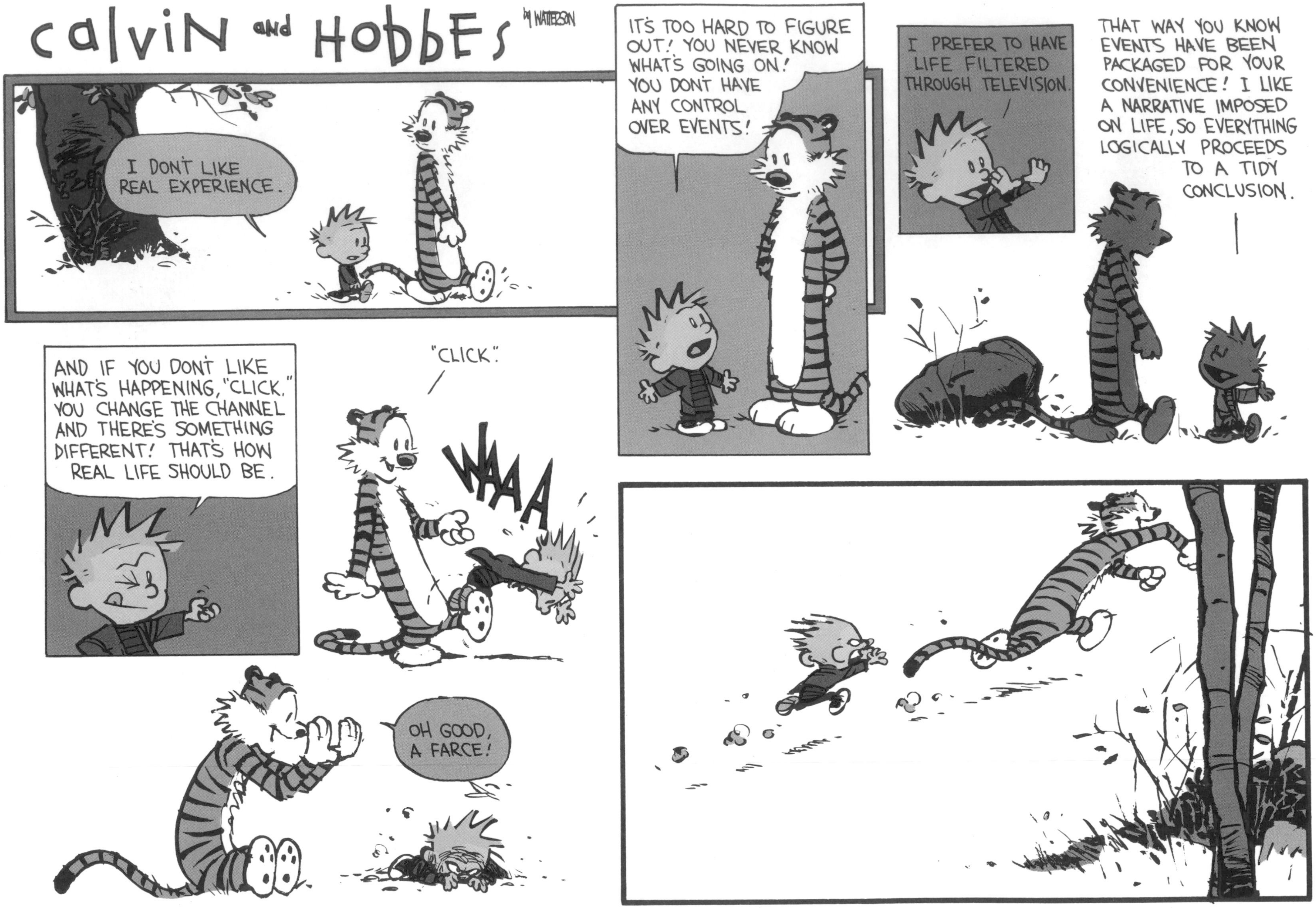

Calvin and Hobbes
by WATTERSON
I DON'T LIKE REAL EXPERIENCE.
IT'S TOO HARD TO FIGURE OUT! YOU NEVER KNOW WHAT'S GOING ON! YOU DON'T HAVE ANY CONTROL OVER EVENTS!
I PREFER TO HAVE LIFE FILTERED THROUGH TELEVISION.
THAT WAY YOU KNOW EVENTS HAVE BEEN PACKAGED FOR YOUR CONVENIENCE! I LIKE A NARRATIVE IMPOSED ON LIFE, SO EVERYTHING LOGICALLY PROCEEDS TO A TIDY CONCLUSION.
AND IF YOU DON'T LIKE WHAT'S HAPPENING, "CLICK," YOU CHANGE THE CHANNEL AND THERE'S SOMETHING DIFFERENT! THAT'S HOW REAL LIFE SHOULD BE.
"CLICK."
WAAA
OH GOOD, A FARCE!

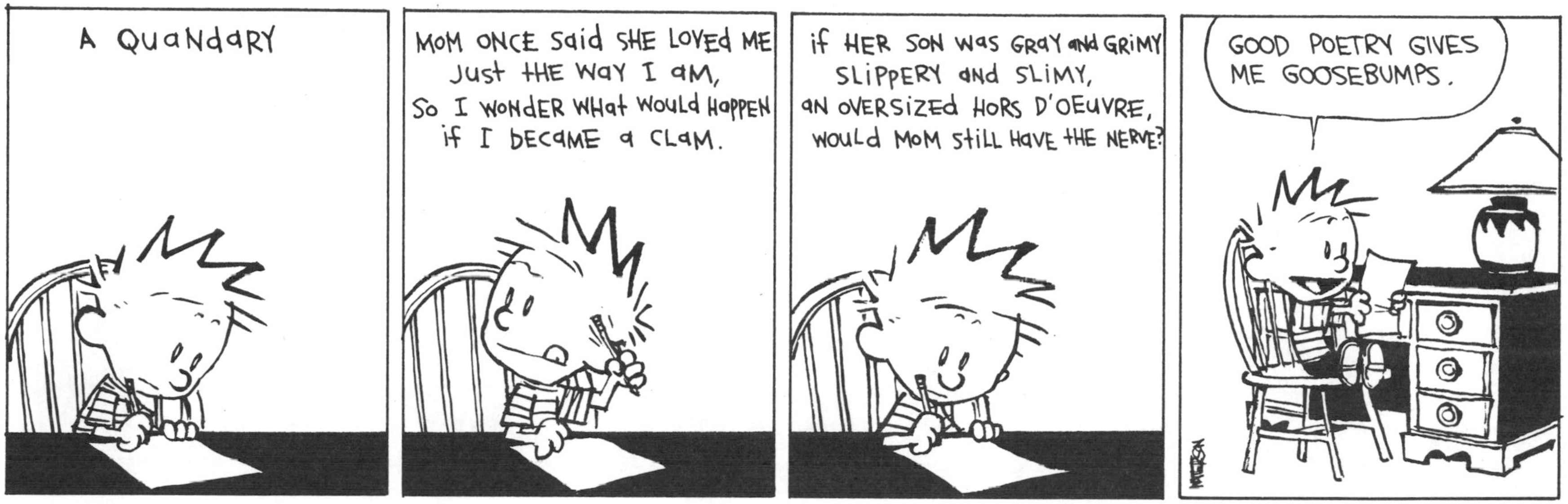
A QUANDARY
MOM ONCE SAID SHE LOVED ME JUST THE WAY I AM,
SO I WONDER WHAT WOULD HAPPEN IF I BECAME A CLAM.
IF HER SON WAS GRAY AND GRIMY SLIPPERY AND SLIMY,
AN OVERSIZED HORS D'OEUVRE, WOULD MOM STILL HAVE THE NERVE?
GOOD POETRY GIVES ME GOOSEBUMPS.

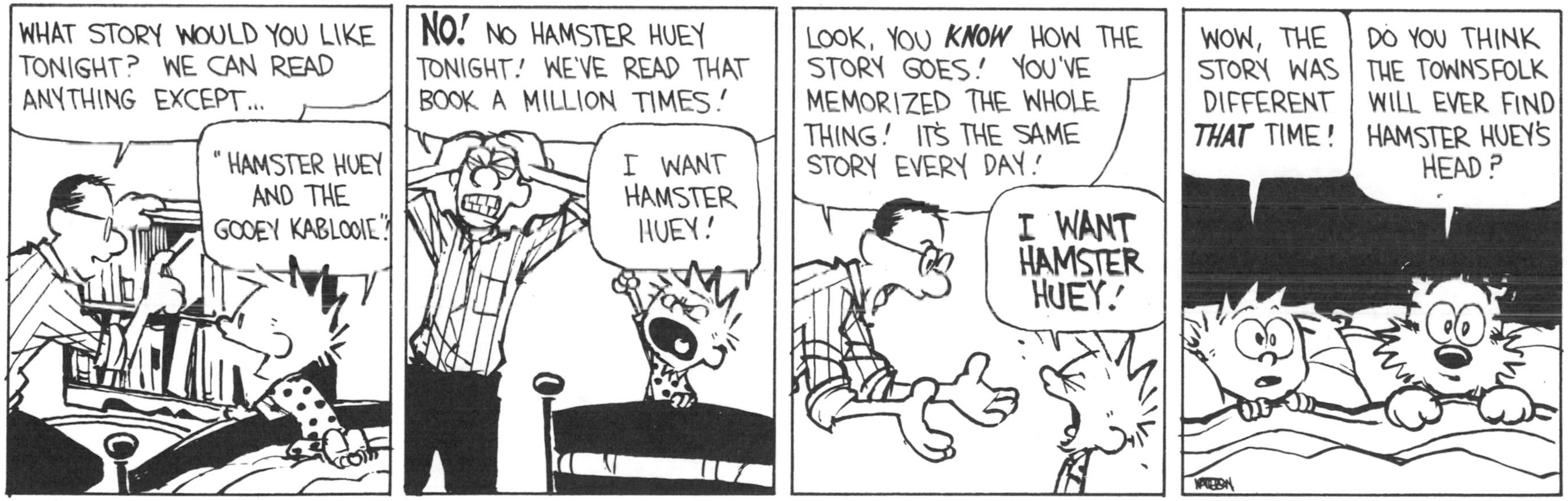
WHAT STORY WOULD YOU LIKE TONIGHT? WE CAN READ ANYTHING EXCEPT...
"HAMSTER HUEY AND THE GOOEY KABLOOIE"!
NO! NO HAMSTER HUEY TONIGHT! WE'VE READ THAT BOOK A MILLION TIMES!
I WANT HAMSTER HUEY!
LOOK, YOU KNOW HOW THE STORY GOES! YOU'VE MEMORIZED THE WHOLE THING! IT'S THE SAME STORY EVERY DAY!
I WANT HAMSTER HUEY!
WOW, THE STORY WAS DIFFERENT THAT TIME!
DO YOU THINK THE TOWNSFOLK WILL EVER FIND HAMSTER HUEY'S HEAD?

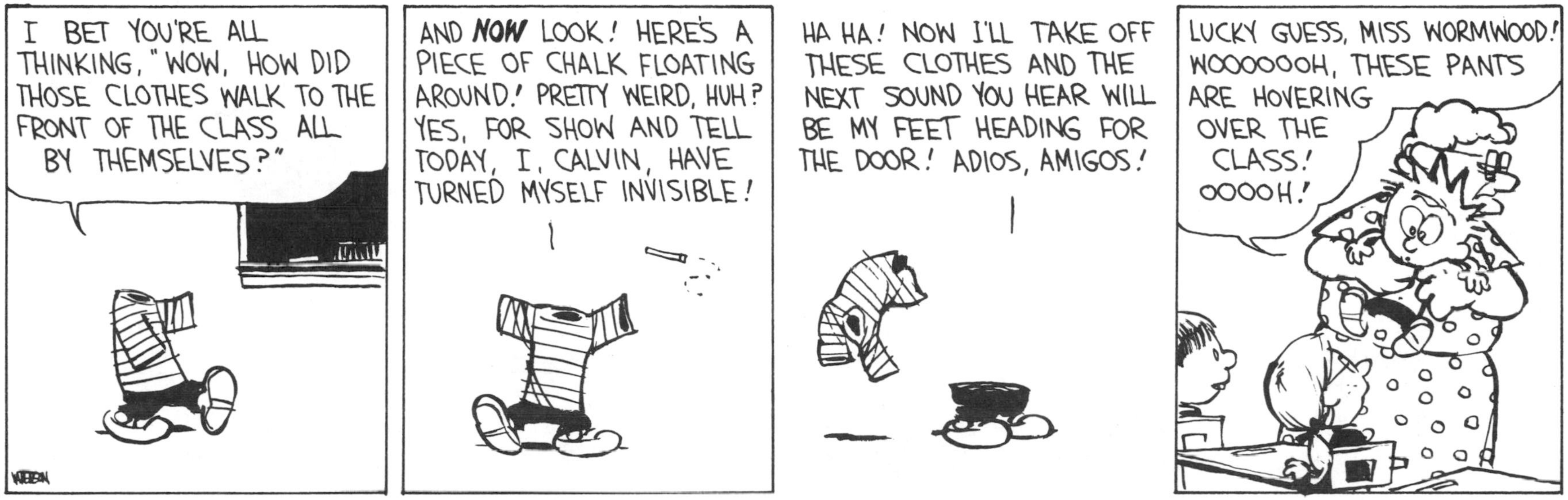
I BET YOU'RE ALL THINKING, "WOW, HOW DID THOSE CLOTHES WALK TO THE FRONT OF THE CLASS ALL BY THEMSELVES?"
AND **NOW** LOOK! HERE'S A PIECE OF CHALK FLOATING AROUND! PRETTY WEIRD, HUH? YES, FOR SHOW AND TELL TODAY, I, CALVIN, HAVE TURNED MYSELF INVISIBLE!
HA HA! NOW I'LL TAKE OFF THESE CLOTHES AND THE NEXT SOUND YOU HEAR WILL BE MY FEET HEADING FOR THE DOOR! ADIOS, AMIGOS!
LUCKY GUESS, MISS WORMWOOD! WOOOOOOH, THESE PANTS ARE HOVERING OVER THE CLASS! OOOOH!

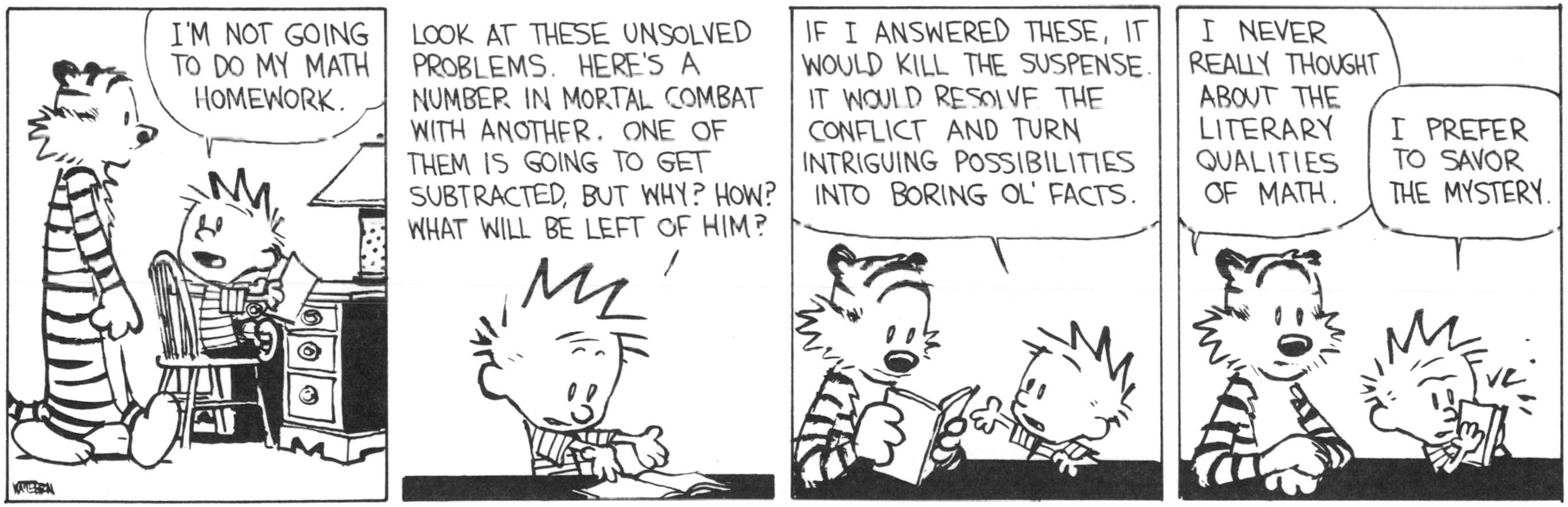
I'M NOT GOING TO DO MY MATH HOMEWORK.
LOOK AT THESE UNSOLVED PROBLEMS. HERE'S A NUMBER IN MORTAL COMBAT WITH ANOTHER. ONE OF THEM IS GOING TO GET SUBTRACTED, BUT WHY? HOW? WHAT WILL BE LEFT OF HIM?
IF I ANSWERED THESE, IT WOULD KILL THE SUSPENSE. IT WOULD RESOLVE THE CONFLICT AND TURN INTRIGUING POSSIBILITIES INTO BORING OL' FACTS.
I NEVER REALLY THOUGHT ABOUT THE LITERARY QUALITIES OF MATH.
I PREFER TO SAVOR THE MYSTERY.

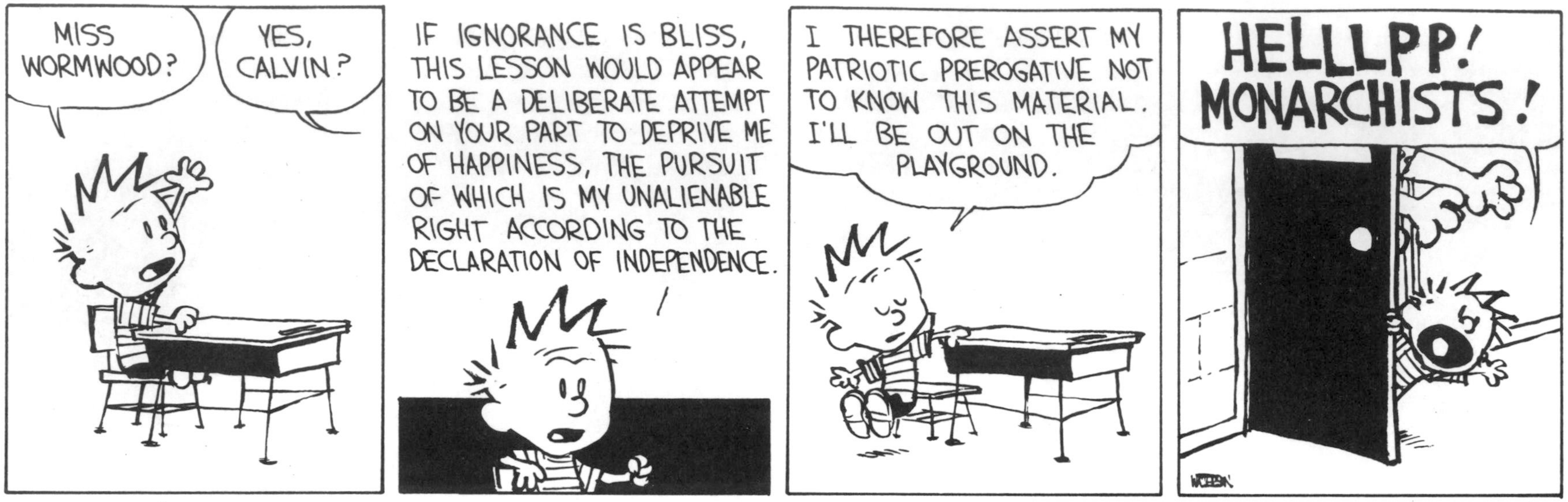
MISS WORMWOOD?
YES, CALVIN?
IF IGNORANCE IS BLISS, THIS LESSON WOULD APPEAR TO BE A DELIBERATE ATTEMPT ON YOUR PART TO DEPRIVE ME OF HAPPINESS, THE PURSUIT OF WHICH IS MY UNALIENABLE RIGHT ACCORDING TO THE DECLARATION OF INDEPENDENCE.
I THEREFORE ASSERT MY PATRIOTIC PREROGATIVE NOT TO KNOW THIS MATERIAL. I'LL BE OUT ON THE PLAYGROUND.
HELLLPP! MONARCHISTS!

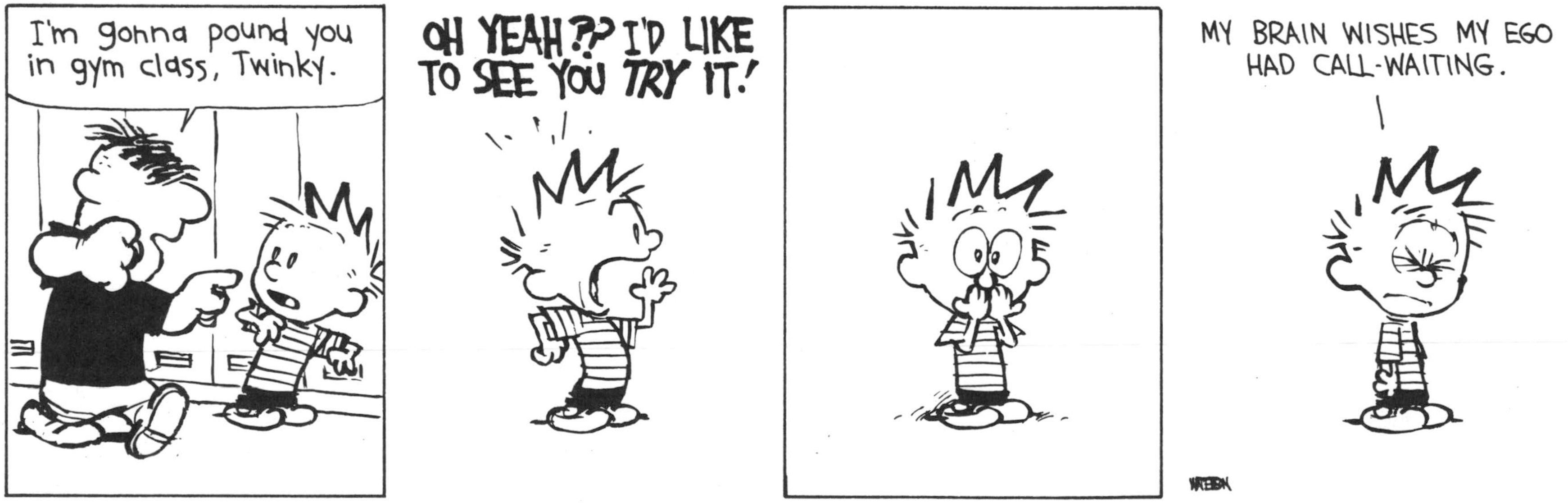
I'm gonna pound you in gym class, Twinky.
OH YEAH?? I'D LIKE TO SEE YOU TRY IT!
MY BRAIN WISHES MY EGO HAD CALL-WAITING.

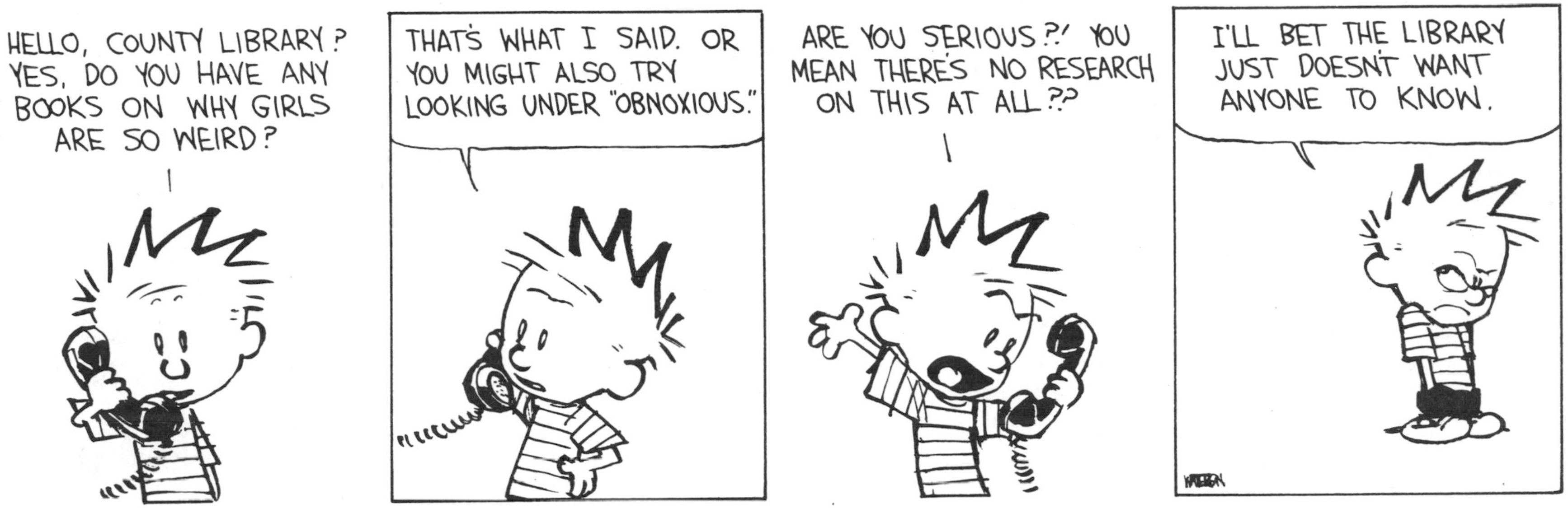
HELLO, COUNTY LIBRARY? YES, DO YOU HAVE ANY BOOKS ON WHY GIRLS ARE SO WEIRD?
THAT'S WHAT I SAID. OR YOU MIGHT ALSO TRY LOOKING UNDER "OBNOXIOUS."
ARE YOU SERIOUS?! YOU MEAN THERE'S NO RESEARCH ON THIS AT ALL??
I'LL BET THE LIBRARY JUST DOESN'T WANT ANYONE TO KNOW.

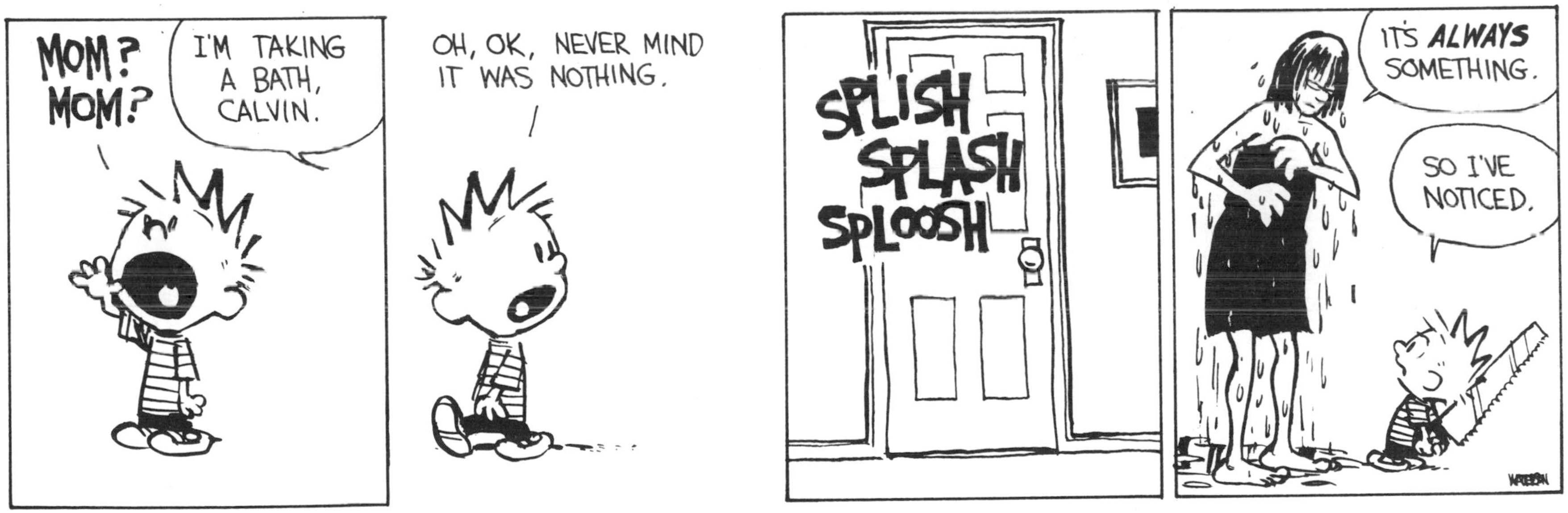
MOM? MOM?
I'M TAKING A BATH, CALVIN.
OH, OK, NEVER MIND IT WAS NOTHING.
SPLISH SPLASH SPLOOSH
IT'S ALWAYS SOMETHING.
SO I'VE NOTICED.

THERE REALLY OUGHT TO BE A FALL OLYMPICS.

IT'S A HIGH PRICE TO PAY, BUT NUZZLING TIGER TUMMIES IS ONE OF THE GREAT PLEASURES OF LIFE.

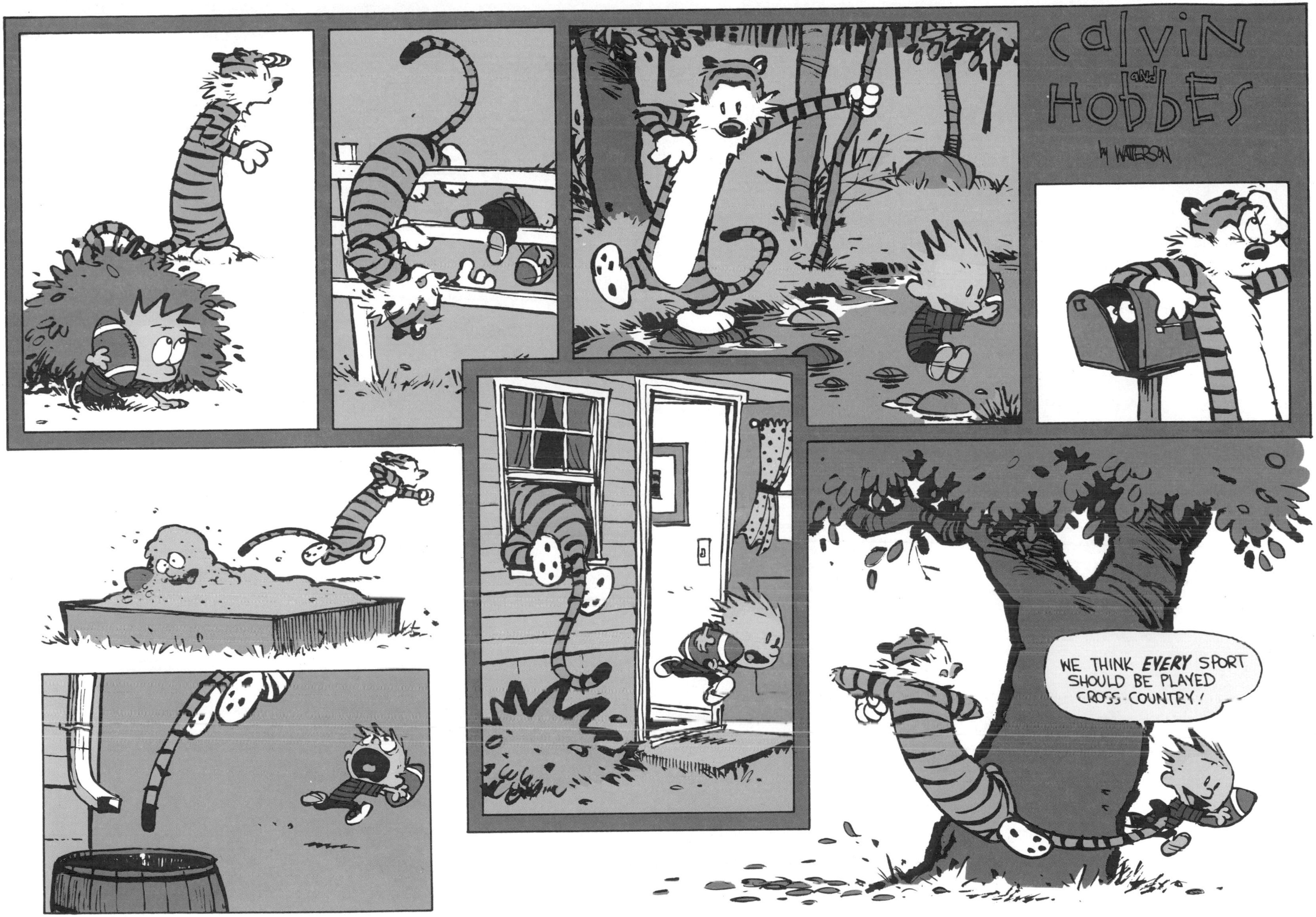
Calvin and Hobbes
by WATTERSON
WE THINK EVERY SPORT SHOULD BE PLAYED CROSS-COUNTRY!

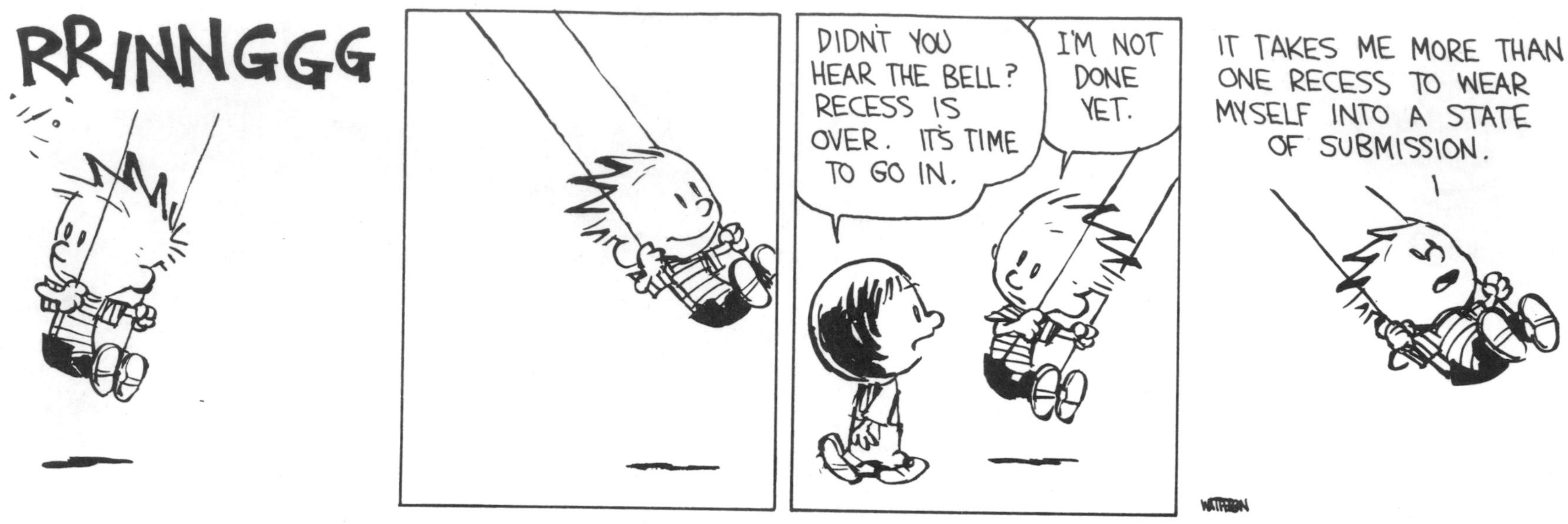
RRINNGGG
DIDN'T YOU HEAR THE BELL? RECESS IS OVER. IT'S TIME TO GO IN.
I'M NOT DONE YET.
IT TAKES ME MORE THAN ONE RECESS TO WEAR MYSELF INTO A STATE OF SUBMISSION.

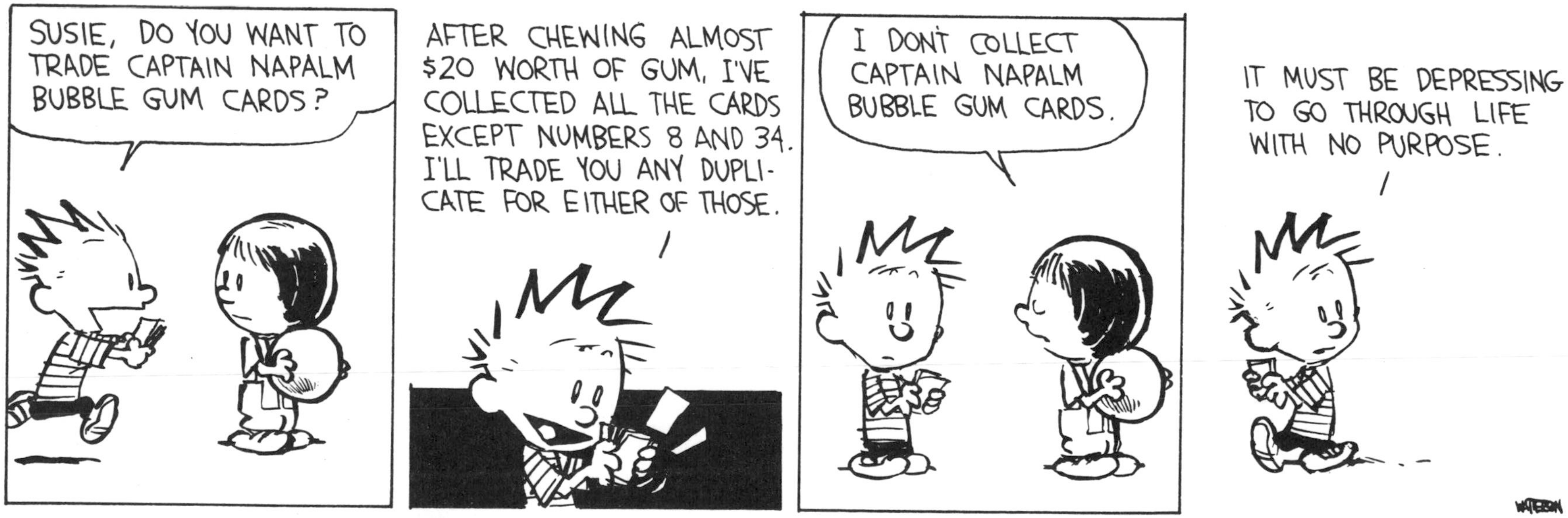
SUSIE, DO YOU WANT TO TRADE CAPTAIN NAPALM BUBBLE GUM CARDS?
AFTER CHEWING ALMOST $20 WORTH OF GUM, I'VE COLLECTED ALL THE CARDS EXCEPT NUMBERS 8 AND 34. I'LL TRADE YOU ANY DUPLICATE FOR EITHER OF THOSE.
I DON'T COLLECT CAPTAIN NAPALM BUBBLE GUM CARDS.
IT MUST BE DEPRESSING TO GO THROUGH LIFE WITH NO PURPOSE.

173

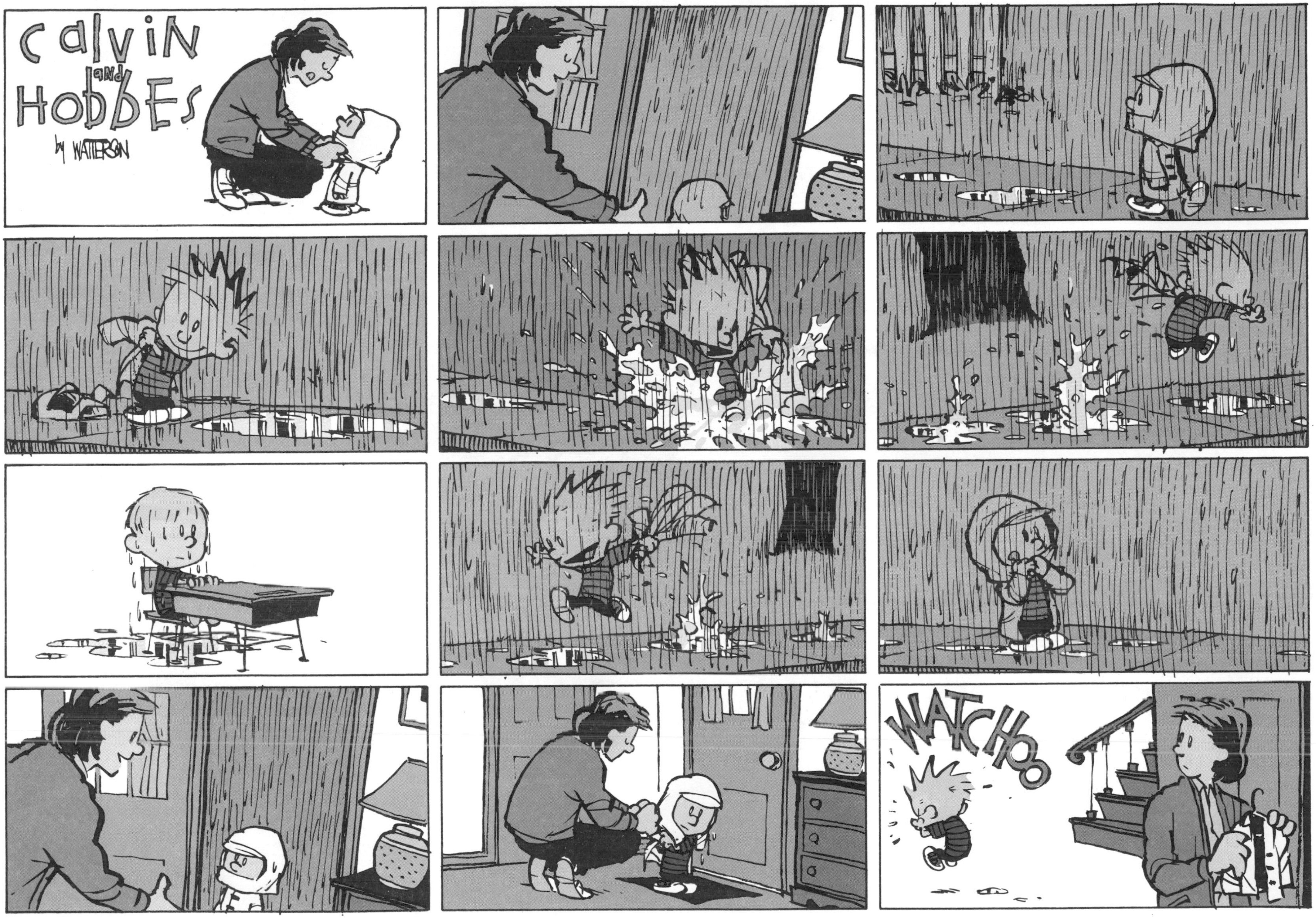
Calvin and Hobbes
by WATTERSON
WATCHOO